W9-AXE-879

THE ILLUSTRATED HISTORY OF THE Third Reich

JOHN BRADLEY

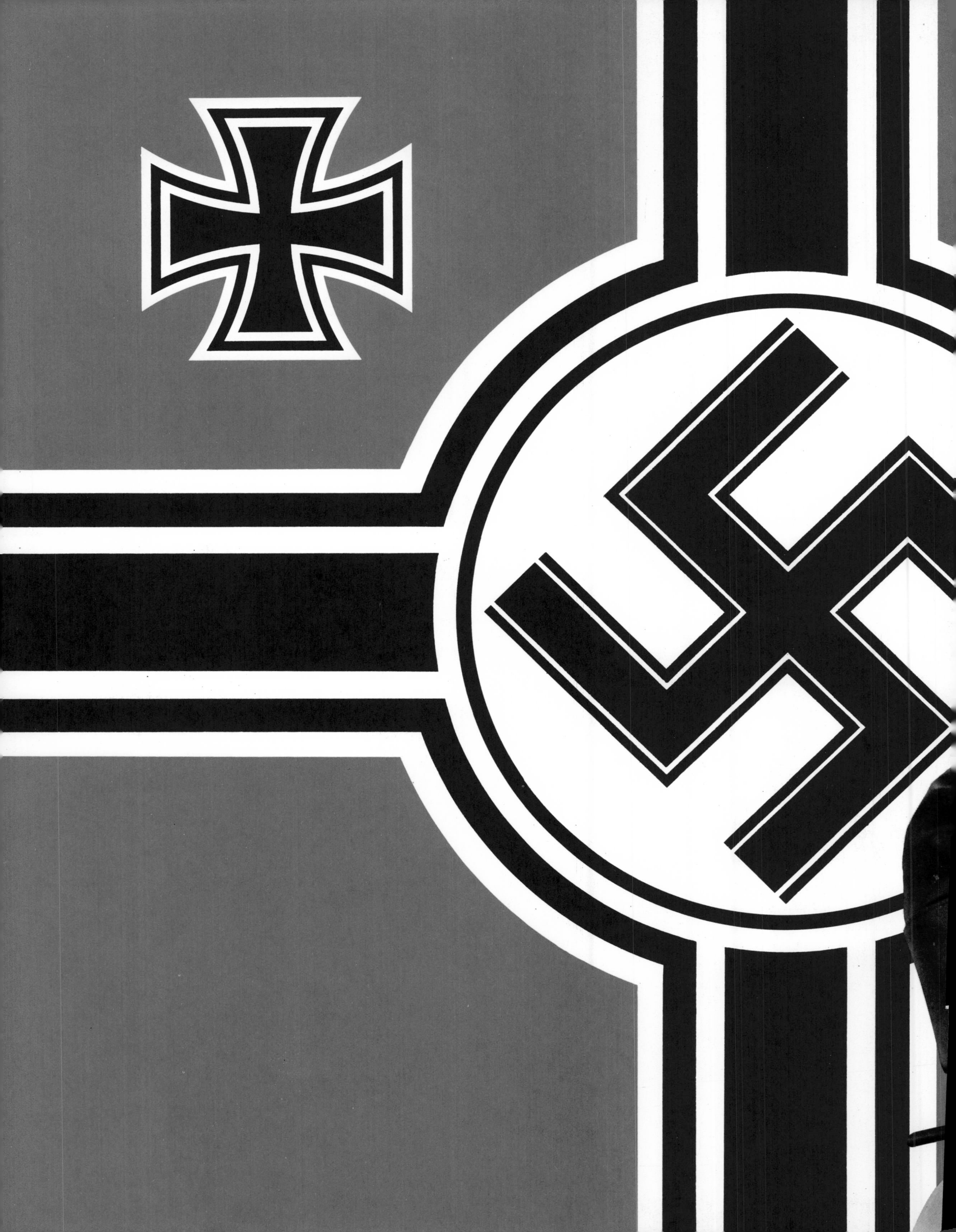

THE ILLUSTRATED HISTORY OF THE Third Reich

JOHN BRADLEY

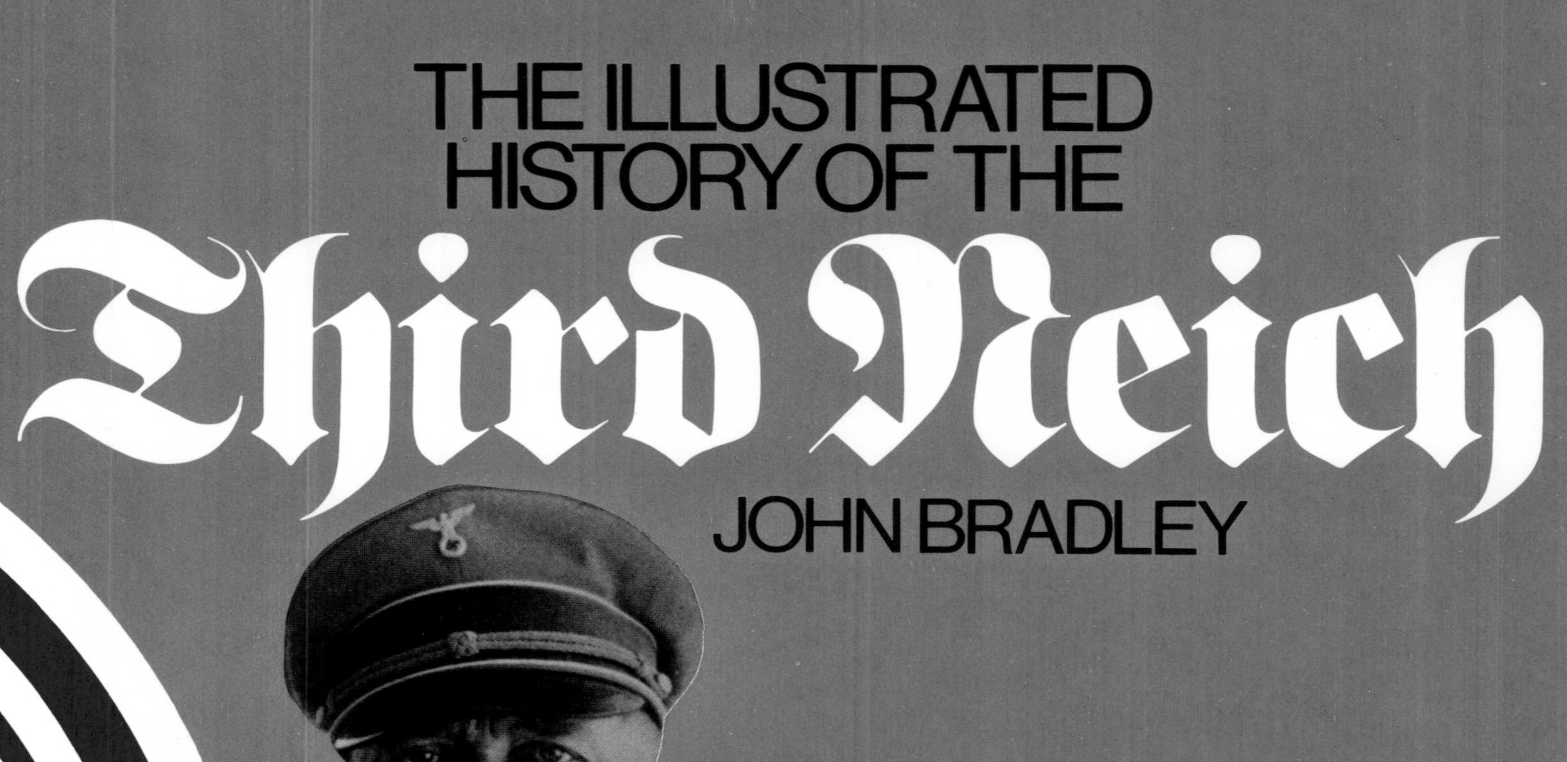

Grosset & Dunlap
A Filmways Company
Publishers New York
A Bison Book

Library of Congress Catalog
Card Number: 77-87811
ISBN: 0-448-14628-2
Produced by Bison Books Limited
4 Cromwell Place
London, England
Published by Grosset & Dunlap
First Grosset & Dunlap edition, 1978

Printed in Japan

CONTENTS

THE YEARS OF HOPE
The Dissolution of the Hohenzollern Empire 8
The Rise of the Nazi Party 34

THE NEW ORDER
Hitler as Chancellor 72
Hitler as Statesman 98

TOTAL WAR
Blitzkrieg in the West 116
On the Eastern Front 150

THE END OF THE REICH
The Empire's Limits 184
Conspiracy and Defeat 218

GLOSSARY 250

INDEX 253

THE YEARS OF HOPE

THE DISSOLUTION OF THE HOHENZOLLERN EMPIRE

Although William II, Emperor of Germany, always claimed that he did much to avoid the war and undoubtedly felt justified in his claim, both he and the German people went to war with enthusiasm. Right up to August 1918 Germans endured the victories and defeats of four years of war with equanimity. Although all the combatants wanted a short war, there had been no decisive outcome in 1914. The Germans had to fight on two fronts. In the West they were probably robbed of a decisive victory because of the questionable decision of a young Lieutenant Colonel called Hentsch, dispatched to the Front by the Chief of the General Staff, Moltke, to halt the offensive and retreat to the Aisne.

However in 1915 and 1916 Germany experienced many successes and reverses: in 1915 it was instrumental in humbling the Russian armies in the East; in 1916 the Russians administered a terrible rebuff. In the same year Serbia and Rumania were practically knocked out of the war, while in the West the trench warfare dragged on. In 1917 Russia finally dropped out, but the United States of America entered the war thanks to the Germans' desperate decision to wage unlimited naval warfare to defeat Great Britain. Despite this setback the year 1918 augured well: in March and May Germany signed separate peace treaties with Soviet Russia and Rumania, and transferred all her available forces from the East to effect a decisive push in the West. The war on two fronts came to an end and Erich Ludendorff's spring offensive brought German armies to within 40 miles of Paris. In the early summer of 1918 Emperor William and the German people thought themselves within sight of victory when suddenly disaster struck.

The whole German nation was intoxicated with the war and its leaders did not discern the danger signs as they appeared: in January 1918 400,000 Berlin workers went on strike, followed by over a million workers in other cities. The strikers wanted the democratization of government in Germany and peace without annexations. Foreign Minister von Kühlmann was dismissed abruptly when he voiced his doubts about the offensives in the West, but his dismissal did not stop American reinforcements arriving in France. In July the Allies launched their counterattacks and on 8 August 1918, the "Black Day of the Ger-

Below: **Gustav Noske addresses sailors involved in the Kiel Mutiny on 7 November 1918, which began the rising leading to the overthrow of the Kaiser on 9 November.**
Bottom: **Representatives of the Entente Allies inspect naval installations at Wilhelmshaven after the German surrender on 11 November 1918.**

Brüder!
Nicht schiessen!

man Army," the morale of the German troops was shattered. On that day alone the British took some 16,000 prisoners of war and the temperamental Ludendorff, Army Chief of Staff and at this stage the real ruler of Germany, lost his nerve. Still it took him over a month to admit defeat publicly, although military disasters multiplied. In the meantime Turkey, Germany's ally in the East, suffered a decisive defeat in Syria, while after the collapse of the Front near Thessalonika, Bulgaria left the war, suing for an armistice. On 29 September 1918 General Ludendorff told the Emperor and his Prime Minister, Hertling, that all was lost if the Allies succeeded in breaking through the Front. He added that they seemed likely to achieve it and as a consequence the German armies would have to retire to the Rhine and a revolution would break out in Germany itself. The omnipotent Chief of the Imperial Staff, Ludendorff, then advised his master to sue immediately for an armistice based on the 14 Points enunciated by President Wilson, to prevent defeat in the field and to concede democratic government in Germany to avoid the kind of revolution which had occurred in Russia.

The next day Chancellor Hertling resigned and the Emperor accepted Ludendorff's advice. He appointed Prince Max of Baden as his Chancellor and he, in turn, obtained the Reichstag's endorsement to carry out internal reforms and sue for an armistice. On his assumption of power the hapless liberal Chancellor had no information concerning the German Army's collapse and tried to delay armistice negotiations, but the Emperor and Ludendorff put pressure on him to speed them up, only to discover that President Wilson had added an unpleasant rider to his original 14 Points: the Emperor had to abdicate and the military leaders had to be replaced. The Chancellor thought that since Germany was now a constitutional monarchy he could save the Emperor, but since Ludendorff showed reluctance to sacrifice himself, Prince Max dismissed him. President Wilson was informed that the military had been brought under control and therefore there was no reason for not concluding an armistice. However the question of the Emperor's abdication was not resolved and this remained a pretext for delaying the signing of the armistice. However shortly after the military debacle became clearly known, German political morale also collapsed.

On 25 October 1918 a press campaign was launched aimed at bringing about the Emperor's abdication. The Emperor was astounded and began to make political mistakes; he left his armies and went to Berlin to make sure that his son would not succeed him. Then on 29 October 1918, he sneaked away from the restless capital back to his doomed armies: his personal fate as well as that of his dynasty was sealed. His Chancellor and his military leader, Hindenburg, had finally lost control over events and both were dragged down. On the very day the Emperor relinquished his power, the German High Seas Fleet was ordered to sail from its bases to engage the British Fleet, but it mutinied instead. In the demonstrations that followed the mutiny, eight sailors were killed, but the authorities who had ordered and carried out the suppression of the mutiny and demonstrations collapsed. At Kiel the mutinous sailors set up a council (soviet) to represent them and were quickly joined by dock workers and garrison troops, who all imitated the revolutionary Russians by forming a joint sailors', soldiers' and workers' council. While these mutinies had shocked the Emperor and his administration, they were not in fact the beginning

Left: **"Brothers! Don't Shoot!" says the placard of a member of the workers' council which occupied the Ulan Barracks in Berlin on 9 November 1918.**
Below left: **Revolutionaries of 1918 pass through the Brandenburg Gate.**
Below: **Members of the Soldiers' and Workers' Council lounge in an anteroom of the Reichstag after its seizure in the Revolution.**

Below : **The Emperor's abdication is proclaimed in the streets of Berlin on 9 November.**
Right : **German soldiers disconsolately troop homeward from the Western Front after the Armistice.**

Above: **Workers of the Mercur aircraft factory protest the "bloodbath" on the Chausseestrasse in December 1918.**
Below: **Guard troops parade through the Brandenburg Gate.**
Opposite top: **Machine gunners on the Schloss Platz in Berlin protect the Royal Palace against demobbed soldiers' attacks in December 1918.**

of a revolution, but simple expressions of war fatigue. When Gustav Noske, a socialist Reichstag Deputy, arrived at Kiel to investigate this "revolution," he quickly recognized the real reasons for the mutiny and was able to put things right. The "revolutionary" sailors, soldiers and workers "elected" him Governor of Kiel, the center of the revolutionary development.

Nonetheless the mutinies spread from Kiel all over the country and soldiers and workers set up their spontaneous councils, particularly in northern Germany. However even this movement was under socialist control: Majority Socialists (right wing) controlled the councils set up in small towns, while Independent Socialists (left wing) controlled those established in the cities. Only in Dresden and Leipzig were the councils under the extremists' control. Imperial civil servants abandoned their posts (just as in Russia after the Bolshevik "revolution"), but the councils themselves, almost without exception, were interested in the maintenance of law and order and the continued administration of the country. However it seemed as if no one was really in power or in charge of the administration, and therefore any fortuitous event could spark off a revolutionary "avalanche" which everyone seemed to fear. Then luck played a hand in Munich, the capital of Bavaria, where the slightly eccentric writer, Kurt Eisner, also leader of the local Independent Socialists, seeing the collapse of the old order, simply walked into the Bavarian

Diet with a crowd and took over. On 8 November 1918 he declared Bavaria a republic and administered the country in a coalition government with the Majority Socialists. Royal civil servants remained in charge, while the new political leaders proclaimed socialism as their ultimate aim. More immediately the Bavarian "revolution" quite unexpectedly achieved power without bloodshed in the most orderly fashion and thus set an example for the other *Länder* of the Reich. However the upheaval in Bavaria was the final straw: Berlin then rose and succeeded in demolishing the state edifice of Imperial Germany altogether.

Early in 1918 strikes in Berlin had frightened both Ludendorff and the Emperor: in November they appeared to be on the verge of demolishing even the reformed Reich. Berlin contained a well-organized shop stewards' movement, which could stage a mass strike on request. Much depended on who would make the request: the Majority Socialists wanted power, but no revolution; therefore they were most unlikely to ask the shop stewards to make a revolutionary demonstration. The Independent Socialists talked of a revolution, but with the exception of Ledebour proved extremely cautious, for they sensed that power was within their grasp. Only the extreme Spartacists (later to become Communists) led by Karl Liebknecht wanted revolution and a violent seizure of power. On 7 November 1918 Phillip Scheidemann, the Majority Socialist leader in Berlin, who was aware of the potential revolution, put an ultimatum to the Chancellor: if the Emperor did not abdicate and make a peace agreement, the Majority Socialists would resign from Prince Max's government and a revolution would take place. Scheidemann knew that on the following day the Spartacists intended to launch their "revolution," and was determined to make use of this threat to seize power himself at the head of his party. The following day, strikes and demonstrations took place, but there was so much confusion that the Spartacists never seemed near to seizing power. However Friedrich Ebert and Scheidemann kept the Chancellor, Max of Baden, informed about the "revolutionary" developments in Berlin, and when the distant Chancellor heard from the two socialist leaders that the Berlin garrison had gone over to the strikers (which was not, strictly speaking, true) he announced the Emperor's abdication and then resigned himself, handing over the seals of office to Ebert and making him his "legitimate" successor. In the meantime Scheidemann had been panicked into proclaiming Germany a republic much to Ebert's annoyance: Scheidemann wanted to forestall Liebknecht, while Ebert rightly thought

Below: **Phillip Scheidemann (second left) and army officers review troops parading on the city of Berlin's Pariserplatz on 12 December.**

that the "revolution" had failed. He assumed the office of Chancellor, promised the German people peace, freedom, law and order together with food supplies and said he would run the country in coalition with Independent Socialists (Haase, Dittmann, Emil Barth) until a newly elected Constituent Assembly had decided the further fate of the German Republic.

Even though Liebknecht's coup had come to nothing and had been preempted by the Majority and Independent Socialists, the extreme left was not prepared to suspend its revolutionary activities, for they realized that neither Ebert nor Haase would carry out their type of revolution, now that they were in power. To prevent the extreme leftists from exploiting justified causes of grievances, Ebert decreed a number of revolutionary measures (eight-hour day; guaranteed work for demobilized soldiers; improved sickness and unemployment benefits); nevertheless Liebknecht and his followers were not satisfied with these concessions and prepared for another attempt to seize power, which forced Ebert to conclude his famous agreement with the Army, to checkmate the extremists and keep himself in power. He certainly did not know that one of his telephones,

Left: **The People's Naval Division in Berlin in December 1918.**
Below: **Members of Munich's Red Guard after their seizure of power in January.**

marked 988, was a secret direct line to the Supreme Headquarters of the Army at Spa, but he was clear on what he wanted from the Army, once General Wilhelm Groener, the new Quartermaster General, got in touch with him this way. Groener pledged the Army's support to the socialist government in its fight against "Bolshevism" which was the term used by the Army to describe "revolution." In return Groener demanded the preservation of the officer corps and a free hand in matters of national security: Bolshevism was to be combatted on the Army's own terms. The pact had far-reaching political consequences for the future republic, but in the short term, it brought no relief to the beleaguered socialist coalition in power. In Berlin the most dangerous of left-wing forces were the Kiel sailors who had quartered themselves in the Emperor's Berlin palace and its stables. This "People's Naval Division" of some 3000 men was under the orders of Otto Wels, the Socialist Governor of Berlin, and was responsible for maintaining law and order in the Unter den Linden district which housed most Ministries of the Republic. However the riotous living of the Naval Division alarmed both Ebert and Wels who had tried to reduce their numbers and get them out of their quarters. A dispute over the back pay of this division led to a march on the Chancellery, where a deranged Lieutenant Dorrenbach placed Ebert and five other Ministers (called then People's Commisioners) under arrest. Ebert immediately asked for Army help to suppress this "left-wing" coup against him and his government through the same "hot line." General Groener immediately complied and sent some 800 soldiers to help the government. They bombarded the sailors, entrenched in the palace, and then stormed it. However, before the sailors could properly surrender they were "relieved" by soldiers and civilians, who had come to their aid after hearing the bombardment. In turn the soldiers were disarmed and sent back to their barracks, while the sailors "voluntarily" evacuated the palace. This inconclusive engagement had far-reaching consequences.

Above left: **Karl Liebknecht, the Spartacist leader, speaks in Berlin's Tiergarten in December 1918.**
Above: **Communist demonstration in Munich in January 1919 in support of the Spartacists Liebknecht and Luxemburg.**

Up to that moment Ebert and his Majority Socialists were going from one political triumph to another. For almost a week, between 16 and 21 December 1918, the All-German Congress of Workers' and Soldiers' Councils was in session in Berlin. Despite the fact that the veteran radical, Georg Ledebour, called the Majority Socialists the "traitors of the revolution" when opening the Congress, it nevertheless endorsed most of Ebert's proposals: the most overwhelming vote went to the election of a Constituent Assembly which would determine the future shape of Germany. While the extremists wanted to seize power in the streets, Ebert had his way and the German "soviets" sanctioned the way to power through the ballot box. However the Army-Navy confrontation turned this political victory sour, because the Independent Socialist members of the government coalition resigned. The extreme left, the Spartacists and a few Independent Socialists now formed a Communist Party, excited by this "double victory," and prepared for an uprising.

Although the left set up a revolutionary committee of 53 to lead the uprising, the strong man of the left was Emil Eichorn, presently the Berlin Police Chief. This telegraph operator from the Soviet Embassy jumped on the revolutionary bandwagon when disorders began in Berlin. On 9 November 1918 he led a mob to the Berlin Police Headquarters and took it over peacefully. The policemen sneaked away, leaving behind their pistols and guns. Eichorn, on assuming office, recruited his own force, mainly from the newly released political prisoners, but also from the mob that came with him, and armed it with the weapons left behind. Overnight he was master of Berlin, because the garrison troops had also disappeared making their way home. Eichorn was confirmed in his omnipotent rôle as Police Chief after the failure of Chancellor Ebert and General Groener to bring regular troops into Berlin to look after the security of the capital and the government; when the troops attempted to do so under the pretext of a parade their morale collapsed and they instantly disappeared in confusion. In fact it was Eichorn who had "rescued" the Naval Division when it was on the verge of surrender: he distributed arms to civilians and soldiers alike. Still the projected left-wing *coup d'état* was clearly beyond his means, although Liebknecht charged Eichorn with the purely military aspects of the coup. Liebknecht had concerned himself so much with military problems that he had failed to prepare a political program for the planned insurrection, despite constant pressure from Rosa Luxemburg, another Spartacist leader. Thus, on the 6 January 1919, when the combined left (Independent Socialists of Ledebour, Spartacists of

Above left : **Premier Scheidemann announces the terms of the Treaty of Versailles.**
Above : ***Freikorps*** **members in Riga in May 1919 were led by Majorgeneral von Manteuffel (center).**
Below : **The III Squadron of the** ***Freikorps*** **march back towards Riga in May 1919.**

Liebknecht and the shop stewards led by Scholz) called for mass demonstrations and an uprising, the political leaders were really unprepared, still debating as to their next move. As for their followers, they had gathered in the center of the city, in spite of the rain and cold, but grew tired of waiting for their leaders and like the Army before them went home. Still, the armed minority of this massive crowd (some 200,000 people turned up) did go through the motions of an armed uprising.

As there was no concerted plan behind the insurrection, armed detachments went to seize the lines of communication, especially the socialist newspaper, *Vorwärts*, and a liberal publishing house. Only one attempt was made to take over a public building, the Ministry of War, by Petty Officer Lemmgen on Liebknecht's express orders. Lemmgen took with him elements of the People's Naval Division, but when challenged for a pass by the lieutenant on duty, he panicked and returned to the Revolutionary Council's Headquarters to have the document duly signed. After witnessing this setback the Naval Division quickly pulled out of the fight declaring itself neutral: the Ministry of War was never taken, and it would probably not have mattered much, even if it had been. However the scale of this uprising was such that the armed forces under government control could not have coped; the newly appointed People's Commissioner for War, Gustav Noske, therefore had to call in the newly formed paramilitary units, the *Freikorps*. As the demobilized Army's morale collapsed, professional army officers began to organize new units consisting of "reliable volunteers" from the demobilized soldiery. They wore Imperial Army uniforms and used the old Army's equipment, but owed allegiance to their officers and the "provisional government."

The regular Army could only deal with the insurgents in the center of the capital. Some 560 regular soldiers ringed off the *Vorwärts* building in which the insurgents were entrenched, lined up a few howitzers and field guns, and bombarded it. The insurgents immediately tried to surrender and sent out a delegation, led by a poet, to talk terms. The besiegers quite uselessly executed the "delegates" except for one, whom they sent back to demand unconditional surrender. However it required more fighting before the insurgents finally gave up. Some 390 of them were treated more leniently: the soldiers beat them up brutally but then released them. After the *Vorwärts* capitulation most of the other insurgent centers also surrendered and ironically it was at this moment that the irregular *Freikorps* forces arrived to take charge of mopping up operations and the total liquidation of the captured political conspirators.

Even as actual fighting was taking place some politicians on both sides were engaged in peaceful negotiations. However with the arrival of these irregular forces, politicians lost initiative and the tough ex-soldiers took over. Liebknecht and Rosa Luxemburg were tracked down and brutally murdered. The *Freikorps* men were using the methods of Bolshevism which they were supposed to combat. The defeated left now turned to another way of fighting; it proclaimed a general strike which the government also decided to suppress. Martial law was declared and *Freikorps* men let loose on the city: several days later, after some 1200 men had been killed, the city was subdued. However insurrections spread from Berlin all over the country and *Freikorps* had to be employed to put them down. In Düsseldorf "only" fourteen people were killed during the disturbances; the insurgents occupied newspaper offices as well as the abattoir, banks and coal mines. In Nuremberg they even succeeded in capturing army buildings, presumably without signed passes. At Mannheim, for some reason, the theaters and law courts were occupied by the insurgents and even the left-wing dominated Bavarian republic had its dose of insurrections. The flamboyant but honest Eisner was assassinated while walking to the Diet to announce his government's resignation. Murder and anarchy then broke loose, power slipping into the hands of more and more extreme leftists, until the Communist Leviné proclaimed a dictatorship *à la soviétique*, thereby signing his own death warrant. His 15,000 men whom he called the Red Army resembled Eichorn's People's Security Forces and were no match for the *Freikorps* men who had arrived under the command of Lieutenant General von Oven and "pacified" Munich and Bavaria after some 557 executions. The German Communist Party was finally defeated both in the military and political sense, and would take a long time to recover. It had gone into military insurrections ill-prepared, responding largely to badly judged Soviet incitement: Radek, Lenin's principal emissary, was in Berlin throughout and even the Bavarian Left was incited by Lenin, after it had lost the local Bavarian election to the Nationalist Bavarian Peoples' Party (however Lenin also lost an election, but he was then decisively in power). On 19 January 1919, while this confused fighting, insurrection and counter-insurrection were going on, Germany voted for a new Constituent Assembly as the all-German Congress of Workers' and Soldiers' Councils had decided. The Majority Socialists won the elections very handsomely polling some 11,509,100 votes which brought them some 187 seats in the Assembly. They were the largest party in Germany, but because their fellow Independent Socialists did badly, polling only some 2,317,300 votes (22 seats) and in any case refused to support the Majority Socialists politically, the latter had to join a coalition with the Center Party (largely Catholics polling some 5,980,800 votes) and the Democratic Party (largely left-wing Liberals polling some 5,641,800 votes) to run the country. Fighting was still going on in the capital, when the government convened the newly elected Constituent Assembly to the historical town of Weimar, where it finally met in the local theater to usher in a new era for Germany.

Right: ***Freikorps*** **troops fight on the Lübeck Bridge in Riga in an attempt to take the Latvian city in May 1919.**

Three months after Ebert had taken control, he ended this power provisorium by being elected by the Assembly the first President (by 277 votes to 51) of the Weimar Republic. His fellow Socialist, Scheidemann, then became Chancellor with the Center Party and Democratic Party having three representatives each in the government. After this act of legitimization the Constituent Assembly proceeded with its two main tasks, drawing up a constitution and concluding a peace treaty with the victorious Allies.

The Weimar constitution was mainly the work of the constitutional lawyer, Professor Dr Hugo Preuss, who was a left-wing Liberal and a republican. The short but turbulent history of the republic led Professor Preuss to the conclusion that little needed to be changed in the system inaugurated by the Imperial Chancellor, Bismarck, in 1870. In fact Preuss only thought of strengthening the old system both politically and administratively, possibly because of the revolutionary experience. The kingdoms of which the old Empire (Reich) consisted were further weakened; they no longer boasted separate armies, railways, foreign ministries, but only dealt with matters of churches and education. Only the largest "lands," as they were now called, retained their diets and ministries dealing with internal affairs. The President, though elected directly by the people, was invested with almost all the

Right: **Enemies of the Leviné pro-Communist regime defend government buildings against the Red Guard in May 1919.**

Far right: **Armed supporters of the Red Guard in April 1919. Bavaria suffered three coups and countercoups in the first six months after the Armistice.**

MÜNCHENER-BÜRGERWEHR.
In Erwartung d. Rotgardisten
als Verteidiger der Residenz,
im Wappengang. 1. u. 2. Mai /19.

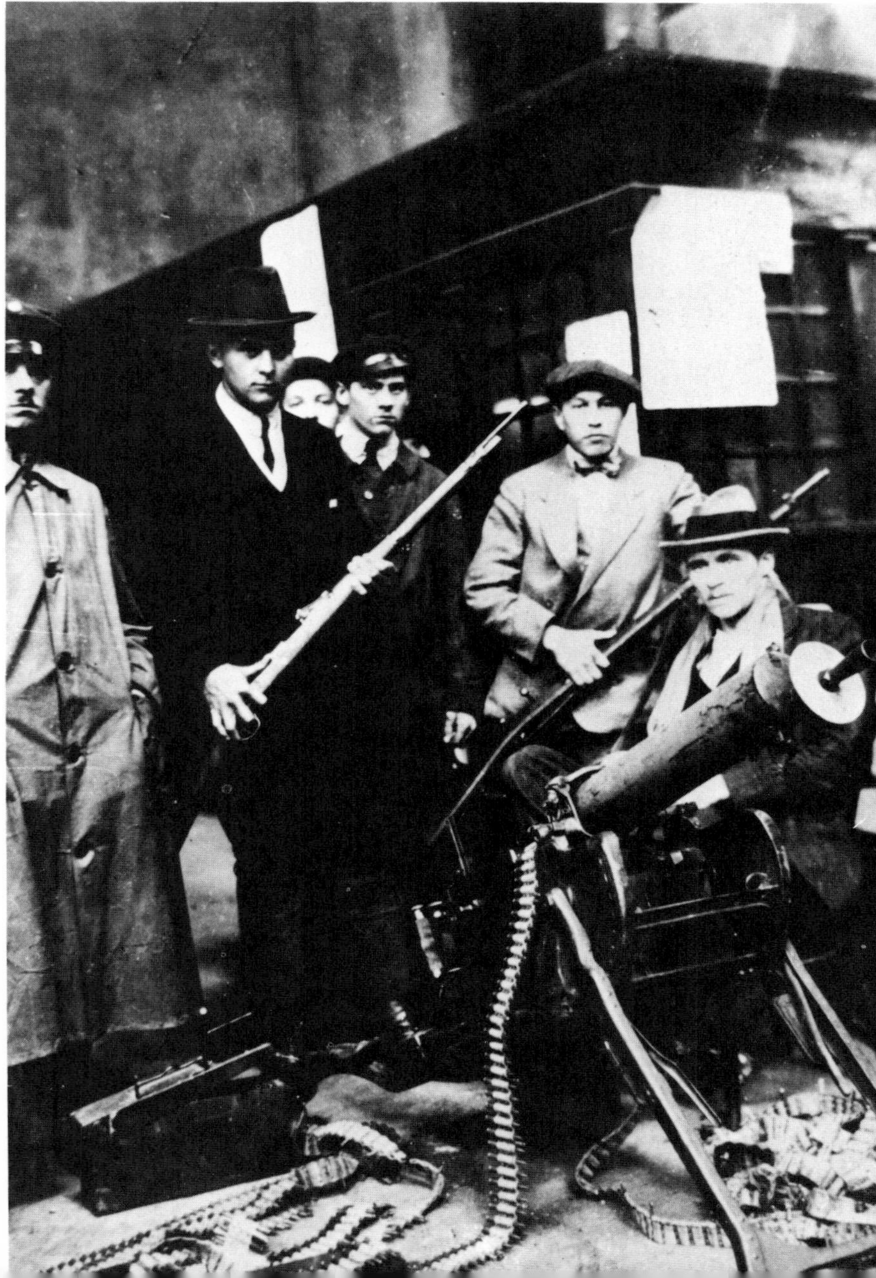

Above: The *Freikorps* fight the Spartacists in Berlin in January 1919.
Right: From the left President Wilson, Premier Clemenceau, Lord Balfour and Premier Orlando in a Paris street during the Peace Conference.
Center right: Communist and other parties' supporters on election day for the Prussian Landtag in Berlin in 1919.
Far right: *Freikorps* poster warns that "Your Fatherland is in Danger" and urges young men to join.

Wahlen
Wählt
S.P.D.
Dein Vaterland ist in Gefahr
Melde Dich!
G. KAV. SCHÜTZEN DIV.
Freiwilligenannahme · Berlin · Nürnbergerstr. 70·71
Bedingungen · Mobiles Gehalt · 5 Mk. tägl. Zulage · Feldverpflegung
freie Bekleidung u. Quartier · kurze Kündigungsfrist · Entlassungsgeld

powers of the Emperor. He was the Commander-in-Chief of the armies and as such appointed and dismissed officers. He also appointed and dismissed the Chancellor and under Article 48 could assume dictatorial powers in an emergency. This power was probably the most dangerous instrument in the hands of the President which Ebert's successors, Hindenburg and Hitler, exploited fully. The President also convoked and dissolved the Reichstag, the legislative assembly which by its vote of confidence controlled the government. Another higher assembly, the Reichsrat, contained the land representation and had the power of veto over the legislative assembly, if it passed legislation which impinged on local interests. Given the electoral system of proportional representation, the constitution would have been difficult to work even in favorable conditions. With the secret Groener-Ebert pact, the indecisive defeat of the extreme left,

Above: **Troops of** ***Freikorps*** **near the Brandenburg Gate in Berlin during the abortive Kapp** ***Putsch*** **in 1920.**
Top right: **Captain Hermann Ehrhardt reviews troops supporting the Kapp** ***Putsch.***

Left: **Security police arrest Communists after a demonstration in Mansfeld, central Germany (now in East Germany) in 1921.**

the enmity of the monarchists still in positions of power, and the implacable hatred of the right-wing nationalists who blamed the Socialists for losing the war, the constitution had no chance of succeeding in establishing a stable political system in Germany.

The other act which the Constituent Assembly was called upon to perform was to conclude peace. On 7 May 1919 the Allies who were meeting in Paris let the Germans know the peace terms giving them 21 days to accept or present modifications. In June the Germans were presented with a final draft of the terms which the Scheidemann government refused to accept. It resigned, but when President Ebert asked the Army's opinion, both the Commander-in-Chief, Field Marshal Paul von Hindenburg and his second in command, General Groener, told the President quite categorically that Germany had to accept the peace terms. The Constituent Assembly then approved the draft treaty by 237 to 138 votes; Gustav Bauer, a Majority Socialist, became the new Chancellor and sent his foreign minister, Hermann Müller, and justice minister Bell to Versailles to sign the treaty which was immediately described by the disappointed Germans as a *Diktat*. Although the result of this *Diktat* entailed territorial losses, reparations and disarmament, the Weimar Republic as such could hardly be blamed for it. Nonetheless during the fateful year of 1919 the *Dolchstosslegende* made its appearance in Germany, largely as the result of the Versailles Treaty, which made the foundation of the Weimar Republic even more unsure than the internal revolutionary unrest. According to this legend the German Army was never defeated on the battlefield. It was Ebert, Scheidemann and the Majority Socialists who "stabbed it from behind" by stage-managing a revolution in its rear. This legend not only forced the Weimar Republic to seek constantly a revision of the peace treaty, but also compromised the very system in the eyes of the great majority of Germans. Most immediately it practically provoked the Kapp *Putsch* in March 1920. The German Army resented most the treaty provision for the reduction of the armed forces to some 100,000 men and officers. They felt quite justified in keeping at least

Left: **Mutilated war veteran bearing the Iron Cross accepts charity in a Berlin street.**
Right: **The Ehrhardt Brigade defends government buildings in Berlin during the Kapp** *Putsch.*

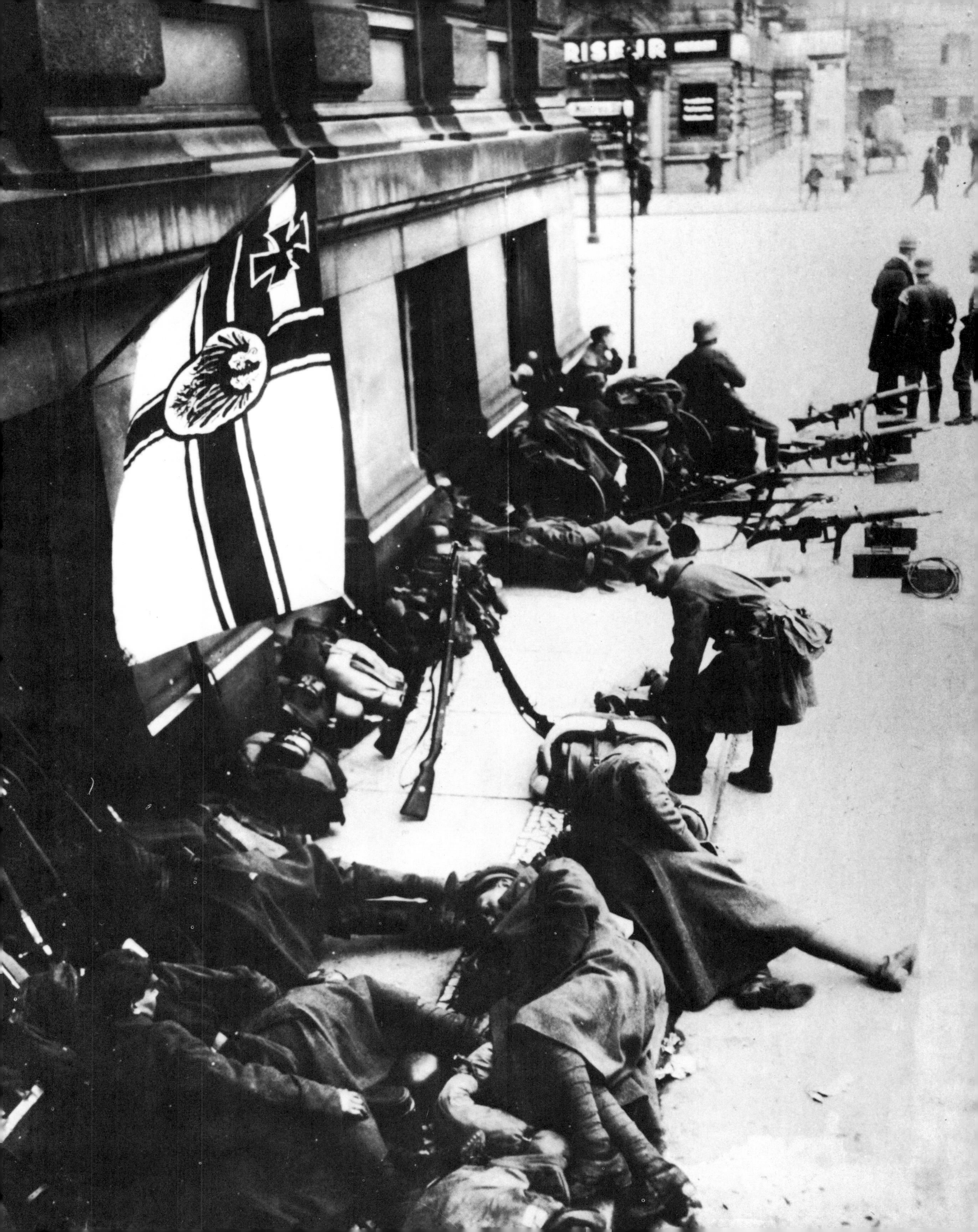

The Hitler Phenomenon

Hitler joined the nascent Nazi Party almost as soon as it was formed. Rather typical of many veterans of the war, he was disillusioned by the strikes, coups, putsches and weak attempts to govern on the part of the Weimar Republic, hampered as it was by the aftermath of Germany's war effort and the unemployment and hardship it brought to most Germans. Of the splinter parties which sprang up, the Nazis were the least significant until the collapse of the Kapp Putsch in 1920.

Above: **A class picture of the school Hitler attended in Linz, Austria in 1901. The future Führer stands in the top row on the extreme right.**

Above: **Klara Hitler, Hitler's mother, who died when he was 18.**

Above: **Hitler's birthplace in Braunau am Inn, Austria near the German frontier as photographed just before Hitler took power in 1933. It became a national shrine and the gas pump was later removed.**

Above: **Humboldstrasse 31 in Linz, Austria, where the family moved after the death of Hitler's father.**

the paramilitary *Freikorps* men in military readiness, not to mention the so-called Black *Reichswehr*, soldiers in labor battalions. While on the one hand the *Freikorps* was needed to suppress left-wing coups and disorders, it was also intended to protect the Weimar Republic from being invaded from the East. The "official" Army was obsessed by this threat from the East, principally from Poland. It considered it imperative to keep the *Freikorps* in being as it could not otherwise guarantee the security of the Weimar Republic. However the *Freikorps* was a political nuisance, for they were, to a man, of extreme right-wing views and political allegiance; in fact they were the very antecedents not only of the SA (*Sturm Abteilung*) and SS (*Schütz Staffel*) but also of the *Stahlhelm* and the green shirts. In April 1920 a right-wing civil servant, Dr Wolfgang Kapp, called on the 12,000 *Freikorps* men stationed near Berlin who were going to be dissolved by the Socialist Chancellor, to support him in seizing power. The *Freikorps* men immediately began their march on Berlin and when the Army refused to help the government to suppress the uprising General Hans von Seeckt uttered his famous "the *Reichswehr* does not fire on the *Reichswehr*" – the government had to leave the capital. Before escaping it did manage to proclaim a general strike against the coup. However Dr Kapp was completely inept and after four days of fumbling, the strike brought down his new government and dissolved this particular *Freikorps*. At the last moment, as the Kapp régime was fading away, and Dr Kapp was about to escape in an aircraft to Sweden, a youthful messenger from Munich arrived at the Chancellery in Berlin. His name was Adolf Hitler and he wanted to co-ordinate his own Bavarian coup with that of Dr Kapp. Hitler returned disappointed, but the Bavarians themselves enacted their coup by bringing down the Socialist Hoffman government and replaced it by a Nationalist right-wing régime headed by Gustav von Kahr.

It is perhaps pertinent to have a closer look at the career of this unknown messenger from Munich. Like all German soldiers after the armistice, Hitler made his way home from a hospital at Pasewalk where he was confined as a result of an injury. On arriving in Munich he found the city and Bavaria in a turmoil. His battalion was under the control of a soldiers' soviet and Hitler left for a spell of guard duties in a prisoner of war camp at Traunstein. He was back in Munich before the left-wing régime collapsed, but only took active part in army duties when the 2nd Infantry Regiment began to investigate the misdeeds of soldiers' soviet.

Soon Hitler was given a job in the Political Department of the Army's district command in Munich. He not only collected political intelligence for the Army but also acted as a *Bildungsoffizier* (educational officer) whose duties, however, smacked of the Soviet political commissar: his main task was to combat dangerous ideologies. However, on the whole, these duties gained him access to politics and political struggle, for the chaos which he witnessed on returning home inspired in him the idea of a political career to put things right. In September 1919 he was sent by the political department to investigate a minute political party calling itself the German Workers' Party. This became ultimately his opening into politics, though he probably hardly realized it, as he sat through a dull meeting of some 25 persons in the Sterneckerbräu beer cellar. Only towards the end of the meeting did Hitler get hot under the collar: someone suggested that Bavaria should secede from the

Below: **Polish supporters struggle with German residents of Upper Silesia during the plebiscite campaign in 1921 which awarded about half of the disputed territory to Poland contrary to the wishes of the electorate.**

Reich and join up with Austria. Hitler, an Austrian who disliked this fashionable idea, tore the poor gentleman who suggested it to pieces and so impressed the audience and the organizing committee by the vehemence of his arguments that they invited him to join them.

In this most fortuitous manner Hitler found for himself a party and followers. His report to the Army's Political Department cleared the German Workers' Party of any subversive aims and on that same day Hitler became the seventh member of the organizing committee. The heart and soul of this party was Anton Drexler, a locksmith, and a newspaper reporter, Karl Harrer, whose "ideology" of combatting Marxism in the trade union movement and seeking a just peace appealed to Hitler. From the very beginning Hitler began to think big and wanted to turn the tiny group into a national movement. Harrer thought him mad and resigned in protest, while his successor as Chairman, Drexler, remained skeptical. However Hitler proved them all wrong when on 1 April 1920 he organized a relatively large public meeting at which he presented the new 25-Point Program. On this day Hitler was launched as a politician; the German Workers' Party, which changed its name to National Socialist German Workers' Party (abbreviated Nazi), was also launched as a national movement and a little paradoxically their ultimate aim was the takeover of the nascent Weimar Republic.

Below: **Supporters of the Kapp regime on Berlin's Pariserplatz in 1920. The right-wing coup failed in Berlin but a simultaneous coup in Bavaria succeeded.**
Right: **The German Workers' Party was founded in January 1919 with a membership of about 40. Their 25 points are printed here and indicate the extreme nationalist as well as socialist character of the early Nazis.**

The Twenty-Five Points of the German Workers' Party, 1920

The program of the German Workers' Party is limited as to period. The leaders have no intention, once the aims announced in it have been achieved, of setting up fresh ones, merely in order to increase the discontent of the masses artificially, and so ensure the contined existence of the party.

1 We demand the union of all Germans to form a Great Germany on the basis of the right of self-determination enjoyed by nations.

2 We demand equality of rights for the German people in its dealings with other nations, and abolition of the peace treaties of Versailles and Saint-Germain.

3 We demand land and territory (colonies) for the nourishment of our people and for settling our excess population.

4 None but members of the nation may be citizens of the state. None but those of German blood, whatever their creed, may be members of the nation. No Jew, therefore, may be a member of the nation.

5 Anyone who is not a citizen of the state may live in Germany only as a guest and must be regarded as being subject to foreign laws.

6 The right of voting on the leadership and legislation is to be enjoyed by the state alone. We demand therefore that all official appointments, of whatever kind, whether in the Reich, in the country, or in the smaller localities, shall be granted to citizens of the state alone. We oppose the corrupting custom of Parliament of filling posts merely with a view to party considerations, and without reference to character or capacity.

7 We demand that the state shall make it its first duty to promote the industry and livelihood of citizens of the state. If it is not possible to nourish the entire population of the state, foreign nationals (non-citizens of the state) must be excluded from the Reich.

8 All non-German immigration must be prevented . . . .

9 All citizens of the state shall be equal as regards rights and duties.

10 It must be the first duty of each citizen of the state to work with his mind or with his body. The activities of the individual may not clash with the interests of the whole, but must proceed within the frame of the community and be for the general good.

We demand therefore:

11 Abolition of incomes not earned by work.

12 In view of the enormous sacrifice of life and property demanded of a nation by every war, personal enrichment because of a war must be regarded as a crime against the nation. We demand therefore ruthless confiscation of all war gains.

13 We demand nationalization of all businesses (trusts) . . . .

14 We demand that the profits from wholesale trade shall be shared.

15 We demand extensive development of provision for old age.

16 We demand creation and maintenance of a healthy middle class, immediate communalization of wholesale business premises, and their lease at a cheap rate to small traders, and that extreme consideration shall be shown to all small purveyors to the state, district authorities, and smaller localities.

17 We demand land reform suitable to our national requirements . . . .

18 We demand ruthless prosecution of those whose activities are injurious to the common interest. Sordid criminals against the nation, usurers, profiteers, etc, must be punished with death, whatever their creed or race.

19 We demand that the Roman Law, which serves the materialistic world order, shall be replaced by a legal system for all Germany.

20 With the aim of opening to every capable and industrious German the possibility of higher education and of thus obtaining advancement, the state must consider a thorough reconstruction of our national system of education . . . .

21 The state must see to raising the standard of health in the nation by protecting mothers and infants, prohibiting child labor, increasing bodily efficiency by obligatory gymnastics and sports laid down by law, and by extensive support of clubs engaged in the bodily development of the young.

22 We demand abolition of a paid army and formation of a national army.

23 We demand legal warfare against conscious political lying and its dissemination in the press. In order to facilitate creation of a German national press we demand:

a) that all editors of newspapers and their assistants, employing the German language, must be members of the nation;

b) that special permission from the state shall be necessary before non-German newspapers may appear. These are not necessarily printed in the German language;

c) that non-Germans shall be prohibited by law from participation financially in or influencing German newspapers . . . .

It must be forbidden to publish papers which do not conduce to the national welfare. We demand legal prosecution of all tendencies in art and literature of a kind likely to disintegrate our life as a nation, and the suppression of institutions which militate against the requirements above-mentioned.

24 We demand liberty for all religious denominations in the state, so far as they are not a danger to it and do not militate against the moral feelings of the German race. The party, as such, stands for positive Christianity, but does not bind itself in the matter of creed to any particular confession. It combats the Jewish-materialist spirit within us and without us . . .

25 That all the foregoing may be realized we demand the creation of a strong central power of the state. Unquestioned authority of the politically centralized Parliament over the entire Reich and its organizations; and formation of chambers for classes and occupations for the purpose of carrying out the general laws promulgated by the Reich in the various states of the confederation.

The leaders of the party swear to go straight forward – if necessary to sacrifice their lives – in securing fulfillment of the foregoing points.

Extract from Raymond Murphy *National Socialism* (Washington, 1943)

1. The Reich Service Flag.
2. The National and Mercantile Flag.
3. The Flag for the Minister of War and Commander-in-Chief of the armed forces.
4. The command flag of the Commander-in-Chief of the German Army.
5. The National War Flag 1933.
6. The National War Flag 1935.

"Die Fahne Hoch" ("Horst Wessel Song")

Text and music by Horst Wessel

Die Fahne hoch, die Reihen fest geschlossen!
SA marschiert mit ruhig festem Schritt.
Kam'raden die Rotfront und Reaktion erschossen,
marschiern im Geist in unsern Reihen mit!

Die Strasse frei den braunen Batallonen!
Die Strasse frei dem Sturmabteilungsman.
Es schaun aufs Hakenkreuz voll Hoffnung schon Millionen,
der Tag fur Freiheit und fur Brot bricht an!

Zum letzen Mal wird nun Appell geblasen!
Zum Kampfe stehn wir alle schon bereit.
Bald flattern Hitlerfahnen uber allen Strassen,
die Knechtschaft dauert nur noch kurze Zeit!

Up with the flag! Close the ranks!
The SA marches at a quiet, steady pace.
Comrades, shot by the Red Front and reactionaries—
Their spirit marches within our ranks!

Clear the streets—for the brown(shirt) battalions!
Clear the streets—for the Stormtroops!
Millions already look to the swastika—full of hope.
For the daybreak of Freedom and Bread is upon us!

The signal sounds—for one 'last charge'!
We stand ready for the struggle.
Soon, Hitler's flag will wave over all the streets:
The days of slavery will be short-lived!

5

6

THE RISE OF THE NAZI PARTY

For the time being the Weimar Republic remained ignorant of the new danger that Hitler and his Nazi movement constituted. Born in a crisis, it struggled from one crisis to another, but somehow, as if by a miracle, it survived them all. The Kapp *putsch* collapsed easily but left a messy aftermath: in the Ruhr the undefeated Communists (Spartacists) organized an uprising against Kapp and refused to dissolve their 50,000-strong Red Army. President Ebert and Premier Bauer, who took refuge in Dresden, had to appeal to the *Reichswehr* and the *Freikorps* (who had forced them out of Berlin) to restore their power in the Ruhr. This time they were obeyed and after a show of brutality the Red Army was dissolved. Similarly Saxony and Thuringia had to be "pacified" by the combined forces of the *Reichswehr* and the *Freikorps*. Obviously the young Republic was shaken to its foundation by these upheavals, but the Majority Socialists had no better idea than strengthening it by another election: on 6 June 1920 they easily won but had to continue in coalition with the Center, because the Independent Socialists tripled their representation to 84 seats and still refused to join their Majority comrades in power. The new Chancellor, Hermann Müller, a Socialist, acknowledged the government's debt to the *Reichswehr* and not only refused to discipline the disobedient generals, but also refused to dissolve the turbulent *Freikorps*. On the contrary he set out to strengthen the Army's position. Gustav Noske was dismissed and his successor, Otto Gessler shielded the Army even from the Reichstag's supervision and control.

As a matter of fact the *Reichswehr*, after the series of crises in 1920, rapidly became a state within the state. Its Chief of Staff, General Hans von Seeckt, not only began its rebuilding (in contravention of the

Treaty of Versailles), but even conducted foreign affairs and extended armament production abroad. Thus the regular Army which was limited by the peace treaty to 100,000 officers and men, consisted only of NCOs and officers, while men were trained in the various *Freikorps* and the Black *Reichswehr*. The general staff was simply re-named as the *Truppenamt*, and Krupps and other armament industries built their factories abroad: submarines were constructed in Spain, tanks and guns in Sweden, airplanes and chemical weapons in Russia, while Holland, Denmark and Switzerland provided the rest of the armaments that were needed by the *Reichswehr*. Actively helped by the German government Seeckt proved immensely successful and by 1924 General Morgan, a member

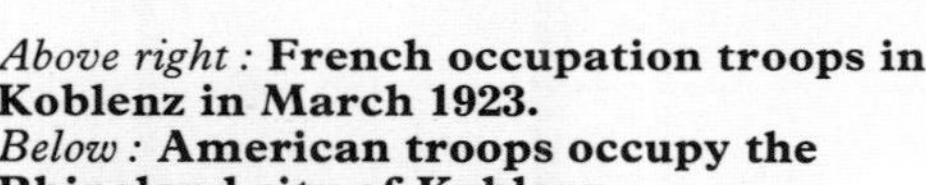

Above right: **French occupation troops in Koblenz in March 1923.**
Below: **American troops occupy the Rhineland city of Koblenz.**

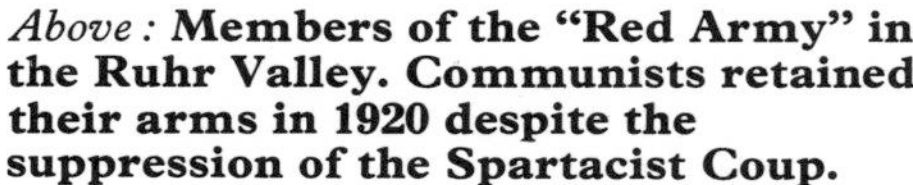

Above: **Members of the "Red Army" in the Ruhr Valley. Communists retained their arms in 1920 despite the suppression of the Spartacist Coup.**

Above: **American occupation troops in Koblenz in front of a police station. The British and Americans did not enjoy their role as occupation troops.**

of the Allied Supervisory Commission, could write that Germany was capable of reaching the maximum war production of 1918 within a year and correspondingly have its Army on a war footing within the same period of time.

However, the consolidation and restoration of the *Reichswehr* did not mean that political unrest came to an end. In fact while large-scale uprisings became rarer, political assassinations continued unabated. In 1921 the Center politician, Mathias Erzberger, was assassinated, while in 1922 Walther Rathenau, then foreign minister, became a victim; between 1919 and 1922, 376 prominent politicians were assassinated. As a result the Reichstag passed a law for the protection of the republic and created a special court in Leipzig to enforce it. Only the *Stahlhelm* was dissolved, and while individual assassinations slowed down, the rival *Freikorps* began to stage pitched battles in the streets, and when French and Belgian troops occupied the Ruhr as a result of reparation wrangles, they waged war on the occupiers.

The next serious crisis which shook the Weimar republic was both of domestic and foreign manufacture: the Germans kept their internal economic situation artificially unstable in order to avoid paying reparations imposed on them by the Treaty of Versailles. As a result of the war Germany had a huge internal debt of some 144,000 million marks; the trade deficit was catastrophic while foreigners refused to invest in the country. Despite this instability the Allies presented a bill of 132 billion marks in reparations, of which two billions were due in 1921. As a consequence the Fehrenbach government, which succeeded the Müller government, resigned, while the new Wirth coalition found support in the Reichstag to accept the reparations bill. However, after long arguments Chancellor Joseph Wirth was granted a moratorium and the Allies convoked a European Economic Conference in Genoa to sort out economic problems as well as reparations. The conference, as expected, achieved nothing apart from a rebuff to the Allies: Germany, thinking that it might have even greater reparations imposed on it, since the Allies proposed a settlement with Soviet Russia which should have assumed responsibility for war-time Tsarist debts, came to a direct agreement with the Soviets, after which the conference collapsed. The French were particularly incensed and were determined to teach the Germans a lesson. In January 1923 the Reparation Commission reported that the Germans had deliberately defaulted over their coal deliveries: French and Belgian troops therefore occupied the Ruhr to enforce deliveries. German resistance was united: the Communist party immediately proclaimed a general strike; passive resistance was widely practiced – and the *Freikorps* conducted open sabotage and ambushed

Below: **Women and children desperately search for lumps of coal during the inflation crisis of 1923. Finding left-over fuel often meant life or death.**

Left: **British troops on the Rhine in Bingen are inspected prior to their departure.**
Below left: **Money is transported by handcart in Berlin during the inflation crisis, when it took millions of marks to purchase a loaf of bread.**
Below: **The Americans raise the Stars and Stripes over the Rhine during their occupation.**

Above: **French troops march to the railway station in Dortmund as the occupation of the Ruhr comes to its inevitable end.**

foreign troops. Disorders spread throughout Germany and the mark collapsed completely. In January 1923 the American dollar was worth 18,000 Deutschmarks, while in November of the same year it fetched four billion Deutschmarks. All this was a deliberate policy of the Weimar Government in the course of which German middle classes were entirely ruined. Only a few speculators gained from the gigantic inflation: landowners were able to repay their mortgages; industrialists who had borrowed money repaid their loans with inflated marks; but on the whole only the German state emerged from the inflationary wave the real economic victor. The war loans were repaid and Germany was in 1923 in the same healthy economic position as Bismarck's Reich in 1871 after a victorious war. However the political consequences of the French occupation of the Ruhr and collapse of the mark finally forced the government to surrender.

The Cuno government, in which the bourgeois Center predominated, and which was effectively responsible for this political and economic ruin, resigned in August 1923 and was succeeded by a grand coalition led by Gustav Stresemann. Although Stresemann remained in power for three short months, he saved the Republic from complete ruin. He called off passive resistance and resumed reparations' payments. As a result the mark was stabilized and within a year the German economy was booming. Next he had to reunite Germany: the lands of Saxony and Thuringia were in open rebellion, while Bavaria was defying the federal government. The *Reichswehr* was sent to the former lands and deposed the left-wing coalitions (Social Democrats and Communists) in power, while in Bavaria only the tiny Nazi party led by Hitler risked an open confrontation and was easily suppressed. The Rheinland separatist republic as well as the Palatinate government lasted as long as the French Army supported them and then were destroyed by the local population. By May 1924 all seemed calm, the Dawes Plan was bringing further relief to the German economy and the government risked an election, which, despite its achievements, proved disappointing. Although the Center remained stable there was a tremendous resurgence on the extreme left and right. Thus the Communist party polled three million votes and had 62 deputies in the Reichstag, while the Bavarian Nationalist Party attracted almost two million voters. Albeit in another election, in December of the same year, the two extremist parties lost some votes, their arrival at the federal level boded ill for the Weimar Republic as both parties proclaimed publicly their aim of seizing power and destroying the Weimar system. Still, in the meantime, between 1924 and 1929 the Weimar Republic enjoyed its "golden age."

Below: **Moroccan troops on the German–Belgian border. Their infringement of German sovereignty as well as their race created tension in 1923.**

174
5. Jahrgang

NEUE BERLINER ZEITUNG.
«DAS 12UHR BLATT»

Verlag und Redaktion: Berlin-Charlottenburg, Berliner Str. 128 — Fernspr.: Wilhelm 7750-64

Sonnabend, den 28. Juli 1923

Post-Bezug monatlich 15000 M. — Anzeigen die neungespaltene Millimeterzeile 3000 Mark

Der Dollar in Newyork = 1 Million Mark.

Markpanik.

Die Scheu vor dem Papiergeld.

Heftige Angriffe gegen die Regierung.

Above: **German housewives in a bread line during the inflation of 1923.**
Top: **Berlin newspaper announces the new dollar-mark exchange rate of 1 : 1 million. It rose to four billion to the dollar before the mark was stabilized.**

Above left: **French Red Cross waiting room at Limburg station after the Ruhr occupation in 1923.**
Above: **Hitler and Ludendorff in a faked photograph, the two "leaders" of the Beer Hall Putsch.**
Left: **The fate of tens of thousands of unemployed and indigent Germans in the inflation crisis of 1923.**

Throughout these five years the country was governed by bourgeois coalitions which made Germany economically prosperous and internationally recognized. Stresemann, who served throughout as Foreign Minister, signed the Treaty of Locarno with the Allies. Germany was admitted into the community of great powers and subsequently into the League of Nations. Foreign investments poured into the country so that it could not only pay reparations but could also prosper itself. In 1925 the Founder-President, Ebert, died of appendicitis and Field Marshal Paul von Hindenburg was elected President; this was supposed to be the final sign of political stabilization. It is true that in the field of creative arts Germany became the world leader: Max Reinhardt produced his operas and theater plays, Walter Gropius's Bauhaus prospered while Fritz Lang among others experimented in film making. Paul Klee and Wassily Kandinsky painted in Germany; Berthold Brecht and a whole pleiad of writers flooded Germany with their left-wing creations. However there was another side to this picture of prosperity – the wholesale moral relaxation in Germany. People felt for the first time that the war was over, that austerity was a thing of the past and they let themselves go. This *joie de vivre* was somewhat negative. All sorts

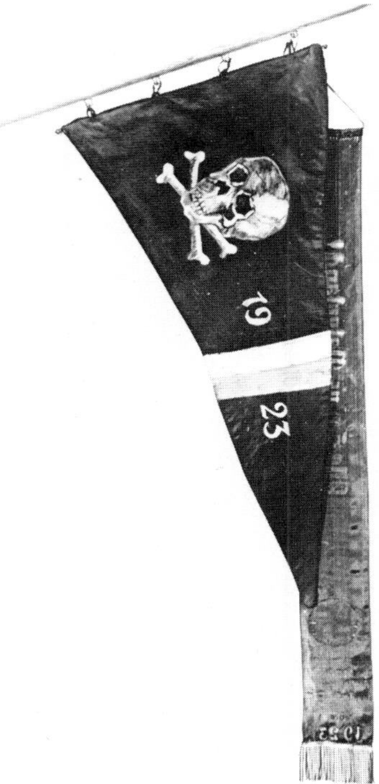

Above left: An early SA flag of 1923.
Above: The Sterneckerbräu beer hall in Munich where the Nazi Party held its first public meetings. The Hofbräuhaus was also used.
Left: Members of the SA in the streets of Neustadt before the Beer Hall Putsch.
Below: The exterior of the beer hall in which the Nazi Party was founded.

of vulgar entertainments sprang up, sexual perversions were in vogue, so that Germany lived out its "permissive" period in the 1920s, while Western Europe had to wait until the 1960s to reach it on the same scale. This permissive atmosphere failed to produce any real leaders, but rather catered for firebrand-miracle workers of Hitler's type. Moreover the first shock of the world depression shattered this perverted dream world and the brutal miracle worker, Hitler, was able to take over without any struggle at all.

There were no obvious indications of the deep crisis which immediately pre-

Left: **The second headquarters of the Nazi Party on the Corneliusstrasse 12 in Munich. The central organization was still funded solely by members' dues.**

ceded the demise of the Weimar Republic. On 29 May 1928 the Social Democrats won a handsome majority in the general election, while the Center only suffered marginal losses. Coalition government continued, though the Communists increased their representation (from 45 seats in 1924 to 54) and the Nazis, for the first time, won national representation in the Reichstag: they polled 810,000 votes and obtained a modest 12 seats. Then suddenly in 1929, after the collapse of the New York Stock Exchange, Germany itself was hit: American investors, who formed the bulk of the foreigners who had financed the five year boom, began to call in the short term loans which they had made in Germany. As a result banks began to collapse and many businesses went bank-

Right: **The SA in 1922.**
Below: **A Nazi Party meeting in Oberwiesenfeld in May 1923; some are wearing *Freikorps* uniforms.**

Above : **Hitler soon after he became a Nazi in 1921.**
Right : **Hitler, one of the many faces in the crowd, watching a parade of Nazis on German Day in Munich in 1923.**
Below : **Nazi rally in Oberwiesenfeld, 1 May 1923.**

rupt. However, the most severe blow was felt in the sphere of employment: by 1930 Germany had 3 million unemployed and their number doubled by 1932. Germany's economy was shattered and lay in ruin, with far-reaching repercussions in politics which overnight became polarized and radicalized; the most spectacular was the electoral rise of the Nazi Party. Compared to 1928 they polled 6.5 million votes in September 1930 (107 seats) and almost doubled their strength in July 1932, when they obtained 230 seats and became the strongest party in the Reichstag.

Thus it took Hitler, who was throughout the leader (Führer) of the National Socialist Workers' Party, twelve years to arrive at the gates of supreme power in the Weimar Republic, and considering the humble beginnings and reverses that Hitler and the party suffered in these twelve years, it was a remarkable feat. On closer examination the miraculous aspect of Hitler's progress becomes more comprehensible when the total irresponsibility and gray inability of the Weimar politicians is taken into account. From the very beginning Hitler and his movement hovered on the extreme nationalist right and made its way up in the political arena on the back of the conservatives. On the other hand, to arrive where it did in 1932, Hitler and the Nazis had to attract to themselves the disaffected working class voters; in this way they obtained real electoral substance, but this took them some ten years to achieve.

As was the case with all the extremist movements and parties, the year 1923 was for the Nazis a fateful landmark. In Bavaria the mood was one of defiance of the central government bordering on rebellion, and Hitler rather ill-advisedly decided to exploit it. In 1923 Hitler's party was not distinguished by its electoral strength but by the oratory of its leader and the organization and toughness of its orderlies, the so-called *Sturm Abteilung* – Storm Troopers. In September 1923 Hitler formed a coalition with other extremist Bavarian organizations, the *Deutscher Kampfbund*, and this made the SA feel that they could seize power in Bavaria provided Hitler smoothed over matters with the "rebellious" authorities. On 26 September 1923 Premier Eugen von Knilling proclaimed a state of emergency in Bavaria and handed over power to the

Below: **Nazis erect barricades in Munich in front of the War Ministry during the Beer Hall *Putsch* of 9 November 1923. Only 3000 people joined Hitler and the *Putsch* flopped badly.**

former Premier, Gustav von Kahr, whom he made a Reichscommissioner. Kahr confirmed General Otto Hermann von Lossow, the sacked Bavarian commander of the *Reichswehr*, as commanding officer and with the aid of the Police Colonel Hans von Seisser the triumvirate continued to govern Bavaria in defiance of Berlin. Then Hitler decided to force the triumvirate into an open rebellion against the Reich government, march on Berlin and seize power.

However, this time Hitler's calculations went awry. After he had tried to seize power locally with his SA, who were ready all round Munich to storm the city (provided the police and the *Reichswehr* did not oppose them), Hitler had finally seized his last opportunity on the evening of 8 November when the triumvirate gathered at a public meeting in the Bürgerbräukeller (a famous beer hall) to spark off the takeover throughout Germany. While Hitler dramatically burst into the beer hall and announced to the Assembly that power was theirs, he failed to impress the triumvirate with his Iron Cross and the spiked helmet which he wore together with a tuxedo; they left the beer hall as soon as they could and took different dispositions from those of Hitler. The commissioner patched up a compromise with Berlin; the general declared the Army neutral and the police commissioner dispatched his security forces to a few strategic places in the city. In the morning, when Hitler with his SA and a large following (some 3000) tried to march and take over the city, one volley from the police put a stop to his deadly comedy. The crowd dispersed in panic, Hitler disappeared and went into hiding, while only the former Chief of the Imperial Staff, General Ludendorff, marched on and was finally arrested by the police.

Hitler's *Putsch* collapsed quickly and though the Nazi leaders scattered – Her-

Far left and left: **These men who fell during the Beer Hall *Putsch* were honored by the Nazis.**
Below: **SA troops enter Munich for the *Putsch* on 9 November 1923.**

Left: **Julius Streicher addresses the reorganized Nazi Party in Weimar in 1926.**
Above: **Ritter von Epp, a Bavarian war hero, who was an early supporter of the Nazi Party.**

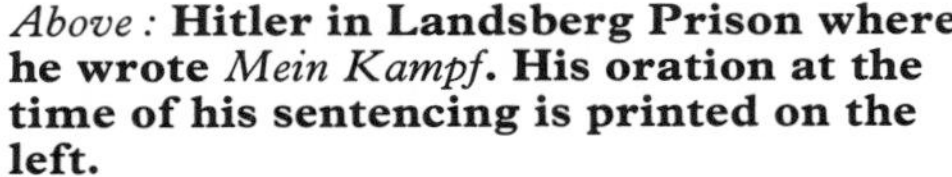
Above : **Hitler in Landsberg Prison where he wrote *Mein Kampf*. His oration at the time of his sentencing is printed on the left.**

Above : **Alfred Rosenberg, an early Nazi Party philosopher of racism, whose *Myth of the 20th Century* was read by Hitler's supporters.**

mann Goering and Rudolf Hess fled to Austria – they were all arrested together with Hitler in his hiding place at Uffing, and on 24 February 1924 they were put on trial in Munich. Paradoxically this show trial served to turn Hitler's defeat into a triumph. Of the ten accused (among whom was Ludendorff) Hitler was easily the greatest orator and propagandist, and he quickly made the prosecuting authorities look as guilty as the accused. Hitler's defense stirred up public opinion, made a hero of him and though he was sentenced to five years' imprisonment, he finally made a national reputation for himself, and in prison gained time for reflection and rethinking of his political strategy and tactics.

Below : **Hitler and one of the Strasser brothers after his release from prison.**

Hitler's sentence and imprisonment were not as harsh as they appeared at first sight. He served only nine months of the sentence and then was freed. While in the old Landsberg prison-fortress, he was treated as an honored guest and not as a prisoner. He was surrounded by his fellow Nazis, was allowed any number of visitors, continued to run the party from prison and in fact dictated his propaganda memoirs, *Mein Kampf*, while at Landsberg. Although *Mein Kampf* became the bible of nazism and surprisingly contained all Hitler's political ideas for the future, it was not taken seriously at all when it came out in the fall of 1925. Not surprisingly, the book was written in rather turgid style – a jumble of half-baked ideas, trends and moods. Politically it was nothing but opportunism with the underlying will to power. The three pillars of Hitler's views were nationalism, anti-Bolshevism and anti-Semitism. While in prison Hitler had read a number of books on Darwinism and the philosophy of history. He immediately incorporated these ideas into his book: the future for him was a titanic struggle for the survival of the fittest: the iron laws of nature were used to excuse brutality, ruthlessness and a complete disregard for the rights of individuals. Such struggle then was necessary to arrest the decay of the Aryan (Germanic) race which he conceived (borrowing heavily from Gobineau) as superior: the decay of this superior race was the responsibility of the Jews and they had to be wiped out before the thousand-year Germanic Reich could be established on earth. The triumph of the Germanic race would be brought about only if the German nation would forsake its imperfect democracy and become united under a leader (Führer) and for this rôle he proposed himself. Hitler's imprisonment and ideological ruminations therein had two significant political results: the Nazis would never again attempt a *putsch* and would at any cost come to power "legally," observing the principles which Hitler lay down for political success: unity under one leader, vigorous opportunistic propaganda and making maximum use of the democratic means that were available. Still the road to power was long and difficult.

While in prison Hitler resigned the leadership of the Nazi party and when he emerged from Landsberg found the party in ruin. Perhaps a little fortunately for Hitler no rival Führer arose from this moribund body politic, so he could smoothly regain the leadership and start anew. Within two weeks of his release Hitler had an interview with the Bavarian Premier, Heinrich Held, and promised him that he would continue his political struggle on a strictly legal basis. Shortly afterwards, the ban on the Nazi party was lifted and it was allowed to hold public meetings and publish a newspaper: the *Völkischer Beobachter* re-appeared on 26 February 1925. How-

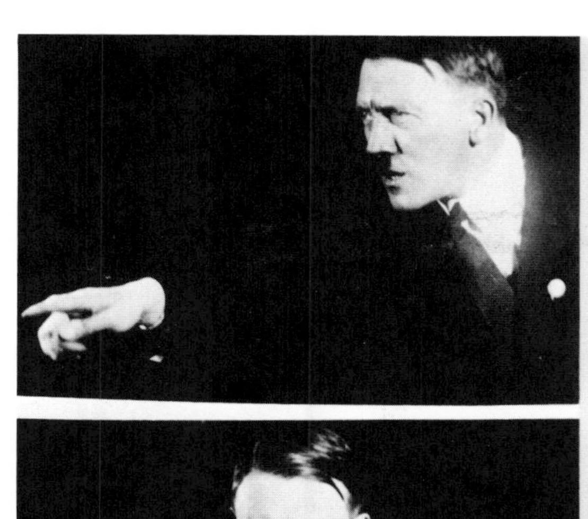

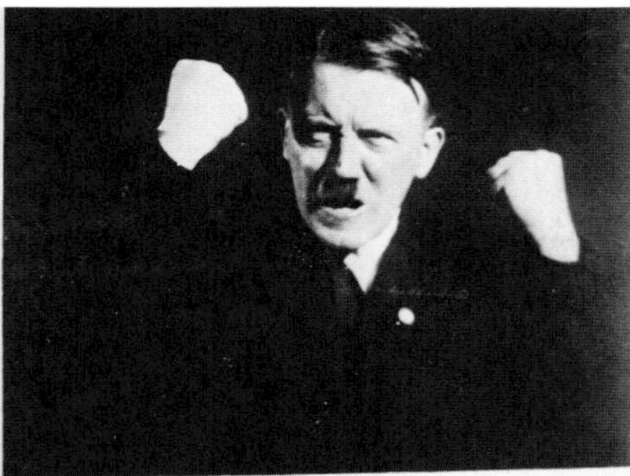

Left : **Hitler in a series of posed shots of his orating posture in the mid-1920s.**
Above : **Hitler honors those Nazis who died in the 1920s.**
Below : **Hitler, with Brückner, Dr Frick, Sauckel and Hierl in Weimar during a rally in 1931.**

ever, Hitler was still out of prison on probation and so had to keep in the background; nevertheless he could continue to re-organize the party according to the ideas he had formulated in Landsberg. Since no one of significance wanted to put these principles into practice, Hitler practically broke with every "reputable" Nazi: Ludendorff, Ehrhardt, Streicher, and Röhm. However, Gregor Strasser remained by him and with his aid Hitler succeeded in remolding the party into his personal instrument of power. Röhm's defection also meant that the SA had to be re-organized according to Hitler's wishes and became firmly subordinate to the political leadership. Nevertheless the SA remained an unreliable instrument and Hitler formed a special bodyguard unit, the SS (*Schütz Staffel*). By 1928 when the Nazis once again fought an election their party membership amounted to some 150,000 and they polled some 2.6 percent of the vote, a clear indication of weakness but also a sign of revival, when compared to the catastrophe in 1924.

In 1929 Hitler and the renovated party at last made the break into national politics. Germany, struck by recession, once again had difficulties with reparations payments and the Young Plan which was to solve these problems was attacked by the German Nationalist right wing. The rather unsuccessful Nationalist leader, Alfred Hugenberg, proposed an alliance with Hitler's Nazis whom he thought he

Above: In the Beginning was the Word, **a stagey painting by H O Hoyer.**
Below: **Hitler with SA leader Victor Lutze on Party Day in Braunschweig in 1931.**

Below: **Hitler, Goebbels and Dietrich at the Berghof in Berchtesgaden.**

Left : **The march past of SA troops in Harzburg in 1931 is saluted by their Führer.**
Above : **Hitler addresses his radio public in 1932 during the election campaign of that year.**

Und Ihr habt doch gesiegt!
Daß wir das noch erleben konnten!
Wann werde ich den Führer sehen

Far left: **Nazi supporters explain why they back the Führer. The grandfather says it was in order to exist. The granddaughter asks when she will see the Führer.**
Left: **Hitler with Franzen and Dietrich Klegges, a local schoolteacher, in Braunschweig in February 1931.**
Below: **Unemployed gather in Hamburg near the docks after the Depression struck Germany in 1930.**
Below right: **Unemployed workers play cards to while away the time. Support from the lost millions of unemployed was the basis for Hitler's rise to power.**

could use. Although the newfangled alliance failed in its referendum bid on the Young Plan (it only got 14 percent of the electorate to vote against the Young Plan), for the first time it gave the Nazis access to propaganda means and they certainly put them to good use. The chain of newspapers controlled by Hugenberg gave Hitler free publicity; Hugenberg's name also added prestige to Hitler who was able to meet businessmen and industrialists, some of whom (Thyssen) began to support his party financially. Thus Emil Kirdorf established and administered for Hitler the Ruhr Treasury, a political fund which enabled Hitler to refurbish his Munich Headquarters, pay permanent party officials (*Gauleiteren*) and win for the first time a regional election (Wilhelm Frick became the first Nazi Land Premier).

Under the impact of the depression the Weimar Republic began to falter politically. From 1930 it moved from parliamentary to presidential government: the coalition government fell apart in the spring of 1930. The 82-year old President, Field Marshal Paul von Hindenburg, appointed as his Chancellor the Catholic Center leader, Heinrich Brüning, who was recommended to him by General Kurt von Schleicher of the *Reichswehr* and the President's *homme de confiance*. Brüning governed the country by virtue of emergency decrees signed by the President and ratified by the Reichstag. The Social Democrats supported this type of govern-

IA17402

Top left: **Nazi supporters brandishing the deposed Kaiser's flag during the 1928 election campaign.**
Above: **Nazi supporters festoon the streets near Berlin's Brandenburg Gate with propaganda leaflets.**
Top right: **Propaganda leaflets of the German Peoples' Party are strewn during the election of 1924.**

Geschlossene Börsen.

Traurige Statistik
Immer mehr Selbstmorde

Bankenschluss.

Golddeckung 35,8 Prozent!

Gehaltszahlung in Raten

Lohnsenkung!

Notverordnung

Arbeitslosigkeit steigt

Owen Young, (below), author of the Young Plan of 1929 to continue to stabilize Germany's currency. The Depression which immediately followed it used the Plan as a cause for unemployment, as these headlines (left) showed: Unemployment rises, banks close, stock exchanges close, etc.

ment in the Reichstag, preferring it to an open right-wing dictatorship. However as soon as they disapproved of any of his measures (for example, the budget) Brüning dissolved the Reichstag and a new election took place which invariably failed to resolve the parliamentary impasse. In September 1930 the Nazis finally achieved their electoral breakthrough; although their election program was ridiculously superficial and naive – they accused France, the November traitors, marxists, freemasons, Jesuits and the Jews of ruining Germany – they nevertheless polled some 6,380,000 votes and had 107 deputies in the new Reichstag, thus making them the second largest party. Only the Social Democrats with their 143 seats beat the Nazis, while Chancellor Brüning's Center gained only 76 seats. Nonetheless the President re-appointed Brüning as Chancellor and he continued until 1932. It was evident that power was no longer in the Reichstag but rather in the President's Chancellery and in the streets and houses of the cities.

Economic depression obviously radicalized German politics and the sinking middle class flocked to the Nazi party. But they were not the only ones: the unemployed joined the SA in scores, while at universities the Nazi Students' Union made surprising headway. They controlled the universities at Erlangen, Jena, Rostock and Breslau. It seemed that elections served only as a pretext for street

Above left: **Hitler leaves the Clou Konzert Hall in Berlin after making an election speech there in 1932.**
Left: **Prussian Interior Minister Carl Severing leaves the polls after the first round of the Presidential election of 1932.**

Left: **Hitler with General Franz Ritter von Epp in 1929. Von Epp was an officer in the District Command in Munich and in March 1933 led a Nazi coup in Bavaria.**
Above: **Hitler in his SA cap in the same year, 1929.**
Below: **A rally in Gera in 1931 as the Nazi movement gathered momentum.**

Above left : **Hitler leaves a meeting in 1927.**
Below : **Hitler and SA Leader Ernst Röhm on Party Day in Nuremberg.**

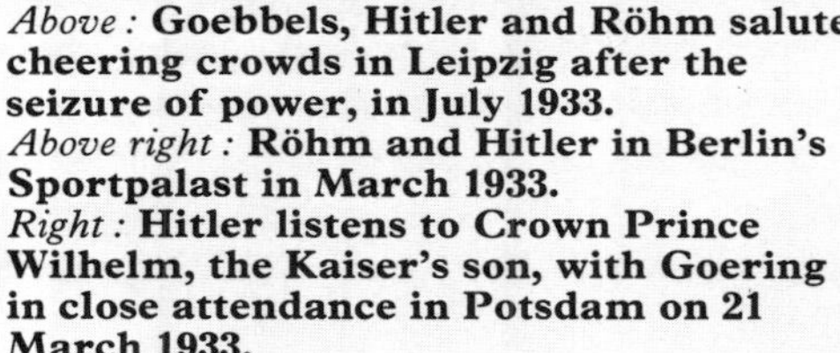

Above: **Goebbels, Hitler and Röhm salute cheering crowds in Leipzig after the seizure of power, in July 1933.**
Above right: **Röhm and Hitler in Berlin's Sportpalast in March 1933.**
Right: **Hitler listens to Crown Prince Wilhelm, the Kaiser's son, with Goering in close attendance in Potsdam on 21 March 1933.**

battles among rival parties, which all had their paramilitary organizations: the *Stahlhelm, Reichsbanner, Eiserne Republikanische Abwehr des Faschismus, Rote Front* and of course the SA which counted some 300,000 or 400,000 members. In 1932 the election result was so surprising that the Nazis simply did not have enough candidates to field (Hitler who was not a German citizen could not stand) and it caused the final economic collapse. Foreign investors fearing political upheavals pulled out of Germany altogether. Some of the Nazis, puffed up by their electoral triumph, wanted to seize power and Hitler had to calm them down. The Berlin SA became overexcited and rebelled against Hitler's leadership; in addition the party had to be purged of the Strasser brothers and their followers. However, Hitler sensed that power was coming his way: he continued to campaign vigorously and to prepare himself and his more loyal followers for the final "seizure" of power.

As in 1924, so in 1930 Hitler achieved national publicity during the trial for treason of three young Nazi officers. In the same year he needed the SA so he re-appointed Röhm to lead them and "prepare them for civil war." In 1931 when parliamentary immunity was lifted, the Nazis left the Reichstag and fought for power in the streets, registering some 50 dead martyrs in a year. Perhaps the greatest national notoriety was achieved by Hitler in the two rounds of presidential election in March and April 1932. On 13 March the old President was almost re-

elected (he was only short of 100,000 votes to get his 50 percent), while Hitler who stood against the President polled 11,339,285 votes, or some 30 percent. On 10 April Hindenburg was finally re-elected, but Hitler increased his vote to 13,418,051, thus becoming clearly the second most important person in Germany. The hapless Brüning, whom Hindenburg blamed for his electoral difficulties, resigned, when the President refused to sign any more emergency decrees which were the only means of governing the German republic. The President then promptly appointed Franz von Papen as his Chancellor, again acting on General von Schleicher's suggestion. However, Papen's government proved even less popular than Brüning's and Germany soon had another Reichstag election. On 31 July 1932 the Nazis scored their greatest success in a free election and emerged the largest party in the Reichstag polling 13,745,781 votes with 230 seats. Hitler now expected power to be handed

Left : **Hitler, his pilot Bauer, and his pianist "Putzi" Hanfstängel leave Munich airport for Berlin in March 1933.**
Below : **Hitler leaves his meeting with President von Hindenburg in August 1932.**

Above: **Hitler, Feder and Goebbels revisit the Sterneckerbräu, where the Nazi Party was founded in 1920.**
Right: **Hitler, von Papen and von Blomberg in the Chancellor's Ju 52 soon after Hitler took power in 1933. Hitler was an enthusiastic supporter of air power and was one of the first of the world's leaders to use aircraft for personal travel.**
Below: **Hitler and Goering shortly before both took office in the Cabinet of January 1933.**

to him by the old Field Marshal, but the old man decided to prolong the agony of the Weimar Republic.

In July 1932, just before the election, Chancellor Papen decided to remove the last obstacles to fully efficient presidential government: he declared a state of emergency in Prussia which was the dominant land in Germany and had been ruled by Social Democrats since 1918. He dismissed the coalition government, took over himself as the *Reichskomissar* and purged the administration and the police, thus preparing a smooth takeover of power in that land by the Nazis. However despite this *coup d'état à main forte* the Nazis were unimpressed and refused to collaborate with Papen who had to dissolve the newly elected Reichstag and hold another election in August. Although in this election the Nazis lost some two million votes, they remained the largest party and Papen once again had to go to Hitler and ask for his support. On 16 November 1932 Hitler again told Papen that he would not serve under him and therefore there was no possibility of a parliamentary majority for the government. By now General von Schleicher had also turned against Papen, who promptly resigned and was succeeded by the general himself. Although Hitler had again been passed over by Hindenburg, he was now firmly convinced that, by hook or by crook, he would come to power.

In fact the President received Hitler and Goering two days after Papen's resignation. He obviously wanted to size up the corporal and lectured him on the sense of soldierly duty and comradeship as well as the "supra-party" government in which Hitler was not included. Two days later the two men met again and exchanged the speeches they had read to each other. Hitler had definitely arrived at the threshold of power, but the old president was so obstinate in his opinions and views that only his innermost circle's intrigues could make him change his mind. At that moment Hindenburg–Hitler relations were still those of a Field Marshal to a lance corporal; however, among other things, Hitler was an excellent intriguer, and he now applied all his talents to this end.

On leaving Hindenburg on 21 November Hitler was told that the door was always open to him and he took advantage of it. First Hitler tackled the Head of the Presidential Office, Dr Otto von Meissner: he wanted Hindenburg to appoint him as Chancellor, but the old man wanted Hitler to head a parliamentary government or nothing at all. Next Hitler had Goering bluster about the non-constitutionality of the exclusion of Nazis from power. Then leading industrialists put pressure on the President to include the Nazis in the government; a letter from them sent to the President included signatures from Dr Hjalmar Schacht, Kurt von Schröder, Fritz Thyssen, Alfred Krupp, Siemens and Robert Bosch. The President was willing to have Nazis included in his government, but by now Hitler wanted all or nothing, and the old man could not make up his mind.

At this stage a dangerous counter-intrigue endangered Hitler's very existence. It seems that everyone in the President's entourage was involved in the plot and Schleicher tried his last trump: if he were made Chancellor he promised the President he would split the Nazis and govern with a parliamentary majority. Schleicher knew full well that Gregor Strasser had never been just a follower of Hitler and as the Head of the Party Administration he was bound to command an important faction of the Nazi party. In fact Strasser's ideology was different from Hitler's – he was more radical and socialist than the latter – but by 1932 Hitler had the bulk of the party solidly behind himself. When it came out that Schleicher had offered to include Strasser in his government as Vice-Chancellor, in exchange for certain concessions, Hitler was at first frightened and threatened to commit suicide if the party split. Strasser, on the other hand, summoned the *Gauleiteren* but only Heinrich Lohse, Robert Ley, Bernhard Rust, Ernst Hasse, Sprenge, Martin Mutschmann and Leoper met him and they all refused to follow him. Hitler saw them after the mini-summit meeting and the result finally gave him the courage to expel Strasser from the party. He charged Ley and Hess to take over Strasser's administrative duties and the crisis was over, as far as the Nazis were concerned.

On 6 December 1932 the Reichstag reassembled and again elected Goering its President; the Nazis commanded a parliamentary majority but were excluded from the Presidential government. However, with the Strasser crisis still on, the morale was low in the party's ranks and financially it was exhausted: it could not afford another election, for that would have meant definite losses and, even if victorious, no definite prospect of power. Then the confident Schleicher, still sure of being able to check Hitler with Strasser, announced his governmental program and thus committed political suicide. He addressed himself directly to the nation, proposed to rearm Germany and re-distribute 800,000 acres of land in Northern and Eastern Prussia; he further promised to be neither capitalist nor socialist. Though the General-Chan-

Far left: **Hitler acknowledges the cheers of a crowd gathered outside the Reichschancellery the night he took power, 30 January 1933.**
Left: **Hitler's first Cabinet formed at 1830 hours on 30 January 1933. Seated are Goering, Hitler and Vice-Chancellor von Papen. Standing are Graf Schwerin von Krosigk, Dr Frick, von Blomberg and Hugenberg.**
Below: **Hitler addresses the public gathered under his window at the Reichschancellery during the torchlight parade which celebrated his seizure of power on 30 January.**

Left: **Julius Schreck closes the door of Hitler's car. Hitler traveled extensively throughout Germany to inspire local parades and rallies.**

cellor was certainly not politically naive, he was maladroit: he offended everyone and satisfied no one. His predecessor, Papen, was bitterly disappointed by the general taking over some of his planned measures, while the President was appalled by the "socialistic" land re-distribution. Thus Papen began a furious intrigue to get back to power since the general was only continuing his own policies: the President was now open to suggestions, since his favorite general had disappointed him so badly.

On 4 January 1933 Franz von Papen secretly met Adolf Hitler in the house of the Cologne banker, von Schröder. They agreed that they would bring down the Schleicher government and rule in coalition. Schröder wrote off Hitler's extensive debts and Papen went off to Berlin to put pressure on the President. As if providence had intervened, on 15 January 1933, an election took place in the mini-land Lippe-Detmold and the results were bound to strengthen Hitler's hand. Goebbels saturated the area with Nazi propaganda and Hitler spoke there in person; the resulting Nazi victory (they polled 39.6 percent) however, did not impress the intriguers, who were now joined by the Nationalist leader, Hugenberg, a sufficiently strong coalition of forces to bring about Schleicher's fall. Then, to bring pressure nearer home, Hitler organized in Berlin SA demonstrations and a huge rally in the Sportpalast where he spoke for hours. Two days later Hitler let von Papen, Dr Meissner and Oscar von Hindenburg, the President's son, know that he was willing to head a parliamentary coalition and the old President was duly informed. By this time General von Schleicher had found out that, like his predecessor, he could not govern without emergency powers and Presidential decrees, and told his erstwhile protector. This time the protector dismissed him with a curt remark that the constitution should not be violated and Schleicher was forced to resign. All this time both Schleicher and Hindenburg knew of the negotiations between Hitler, Papen and Hugenberg, and the old President was getting rather confused. While encouraging Papen to deal with Hitler he still hoped for a Papen government. On 26 January 1933 Hindenburg received leading Army generals who had warned

Left: **Hitler, with Goebbels behind, addresses thousands before him and millions at home during one of the 1932 elections.**

Above left : **Hitler greets some young admirers.**
Above : **SA cyclists parade past Hitler in Dortmund in 1933.**
Far left : **Members of the League of German Girls march for Hitler.**
Left : **Hitler Youth trumpet the Führer's arrival at a rally.**
Below : **Flags decorate Nuremberg on Party Day in 1933.**
Overleaf : **The SA at Luitpoldsheim in Nuremberg on Party Day.**

1

Adolf Hitler

2

1939

3

15
NAT.SOZ.DEUTSCHE ARBEITERPARTEI
STURMABTEILUNG

4

5

6

7

9

8

. Standard of Hitler's Bodyguard Regiment
.eibstandarte Adolf Hitler in the Waffen SS.
2. Infantry battalion flag of the Liebstandarte
Adolf Hitler Division of the Waffen SS.
3. Standard of the 15th Cavalry Regiment of the
SS (Munich).
4. SS armband.
5. Armband of a member of the NSDAP (Nazi
Party).
6. Armband of the Hitler Youth.
7. Battalion flag of the 1st SS Regiment 'Julius
Schreck'.
8. Company flag of the 1st Company of Hitler's
SA bodyguard.
9. 'Germany Awake' was the slogan on the flag
of the SS Regiment 'Julius Schreck'.
10. Political leaders' armband.
11. Armband of the Kyffauserbund, the Old
Comrades Association for veterans of World
War I.

10

11

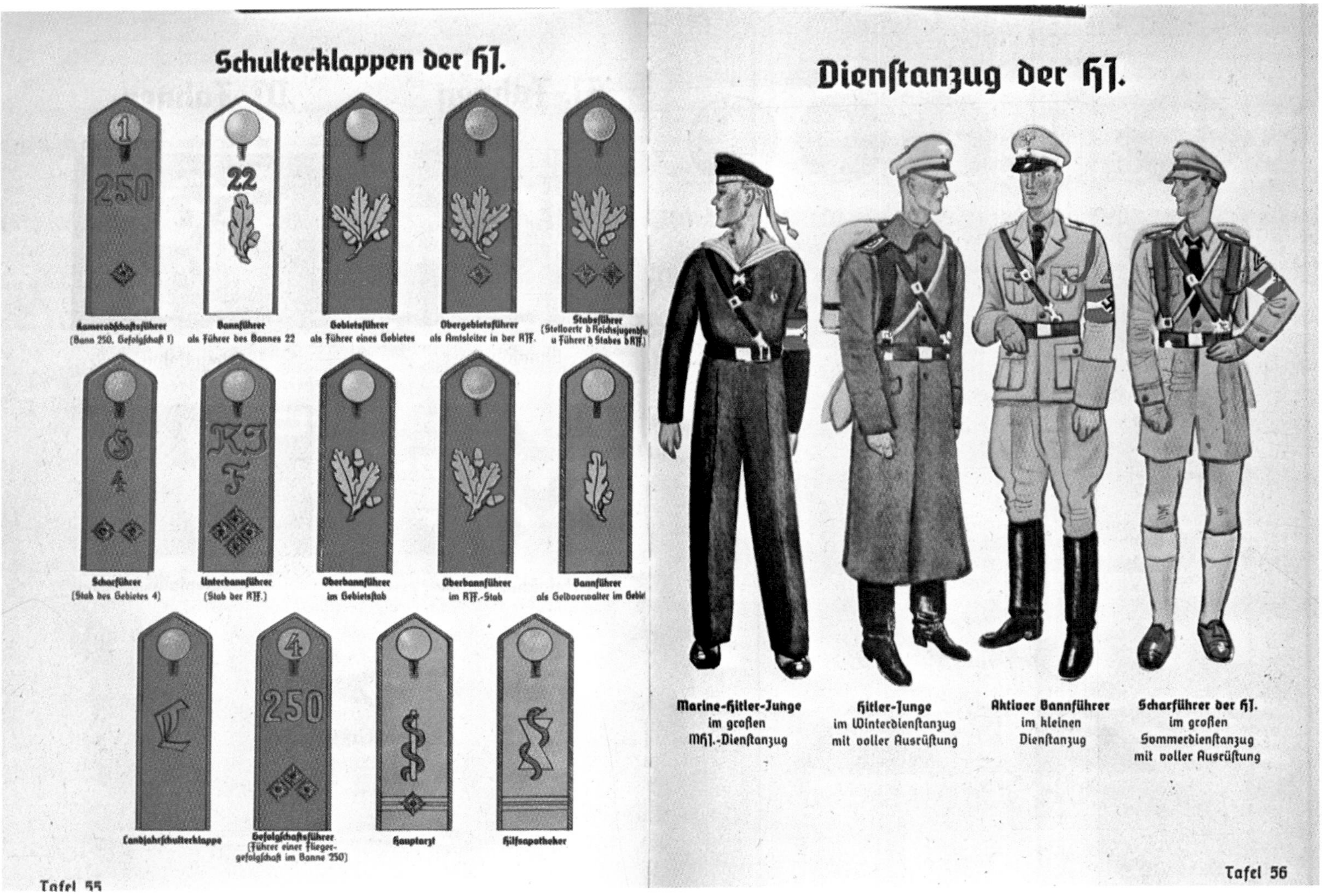

Schulterklappen der HJ.

Kameradschaftsführer
(Bann 250, Gefolgschaft 1)

Bannführer
als Führer des Bannes 22

Gebietsführer
als Führer eines Gebietes

Obergebietsführer
als Amtsleiter in der RJF.

Stabsführer
(Stellvertr. d. Reichsjugendfhr. u. Führer d. Stabes d. RJF.)

Scharführer
(Stab des Gebietes 4)

Unterbannführer
(Stab der RJF.)

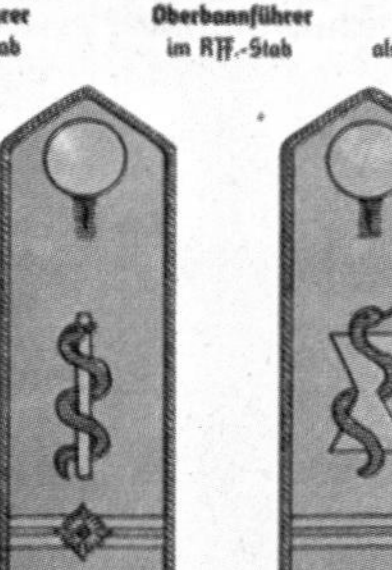

Oberbannführer
im Gebietsstab

Oberbannführer
im RJF.-Stab

Bannführer
als Geldverwalter im Gebiet

Landjahrschulterklappe

Gefolgschaftsführer
(Führer einer Flieger-gefolgschaft im Banne 250)

Hauptarzt

Hilfsapotheker

Tafel 55

Dienstanzug der HJ.

Marine-Hitler-Junge
im großen
MHJ.-Dienstanzug

Hitler-Junge
im Winterdienstanzug
mit voller Ausrüstung

Aktiver Bannführer
im kleinen
Dienstanzug

Scharführer der HJ.
im großen
Sommerdienstanzug
mit voller Ausrüstung

Tafel 56

him against another Papen government "whom the Army would have to defend against the majority of the nation." Misunderstanding them Hindenburg declared quite firmly that he would never appoint the Austrian lance corporal his Chancellor. Still two days later Hindenburg sent Papen to Hitler with an offer of Chancellorship and the Ministry of the Interior.

It is not quite clear who finally persuaded the imperial Field Marshal, and President of the Weimar Republic *malgré lui*, to accept Hitler as Chancellor, but it seems clear that the old man saw no danger in the Nazis holding two key positions in his own Presidential government provided they were hemmed in by ultra-conservatives and Nationalists: those reliable elements would not only control the wild Nazis, but would also make use of them against the left, principally the Communists. Still, even with this mistaken all-pervading confidence that the Nazi tiger could be easily ridden, the final appointment was a touch and go affair. Hitler did not mind having only two other Nazis in the government (Wilhelm Frick as Minister of the Interior and Goering as Prussian Minister of the Interior) but he wanted an immediate election which he was certain to win since he would have the state controlled communication media under his own control. Hugenberg resisted this demand till the last moment and only gave in in the President's ante-room, while waiting to be sworn in on 30 January 1933. Ultimately with him Papen was sworn in as Vice-Chancellor and Commissioner for Prussia, General Werner von Blomberg as Minister of Defense, Count Schwerin von Krosigk as Minister of Finance, Baron Konstantin von Neurath as Minister of Foreign Affairs: nine Nationalists to three Nazis. Thus after long years of weak and unpopular government Germany had a strong and broadly based ruling body and throughout the country popular enthusiasm was expressed in massive torchlight processions. In Berlin the SA and the *Stahlhelm* marched with their torches for hours on end and this victory parade not only satisfied the new Chancellor, Hitler, who watched it and greeted it from the window of the Chancellery building, but also the old President, who watched it from his window beating time with his stick to the accompanying martial music.

Above left : **Insignia and uniforms of the HJ (Hitler Youth).**
Below left : **The HJ listen intently.**
Below : **Bavarians at a Nazi rally.**
Above right : **Poster appeals to children to support Hitler.**

Apart from these two immediate causes for the Weimar Republic's collapse, many others, of equal importance, must be listed when analyzing the end of the democratic régime in Germany. Of capital importance for democracy in Germany was the fact that it was born in an acute crisis, namely as a result of a lost war. It can be said that it was in fact adopted in order to avoid the harsh consequences of the defeat. In this respect the Germans were disappointed, for the peace treaty appeared to them as harsh considering that it came from one democracy to another – then they were quickly disappointed by the working of their democratic system as well. To start with the régime could only survive thanks to the imperial power, the Army. It continued to exist largely because the imperial civil service kept it from lapsing into complete anarchy. In fact all the pillars of imperial power continued as before, generally hostile to the new democratic republic.

Compared to these shaken but still solid imperial powers, the new democratic institutions, especially the Reichstag, proved very quickly disunited, often irresponsible, sometimes corrupt, and basically unable to tackle real problems in Germany. Parliamentarians turned out to be a drab lot incapable of giving leadership or even inspiring confidence. The first President lacked luster, honest trade unionist that he was; the second was a nostalgic imperial servant.

The system made up of the most diametrically opposed forces might have survived, had it not to face two of the most acute world crises, the world economic depression and a general crisis of parliamentary democracy all over the world. Its inability to cope provoked the most virulent nationalism that Germany ever experienced. The final result was the Nazi whirlwind and Hitler. The year 1933 was a landmark for Germany and the world.

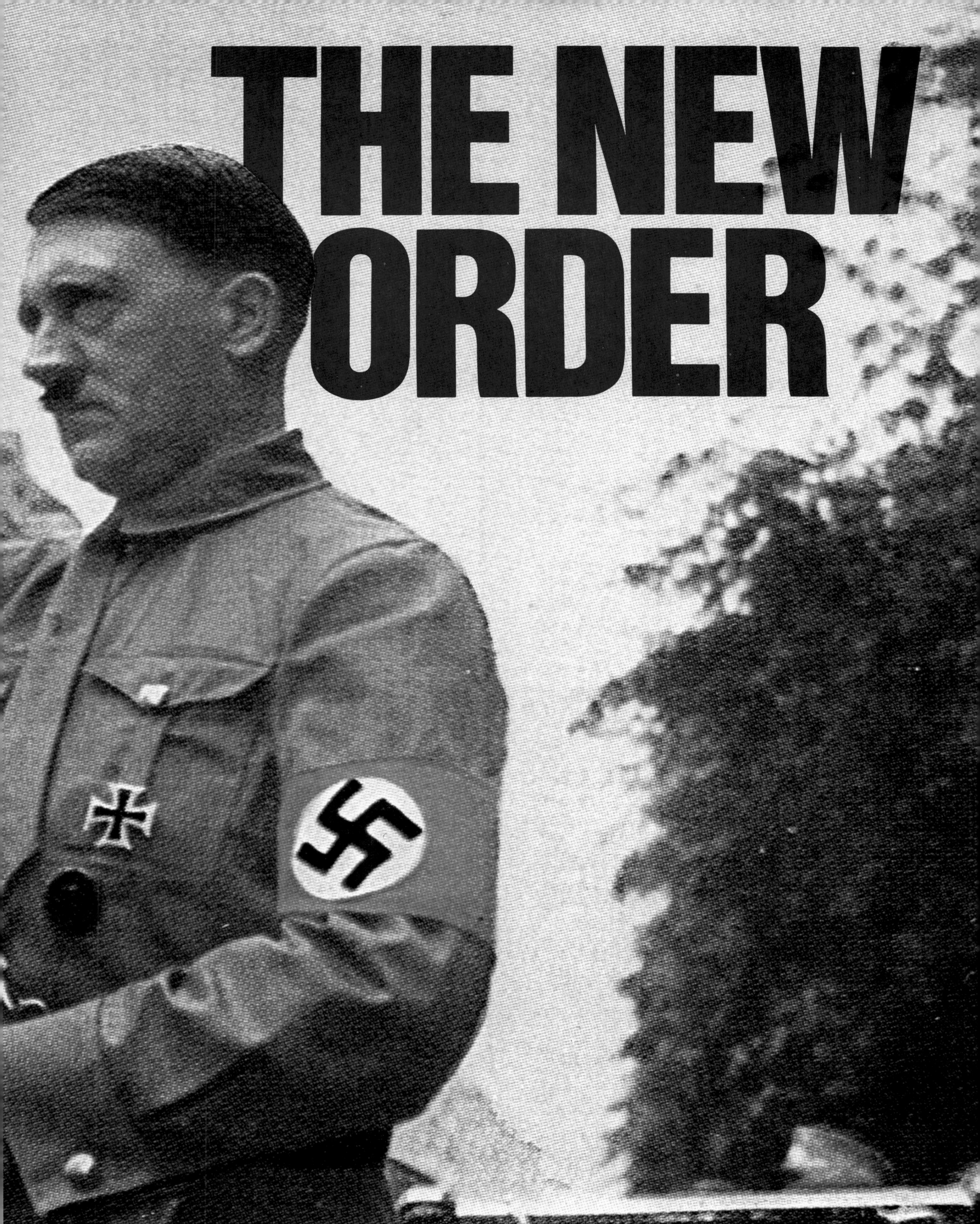
THE NEW
ORDER

HITLER AS CHANCELLOR

Paradoxically although much rejoicing followed Hitler's appointment as Chancellor, there was hardly any despondency among the opposition. After all Hitler was a "legally" appointed Chancellor and it was argued that when he had failed to solve Germany's problems he would be "legally" dismissed like so many of his predecessors and replaced by someone else. With hindsight this was another collossal miscalculation that German politicians were committing, similar to the ridiculous miscalculation of Hitler's allies that good use could be made of the Nazis. Only much later did people realize that once in power it would take a gigantic upheaval to get the Nazis out. Indeed the very first measures taken by the Nazis after they came to power were certainly meant to perpetuate their power: Goering, who was the Prussian Minister of the Interior and therefore responsible for immediate security in Berlin and elsewhere, dismissed 22 out of 32 police presidents; thousands of policemen were simultaneously purged and members of the SA drafted instead. (Goering, however, dismissed them as soon as they had performed their "dirty" duties). In addition Goering issued orders

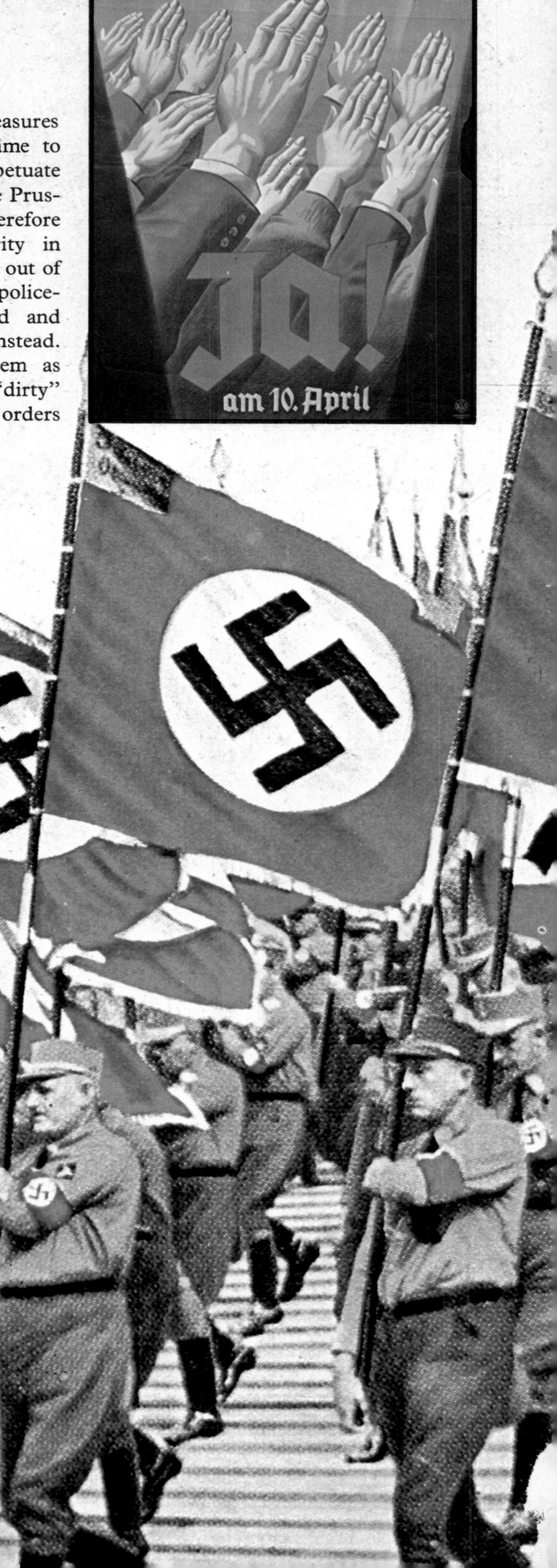

Left: **Election poster of April 1933 urges voters to opt for a Greater Germany in choosing Hitler. It was the last free election in Germany until after the war.**
Below: **The SA parade their banners in Nuremberg on Party Day in 1933.**

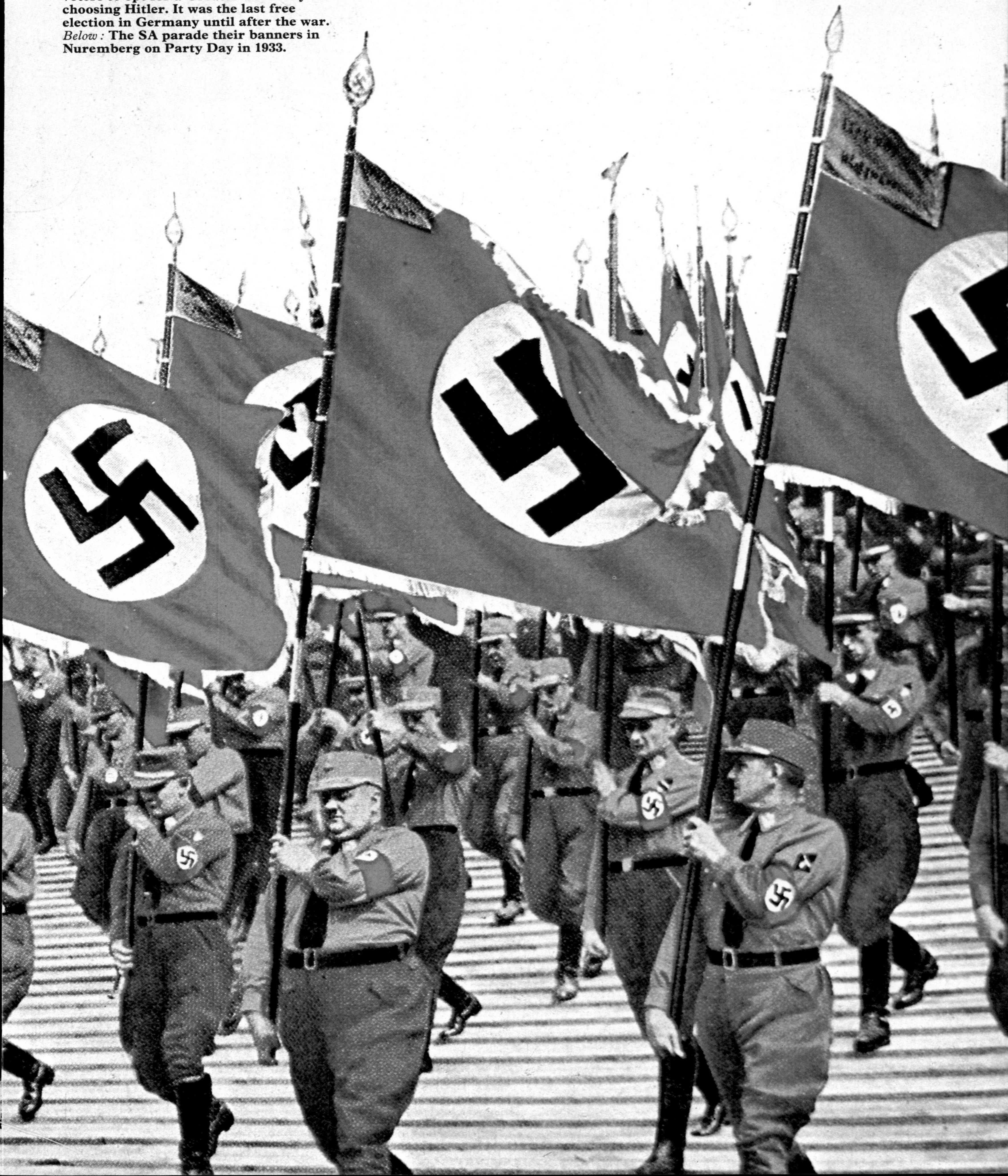

Above left: **"The Eternal Jew" was the title of this blatantly anti-Semitic propaganda film.**
Above: **President von Hindenburg and his Chancellor.**
Left: **Hitler, von Hindenburg and Goering at the Battle of Tannenberg memorial in August 1933.**

to the police to show no mercy to the enemies of the state and use firearms if necessary. On 26 April 1933 he also established the Secret State Police (the notorious Gestapo) to carry out arrests and interrogations of political suspects, which henceforth held all the power of the judiciary in its own hands making the latter (courts, procurators) superfluous. Still, while making sure that they could not be ejected from power, the Nazis were careful not to offend their coalition partners. Of the 50,000 auxiliary policemen drafted in by Goering, 10,000 were drawn from the *Stahlhelm* and Admiral von Leventzow, a non-Nazi became the Police President of Berlin. However even with these carefully calculated moves Goering quickly offended his conservative allies. Baron von Neurath called him a dreadful thug – a real fascist, and Papen complained that he could not control him at all. Thus, for example, Goering put the head of the Berlin SS, Kurt Daluege, a refuse disposal engineer, in charge of the Prussian police force and appointed Rudolf Diels, a cousin by marriage, as head of the political section of the police (future Gestapo). In vain did Papen protest. It was obvious that the Nazis were in politics for good and would not observe the rules of the Weimar Republic.

With some 3 million members of the SA, Hitler and the Nazis could even challenge the *Reichswehr* if such a situation arose. In

Right: **"Blood and Soil" was one of the slogans used for a Farmers' Day celebration in Goslar in 1937. This program encouraged people to stay on the land.**

the event, Hitler absolutely refused to do anything against this instrument of power, once he held it under his control. The new Defense Minister, General von Blomberg, was a bitter enemy of the dismissed Schleicher and was influenced in favor of the Nazis not only by his Chief of Staff, but also by his chaplain. In any case many army officers were most enthusiastic about the Nazis, (among these were the future conspirators against Hitler, Ludwig Beck and Henning von Tresckow). Moreover less than a week after becoming Chancellor Hitler convoked his generals and representatives of the Navy and spoke to them about future policies. He repeated his old dictum that the *Reichswehr* would be the only armed body of the state and then unfolded to them his vision of the expansion in the East and its merciless germanization. All the assembled officers pledged him, there and then, their enthusiastic loyalty. On 1 March 1933 General von Blomberg issued a directive to the officers' corps in which he openly supported the Nazis and he renewed this support in June 1933. Keeping the Army satisfied became Hitler's primary task and for it he was prepared to sacrifice even his own party and its armed force, the SA.

More immediately Hitler and the Nazis applied themselves to the business of elections and Goebbels and the SA monopolized the means of communication and won the streets. Fifty-one people were killed during the election campaign, which was no more nor less turbulent than the previous ones. However the Nazis were given an additional pretext for smashing their opponents when less than a week before the election the Reichstag building was burnt down. Controversy still surrounds the burning of the Reichstag, but there is a large consensus among historians that the fire was started by a half-crazed Dutch former Communist, Marinus van der Lubbe and that the Nazis made use of it to claim that it was part of an anti-state conspiracy which had to be suppressed. On the following day the President signed an emergency decree for the protection of the people and the state which in fact suspended all civil liberties. Van der Lubbe was arrested in *flagranti delicto* and other suspects followed. The Communist Deputy Torgler presented himself to the police while the Bulgarian Communist agents,

Right: **Hitler and Goebbels at a rally in Stuttgart in 1933.**

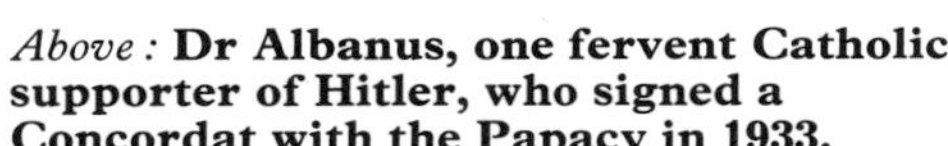

Above: **Dr Albanus, one fervent Catholic supporter of Hitler, who signed a Concordat with the Papacy in 1933.**

Above: **Hitler, Siebert and the Papal Nuncio Vasallo di Torregrossa attend the opening of the House of German Art in October 1933.**

Georgi Dimitrov, Popov and Tanev were easily apprehended, although they were the secret agents of this international Communist conspiracy. It is certain that the conspiracy existed only in Nazi minds – Torgler and the three were found not guilty subsequently – but Goebbels used the pretext to suppress the Communist and Social Democratic press. Still the election results proved disappointing. The Nazis polled 44 percent and their nationalist allies 8 percent. Though they had an arithmetic majority in the Reichstag, they did not have the two-thirds majority necessary to change the constitution in order to govern Germany in their own way. However the emergency decree came to their aid and they disqualified the 81 elected Communists from sitting in the Reichstag.

The formal death of the Weimar Republic came two weeks after the election. On 23 March 1933 the newly elected Reichstag assembled temporarily in the Kroll opera house to pronounce itself on the one major piece of legislation, the Enabling Bill, which would give Hitler's government full powers for four years to destroy "the red peril and consolidate the national revolution." In the absence of the Communists only the Social Democrats, who were admitted to the vote, opposed the bill. Their leader, Otto Wels, made a dignified speech in which he warned the assembled politicians and Germany at large. However, when the vote was taken, all the other parties, even the Catholic Center, voted for it: 441 to 94. Thus the Weimar Republic was voted out of existence, the Reichstag voted itself out of power (in 1937 the Act was formally renewed) and the politicians voted themselves out of politics. Wels left immediately for exile, followed by Brüning and Monsignor Kaas; others swiftly disappeared into concentration camps set up specially to house the victims of the Enabling Act. But it must remain on record that Hitler was legally given a free hand to deal with his opponents and friends.

The first moves to consolidate power in the Nazi hands came even before the Enabling Act was passed. On 8 March 1933 a Nazi Reichskommissar, Franz Ritter von Epp, took over power in Bavaria ousting the elected Catholic Premier, Heinrich Held. Held only managed a token of resistance, when he appealed to the Munich district Army Commander, General Wilhelm von Leeb, who declined to act on his behalf after receiving orders from Berlin. On 10 March a *Reichsstatthalter* (Governor) had taken over Saxony, Wür-

Below: **Horst Wessel leads storm troopers in Nuremberg in 1929. After his death he was immortalized as a martyred hero.**

Left : **Poster commemorating the 10th anniversary of the founding of the Nazi Students' League in 1936.**
Above : **A rally in Coburg in 1932 with stewards of the SA.**
Below left : **Goebbels arrives to a garlanded welcome at the grassy Königsberg airfield.**
Below : **Some of the 100,000 SA men who gathered at Nuremberg for Party Day.**

Left: **"If you save five marks a week, you can own your own car" says this poster urging the German public to save for their new Volkswagen.**
Above: **Poster rallying support for the Nazis from the whole family.**

temberg and Thuringia, while the mini-lands followed suit at the end of the month. Since Prussia was already under Goering's unconstitutional control, the German federation was in fact dissolved and the process which was called the *Gleichschaltung* (Streamlining) resulted in fact in the Nazification of these administrative units and historical states. Local Nazis – sometimes *Gauleiteren* – were appointed Governors with powers to dismiss and nominate civil servants and police officers. Next in the *Gleichschaltung* came the trade unions. The Catholic Trade Union leader, Stegerweld, was beaten up during the election campaign as well as many other lesser trade unionists. The violence exhibited by the SS and SA towards trade unionists prompted the Trade Union Congress Chairman, Theodor Leipart, to issue a letter of protest and an appeal for protection to the President. No protection came from the Head of State, but Nazi vengeance was swift. They had previously declared 1 May as the National Labor Day. It was celebrated by all and sundry without political distinction. However on 2 May the SA broke into and occupied all left-wing trade union offices, arrested their leaders and officials and sent most of them into concentration camps. In June 1933 Christian trade unions received the same treatment and the Nazis instead, created the German Labor Front. Both employers and employees were forced to join this front whose function was to conciliate rather than advance demands.

Once Hitler finished with the Reichstag he had no use for the parties of which it was composed. The Communist party was dissolved before the election and its elected deputies were put *en masse* into "protective custody" and sent to a concentration camp for the duration. On 22 June 1933 the Social Democratic party was dissolved as an anti-state, subversive body and its property confiscated. A week later the German Nationalist Party attracted the wrath of the SA by organizing its own paramilitary formations. When the SA moved against these Green Shirts, the Nationalist leader, Hugenberg, resigned from the government and the party dissolved itself. Early in July the Catholic Center went into voluntary liquidation, followed by the People's Party and Bavarian People's Party. Thereafter the government decreed (Act of 14 July 1933) that Germany was a One-Party state and the formation of any other party was judged a treasonable act punishable by imprisonment. The ease with which Hitler disposed of the trade unions and political parties conclusively proved how decayed these bodies must have become and how badly led they must have been.

Gleichschaltung was carried out not only in the power sphere but affected the whole of national life. As was usual with Hitler even racial *Gleichschaltung* was sanctioned by the law, albeit retrospectively. On 1 April 1933 the vitriolic anti-Semite Julius Streicher proclaimed a nation-wide boycott of Jewish shops and was most efficient-

Right: **"Mother and Child" was the slogan on this poster. The Nazis encouraged large families and paid bounties to those willing to have children.**

ly backed by gangs of SA men who enforced it. In response to these pressures some 235,000 Jews departed from Germany leaving the field of German science somewhat denuded. However in Germany Jews were expelled wholesale from all the liberal professions, be it medicine, law, journalism, fine arts, radio, cinema, music or civil service. Jewish university professors had their lectures disrupted by fanatical students and simply had to abandon their profession. Still the complex anti-Jewish legislation was passed only on 15 September 1935 (the Nuremberg Laws) and Jewish property was "legally" confiscated on 3 December 1938. From the very beginning the Jews were subjected to naked terror which increased with time (Crystal Night 1938), until it culminated in the "final solution" in 1941 when they were to be all physically liquidated.

Only with the Communists was Hitler prepared to go as far as with the Jews, but even with them the *Gleichschaltung*-liquidation was applied gradually so as not to alarm domestic or international public opinion. The ultimate fate of the Christian Churches would probably have been the same as that of the Jews and Communists. During the war Alfred Rosenberg made it clear when he drew up the National Reich Church Program which proposed to replace the Bible by *Mein Kampf* and the Cross by the swastika – only a few rites were to be retained albeit in adapted form. The Catholic Church, which on the whole resisted the Nazis more successfully than the Protestant Churches, was treated with disdain. When Schulze, Cardinal-Archbishop of Cologne, protested against SA and SS brutalities in 1933, he was ignored. On 20 July 1933 Hitler signed a Concordat with the Vatican and immediately broke it: arrests of priests and nuns continued unabated, while many Catholic laymen found themselves in the numerous concentration camps. By 14 March 1937, Pius XI openly lamented the state of the Church in Nazi Germany.

With the Protestant Churches, which were disunited, the damage inflicted by the Nazis was immeasurably greater. In 1933 the Conference of Protestant Churches was declared illegal and the German Christians, a group of some 3000 pastors

Right: **Hitler votes in Königsberg in the election of April 1933. On the right is Sepp Dietrich, his personal bodyguard, who became an SS General and commanded the Sixth Panzer Army during World War II.**

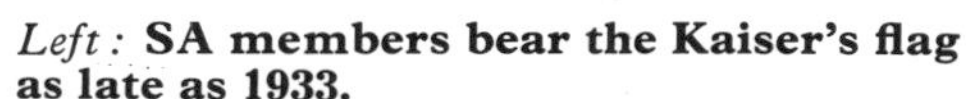

Left : **SA members bear the Kaiser's flag as late as 1933.**
Above : **"All Germany Listens to the Führer" was the slogan on this poster.**
Above center : **"Workers Choose the Front Soldier Hitler."**
Above right : **Women with unemployed husbands and hungry children were encouraged to vote for Hitler with this poster.**

(out of 17,000), were encouraged to take over; this was supposed to be a church *Gleichschaltung*. While the German Christians supported Nazi racial policies only, another group, the Confessional Church wanted to go the whole way and support the Nazis in everything. They argued that Luther was not only a Jew-hater but also an upholder of political power; since power was now in the hands of the Nazis they had to be supported. Soon, however, the Nazis and their sympathizers overreached themselves when they wanted to impose on the synod gathered at Wittenberg a new Reich bishop. Pastor Martin Niemöller, formerly a German Christian, formed a resistance group which gradually neutralized the other factions. By 1937 the Protestant Churches began a process of re-unification and the Nazis arrested and imprisoned not only Niemöller but over 800 pastors as well. By the spring of 1938 most of the remaining clergy swore allegiance to Hitler and the Protestants were deemed "coordinated."

In the sphere of culture the *Gleichschaltung* was instant. On 10 May 1933 bonfires were started with proscribed books of anti-Nazi writers. In September 1933 the Reichs Chamber of Culture was set up under the new Minister of Propaganda, Dr Goebbels, and henceforth all manuscripts had to be submitted to the ministry before they could be published. As a result almost all the writers of any standing emigrated and Germany was left with party hacks whose works were foisted on the public – at this time Hitler's *Mein Kampf* finally sold in millions and he became a writer-millionaire, which was rare in Germany. Although composers were much less bullied they were forced to sever all relations with Jewish and anti-Nazi friends; otherwise they found themselves unperformed. In fine arts in which Hitler took a personal interest some 6500 "decadent" paintings were removed from German museums and art galleries. Later on Hitler personally selected German paintings which were exhibited in the House of German Art in Munich but attendance was low. On the contrary the Ministry of Propaganda's exhibition of "degenerate" art proved so embarrassingly popular that it had to be closed down.

The left-wing press was suppressed even before the March election; when Goebbels set up his Propaganda Ministry all the newspapers were published under the auspices of this Ministry: daily instructions supplemented by oral orders were issued. After 230 years the *Vössische Zeitung* closed down as it found it impos-

Right : **Goebbels leaves a polling station in Berlin after voting in the 1933 election. The posters proclaim "Führer, We Follow Thee."**

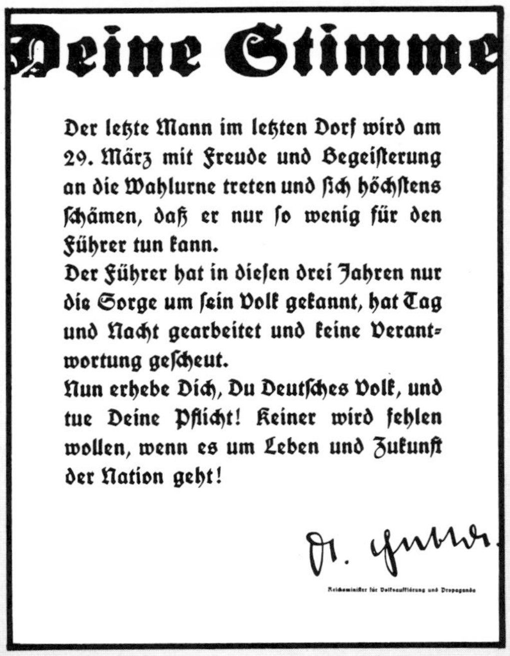

Deine Stimme

Der letzte Mann im letzten Dorf wird am 29. März mit Freude und Begeisterung an die Wahlurne treten und sich höchstens schämen, daß er nur so wenig für den Führer tun kann.

Der Führer hat in diesen drei Jahren nur die Sorge um sein Volk gekannt, hat Tag und Nacht gearbeitet und keine Verantwortung gescheut.

Nun erhebe Dich, Du Deutsches Volk, und tue Deine Pflicht! Keiner wird fehlen wollen, wenn es um Leben und Zukunft der Nation geht!

Dr. Goebbels

Reichsminister für Volksaufklärung und Propaganda

Above: **Poster signed by Goebbels tells Germans that it is their duty to support Hitler in the 1935 election.**
Right: **Goering, Darré, Hitler and Krause at a rally in Bückeburg in 1934.**

sible to work in such conditions. As newspapers became "co-ordinated" and their contents hardly differed from that of the official party newspapers *Völkischer Beobachter*, their circulation steeply declined and they went bankrupt. Subsequently they were bought by the giant party publishing house, the *Eher Verlag*, and the party enjoyed a practical monopoly of the press.

In education, although purges were immediately put in hand, the Nazis tried to implement long-term policies. Bernhard Rust, the teacher-*Gauleiter*, became Reichsminister of science, education and popular culture and immediately ordered all textbooks to be re-written in the Nazi spirit; overnight he had changed school and university curricula. However the teaching profession was hardly touched by the Nazis – after the initial expulsion of Jewish and left-wing elements – and faithfully served the Nazis throughout their reign. Professors of medicine became particularly compromised – some of them serving not as savers of life but exterminators of the feeble, incurable and "inferior" races (Gypsies, Jews). Hardly anyone opposed the Nazis who ordered these abject timeservers to invent Germanic physics, mathematics, jurisprudence and even natural sciences. In 1937 the Civil Service Act made the teaching profession the executor of the will of the Party-state and the perilous state of education was exemplified by the halving of the student population in the six years that followed the Nazis' seizure of power.

In youth organization the *Gleichschaltung* meant a wholesale takeover of all youth organization by the Nazi youth movement, the *Hitler Jugend*; the half-American Baldur von Schirach became its leader. The Nazis seized the national offices of the Youth Association and dissolved the Catholic Youth Association; the rest were incorporated into the *Hitler Jugend*. By 1938 the *Hitler Jugend* amounted to some 7 million members; since some 4 million young people stayed out of this organization, its membership became compulsory. All youth, boys and girls between 6–18

Above: **Hitler queries Dr Todt about the construction of the autobahn while Hitler's aides Krause and Brückner listen intently.**
Below: **Hitler inspects the new section of the Leipzig autobahn which represented over 1000 miles of motorway constructed by 1937.**

Above left: **Hitler inaugurates the construction of the autobahn in 1933 as Julius Streicher, Dr Todt, whose** *Organisation Todt* **supervized construction, and Dr Ley observe.**
Above: **Architectural design for Berlin at Munich's House of German Art in 1938.**
Left: **Model for the entrance to the autobahn near Salzburg on the Austrian border.**

had to join and were organized in a para-military manner, indoctrinated and marched up and down Germany. The results of this youthful indoctrination are incalculable even nowadays.

In the economic sphere the Nazis, owing to Hitler's own confusion, did not have the least idea how to create a boom. Here Hitler had the good fortune of reaping the results of measures taken by his predecessors, Brüning and Papen, and of putting in charge of the economy an experienced expert, Dr Schacht. Still the resulting economic order was somewhat new and the Nazis claimed uniquely their own. Thus no nationalizations were operated in Germany, but the capitalists lost their freedom of investment and fixing prices and wages. In addition Dr Schacht proclaimed two four-year economic plans, one to run from 1933–7 whose aim was to revive the economy and eliminate unemployment. The second was to run from 1937 to 1941 by which time Germany was to achieve autarky. In effect Dr Schacht began to revive the economy by large-scale public works (prepared by Brüning and put into effect by Papen). Schacht's original contribution was the way in which he financed the program: he issued special bills of exchange repayable in five years and easily achieved his objectives. While in 1933 there were six million unemployed, in 1935 there was one million left and by

1939 there was a labor shortage. To start with, the unemployed were put into the *Arbeitsdienst* (Labor Service) and they began to build a new system of expressways. Subsequently Schacht had it easy because the Nazis cowed trade unions; he could direct labor wherever it was needed and had wages and prices under his control. The economy was also helped by the re-introduction of military service, expansion of the civil service and party administration, while women vacated many jobs when they began to get increased family allowances. Although there were large investments in equipment, the fastest expanding sector of the economy became the armament industry, for Hitler immediately rejected the Versailles Treaty limitations. Naturally a lot of money had to be printed, but with import restrictions and confiscation of Jewish capital the first four-year plan was a success. However from the very beginning in 1933, this was a war economy, which some argue, inevitably led to war: therefore in political terms the economic success was reversed. During the second four-year plan (Schacht resigned in 1937 and was replaced by a party hack, Walter Funk) serious failures became apparent; still by 1939 Germany was better prepared for war than any of its enemies, whose economies, either capitalist or Communist, did not undergo the Nazi treatment.

In agriculture the Nazis proved inconsistent and even less successful than in industry. In 1933 farmers solidly backed the Nazis after a decade of slump, but when Walter Darré became Minister of Agriculture and began to exercise pressure in favor of the agricultural interests coming down, he was promptly silenced by Hitler and the Nazis never touched that problem again, although loan repayments were most oppressive and amounted to some 14 percent of the farmers' income. The Nazis also failed to distribute land to smallholders leaving the large feudal estates intact. Darré did enact two useful laws: one prevented further division of land (Hereditary Farm Act) and the other regulated farm production (Reich Food Estate Act). But after the numerous promises that he had made to the farmers his achievements were minor indeed. Although agricultural production aimed at self-sufficiency, Germany by 1938 still depended on imports (some 17 percent of its consumption).

The Nazification of the government was the smoothest of all. On 14 March 1933 Hitler named his new cabinet, and he retained all the non-Nazi ministers, as he

Above : **Hitler proudly points out aspects of his model of Berlin, with Heinz Hoffman and Robert Ley on the Führer's left.**

Below : **Hitler gloats over his model of Berlin in 1938 in the presence of an Italian general, Altolico, and an architect, Dr Dolmetscher.**

Above: **Hitler and Röhm study a document a few months before Hitler gave the order to have him purged. Röhm was shot by two SS men.**
Left: **Munich's Königsplatz was the scene of a Nazi rally commemorating the Beer Hall** *Putsch* **on 9 November 1935.**

Above: **Ernst Röhm, SA Chief of Staff, who was killed in the Night of the Long Knives of 30 June 1934. The plot to eliminate Röhm was masterfully executed.**

had promised, particularly to Hugenberg. The only addition seemed Dr Goebbels who headed a new Ministry of Propaganda and Culture. Significantly Papen, although he retained the Vice-Chancellorship, lost the *Reichskommissariat* of Prussia. Hitler made himself *Reichsstatthalter* of Prussia; he then delegated all powers to Goering. The Nazis were formally in charge of the most important state which Goering properly Nazified. In 1933 it was still unclear how this "nationalist" coalition would work, and Hitler only made it clear after June-July 1934. As it was, he did not need the President, since he had full powers to rule by decree himself, and he only rarely bothered to see him. Since he conceived the full powers as being given by the Reichstag to him personally, he not only dispensed with the Reichstag, but also with individual Ministers. After all it was the Nazi Party backed by the crude force of the SA and SS which was running everything in Germany, so why should Hitler trouble himself about his political allies? The government continued to meet erratically but no vote was taken on policies invariably announced by the Führer. In June 1933 Hitler had to get rid of Hugenberg who thought that the government should be run differently and also dared to protest to the President. Hugenberg's Ministries were handed over to the Nazis. Darré took over the Ministry of Food and Agriculture, while Dr Kurt Schmitt was given the Ministry of the Economy. Subsequently Gereke and Seldte were also dismissed and Hitler strengthened his hand in the government, lest he needed it, by appointing Rudolf Hess and Ernst Röhm as Ministers without Portfolio. If Hitler paid not the slightest attention to the ministers of his cabinet, the appointment of Röhm was nevertheless of great significance. Röhm, the Head of the SA, the thugs who were *de facto* Nazifying Germany, was left out of positions of power until December 1933. Throughout the summer of 1933 he complained about Hitler's *Machtergreifung und Evolution*, while he would have preferred *Revolution*. Since his SAs were doing most of the dirty work he wanted some recompense for his underpaid three millions. Above all he wanted their position regularized by having them included in the *Reichswehr* with corresponding ranks. Thus his appointment could only mean that he was intended to counter-balance the Minister of Defense, von Blomberg, and ultimately perhaps take over from him. In addition, the SA as a whole, while very busy enforcing the Nazification of Germany, mumbled increasingly loudly about the second revolution along socialist lines, so dear to Hitler in the early days of his movement.

Thus difficulties with Röhm and his SAs were the only real problem that Hitler encountered after coming to power: it could not be ignored and it would not go away as others had done. After much hesitation Hitler decided to solve the problem by force. The SA had always been turbulent, uncontrollable, mutinous and above all they began to irritate the only institution that Hitler wanted to leave intact and non-Nazified, the *Reichswehr*. By the end of 1933 violence was no longer needed from the SA and Hitler thought that Röhm would be satisfied with his ministerial position. For the time Röhm seemed content, but the SA as a whole continued to voice ideas about a real Socialist revolution. The objects of their hatred were threefold: the middle class,

Left: **Berlin's police force parade their swastika banner in the Lustgarten in 1935.**
Right: **Hitler in a planning session in 1935 with his deputy, Rudolf Hess, on his right. Also present are von Epp, Sauckel and Funk.**

HAUS ELEPHANT
Koch

Left: **Hitler guarded by the SS enters the Reichstag to deliver a speech in February 1938.**
Above: **Hitler, with Sepp Dietrich behind him, salutes the Leibstandarte, his personal guard, after its formation in 1935.**

the Junkers and the *Reichswehr*. On 28 February 1934 Hitler deemed it politic to issue a warning to the SA and also make his position clear *vis à vis* the *Reichswehr*: "the revolution was finished and the only people entitled to bear arms were the *Reichswehr*." However instead of calming down the situation, Hitler's declaration only irritated the SA to such an extent that the *Reichswehr* became restless. Tensions culminated in June 1934 and at the end of that month Hitler decided to solve the SA problem once and for all: the Night of Long Knives took place.

It was the SA who always dreamt of using their long knives on their petty opponents, the bourgeoisie, Junkers and officers. As it turned out it was their party comrades, the SS, who put their knives to good use on them. In June 1934 rumors of another revolution reached such a pitch that the Vice-Chancellor, Franz von Papen, decided to make a public declaration on the subject. While Hitler was on a lightning visit to Mussolini in Venice, Papen addressed the University at Marburg in a speech in which he claimed that there would be no more revolution and henceforth the Christian principles would be applied in national life. This open call excited the SA no end, but also disquieted the dying President and the Army. On his return from Italy Hitler went directly to Neudeck where the President was in residence, ostensibly to report on his foreign visit but really to calm the President and the Army. Blomberg, who was also at Neudeck, told Hitler that the Army "would restore order if necessary." However Hitler now decided to take the matter into his own hands.

It was at this time that Reichsführer SS, Heinrich Himmler, (who was an unknown in politics) told Hitler that Röhm was plotting his downfall and offered Hitler the SS to liquidate the plot. Whether Hitler believed him is immaterial, but since he had to solve the SA problem, he gratefully accepted Himmler's offer. The rumor of the Röhm plot was skillfully released; the Army also knew about it. On 25 June General Werner von Fritsch, the Army's Commander-in-Chief, put his troops on alert to prevent the SA from seizing power, but Hitler already had matters well in hand. All the actors in this bloody drama were affecting innocence and Röhm agreed to meet Hitler at Bad Wiessee on 30 June 1934; in the meantime he sent his SA troopers on a vacation. Hitler gave plenary powers to Goering and Himmler who, aided by Reinhard Heydrich, drew up the lists of people to be liquidated in the coming purge, for at the last moment Hitler decided not only to square his accounts with the SA, but also to avenge himself on all the other opponents from the past: the conspiracy was enlarged and included even foreign powers (France). On 29 June General von Blomberg stated in the *Völkischer Beobachter* that the Army was behind Hitler, as if to reassure him. At the same time Goebbels confirmed the conspiracy by accusing the Berlin SA leader, Ernst, of planning a *putsch*. On 30 June the purge was launched.

On that day Hitler, accompanied by Victor Lutze, the SA Hanover leader, who was earmarked to take over from Röhm, and by Dietrich, his press spokesman, left by plane for Munich. In Munich, where the *putsch* was supposed to take place, the SA did march in the streets on the previous evening, invited to do so by forged handbills. The SA leaders were

Far left: **Hitler and Hess review a parade of the Leibstandarte Adolf Hitler in Weimar in 1936.**
Left: **The Leibstandarte Adolf Hitler goosesteps past Hitler on his birthday, 20 April 1938.**

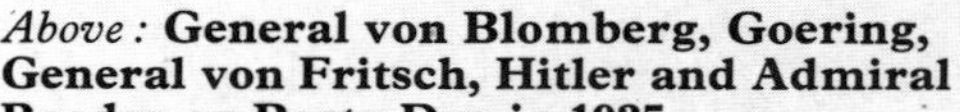

Above: **General von Blomberg, Goering, General von Fritsch, Hitler and Admiral Raeder on Party Day in 1935.**

somewhat confused, but ultimately managed to get the troopers off the streets. On landing in Munich Hitler ordered the arrest of the SA Munich leader, Schneidhuber, and he himself rushed off to Bad Wiessee, where the top SA leaders were waiting for him. As they arrived Hitler's SS bodyguard found the SA leaders, who were all homosexuals, installed in a comfortable hotel, sleeping, some of them with their male companions. The SS shot Edmund Heines dead on the spot, arrested the rest and drove them off to prison in Munich. On that day some 150 leaders were arrested and summarily executed; SS execution squads were kept busy throughout the three days of the weekend. Röhm refused to commit suicide and was executed by two SS men. Three *Obergruppenführers*, Heines, von Krausser and Schneidhuber, died executed as did the SA leaders from Saxony and Pomerania, Hayn and von Haydebreck; Ernst of Berlin was taken off a boat at Bremen before he had time to leave for his honeymoon and was executed in Berlin semi-conscious and with a *Heil Hitler* on his lips. However Hitler seems to have made use of this opportunity to rid himself of anyone who had annoyed him in the past: General von Schleicher and his wife, General von Bredow and Gregor Strasser who allegedly were the pivots of the Röhm conspiracy. Vice-Chancellor von Papen had his office wrecked; two of his staff, Edgar Jung the author of his Marburg speech and Herbert von Bose, another of his advisers, were executed in the office; Papen himself was kept for four days under house arrest protected by the dying President. Immediately after the purge he resigned from the government and was sent by Hitler to Vienna as his special envoy. Many Catholic leaders were assassinated, among them the chairman of the Catholic Action, Erich Klausener. The victims also comprised Fr Stempfle, who once corrected grammatical mistakes in the proofs of *Mein Kampf*;

Right: **Hitler and his henchmen listen to a speech on Party Day in 1938, Streicher, Goering, Kerrl and von Epp sit to the Führer's right; Goebbels, Ley, Schwarz, Himmler and Lutze on his left.**
Below: **Spades are presented by the Reichs Labor Corps on Party Day in 1935.**

Ritter von Kahr, retired *Reichs Kommissar* of Bavaria, who refused to join Hitler's *putsch* in 1923; and by some terrible mistake the music critic of a Munich newspaper, Dr Willi Schmid. In his speech to the Reichstag which Hitler summoned on 13 July, he claimed that 77 conspirators were executed. In spite of this claim there must have been many more executions: in Silesia 44 people were shot at Breslau, and 32 in the rest of the province. At Hirschberg a group of Jews was executed for no other reason than to amuse the local SS leaders. German emigré sources put the number of victims at 400; nowadays it is thought that over 1000 were assassinated during this fateful weekend.

As soon as the bloodletting was over, on 2 July President Hindenburg from his death-bed thanked Chancellor Hitler for saving Germany from the conspiracy. On 3 July General Blomberg echoed the gratitude of the *Reichswehr*. On the same day a governmental decree counter-signed by the Vice-Chancellor laconically justified the executions as self-defense thus making them legal. At the time this bloody purge was considered as the President's victory over the rowdy SA; if it was Hindenburg's victory it was shortlived, for he died on 1 August. It was also thought a victory for the *Reichswehr*; in fact with hindsight it appears a Pyrrhic victory. On Hindenburg's death Hitler fused the Presidency with the Chancellorship and the *Reichswehr* swore allegiance personally to him. It is true that the SA never recovered after the purge; their elimination, in reality, marked the rise of a much more dangerous body, the SS. In the end the SS succeeded where the SA failed: by 1945 there were 33 SS divisions of this Party Army – invariably better equipped than the Army itself. After the attempt on Hitler's life in July 1944 the Army came under direct control of the SS; they supplied the "politruks" who controlled all officers and the *Heil Hitler* salute was used by order of General Heinz Guderian, then Chief of Staff.

Thus the real victor of this prefabricated upheaval was Adolf Hitler. With the naked terror he unleashed, his opponents and allies alike were completely panicked. Of the conservatives only Baron von Neurath and Count von Krosigk were left in the government which henceforth rarely met. Hitler became a real dictator making all decisions, important and unimportant, himself. On paper everything in Hitler's Reich seemed institutionalized and legalized; in reality there was so much flux and confusion that Hitler could actually exercise this type of personal dictatorship most effectively. In the first year of power the Nazis passed possibly more laws than any other régime; even assassinations were legalized. However much of this legislation was retrospective and Hitler's decisions were supreme even if they ran against the law: *Führer unmittelbare Entscheidung*. No one could make headway in this legal confusion and this was possibly the real key to Hitler's personal power.

Thus *Gleichschaltung* had as its ultimate result the growth of the Führer's personal

Left: **The Wehrmacht troop their colors past an enthusiastic crowd at a Party Rally in Nuremberg in 1935. These rallies were held in September every year before the war.**

Above: **A crowd gathers outside the Chancellery to congratulate Hitler on his birthday in 1935.**
Below: **Goebbels' daughters, Helga and Hilde, congratulate Hitler on his birthday.**

Below: **Children salute the Führer in a posed shot, one of thousands taken to convince German parents of Hitler's universal appeal.**

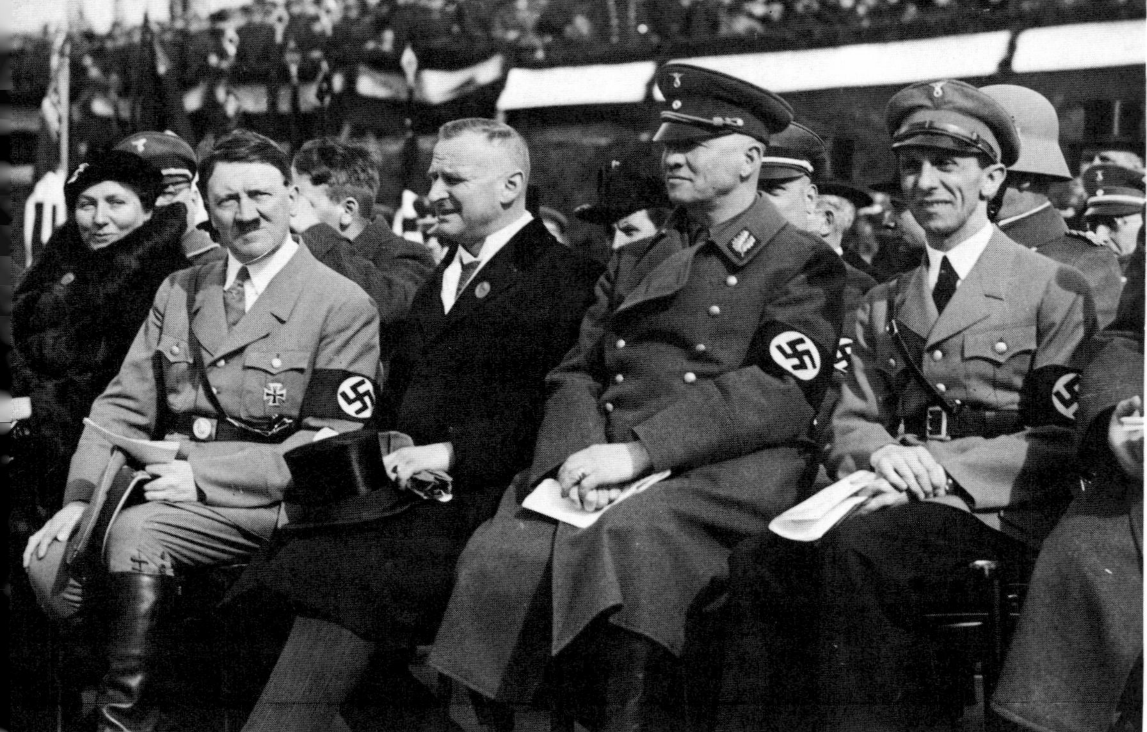

Above left: **Winifred Wagner, Hitler, Mayor Gördeler, Gauleiter Mitschmann and Goebbels at the Richard Wagner Memorial in Leipzig in 1934.**
Above: **Hitler and Streicher (right) attend a performance of** *Die Meistersinger* **at Nuremberg Opera House.**
Left: **Hitler, Goebbels consult a map on motor journey in 1932.**
Below left: **Hitler does not seem to be enjoying his birthday flight in 1932.**
Below: **Hitler and Goebbels leave their Ju 52 on a journey to Bavaria after the seizure of power.**

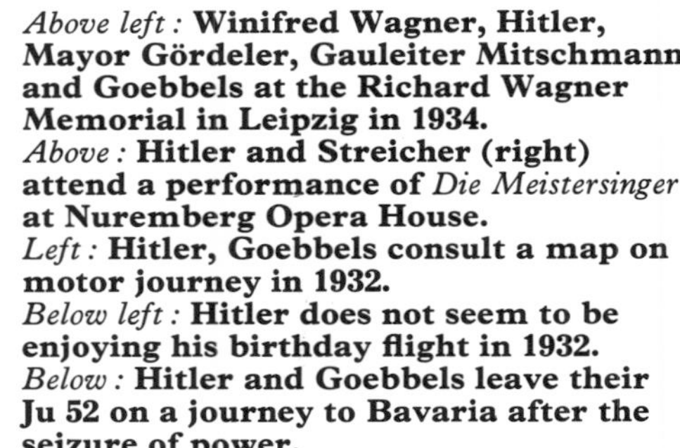

power. It could not be said that the Nazi Party was in power in the sense that Communist parties are in power in contemporary USSR or other Communist countries. Apart from the Führer's activity quite a lot seemed to be happening in Nazi Germany, but no one could say who was in charge, for obviously Hitler could not do nor be responsible for everything. This fact then serves to illuminate the Nazi revolution: it stirred up the people and many changes occurred spontaneously in an uncontrolled manner, the Nazi Party in a sense jumping on the bandwagon. Hitler for personal and power reasons wanted this type of development, providing it did not exceed certain limits. In contrast to Communist parties he did not want a huge bureaucracy to initiate and administer changes; therefore institutional chaos was the order of the day and he suffered it gladly.

Above : **Hitler visits a rural family in East Prussia during an election campaign trip in 1932. He spent much time campaigning in the countryside.**

Frequent changes in policies and redistribution of power among his followers were the means Hitler used to perpetuate this controlled chaos and to balance the power struggle among his subordinates thus making his personal power absolute. In the civil service Hitler invariably exploited tensions between the professionals and the party zealots to keep them all under firm personal control, and thus sacrificing administrative efficiency. The other means Hitler used were the badly defined legal competence of various state and party organs: the ambiguity of relations between state and party, state and government; the interdependence of industry, government and civil service; and finally the rivalries of the various types of state and party police forces. In the resulting chaos Hitler could operate quite effectively, so the National Socialist state was a jumble of overlapping conflicts and inefficiency. Thus there was the most flagrant overlapping between the Wehrmacht (as the *Reichswehr* was now called) and the Waffen SS, the Party Army, fatal for both; between the OKW (*Oberkommando der Wehrmacht* – created by Hitler) and the General Staff; between the Ministry of the Interior headed mainly by Frick and the powers of *Gauleiteren* who usurped most of Frick's powers; in the sphere of propaganda Bernhard Rust and Rosenberg proved much less successful *vis à vis* Goebbels. In the economic sphere the most shocking overlapping occurred between Dr Schacht, Dr Robert Ley and Hermann Goering; while in foreign affairs, after von Ribbentrop succeeded von Neurath, Hess and Rosenberg practically annulled state efforts.

After the elimination of the SA in the summer of 1934 Hitler more or less institutionalized this balance of power (or chaos) and turned almost exclusively to a new sphere of interest, international affairs. Perhaps a little more surprisingly he was to prove most successful as well. However since he could not employ the same divisive tactics in the international power struggle as in Germany, by 1939, when his gambler's luck finally ran out, Hitler once again launched Germany into a major war.

Below : **Hitler arrives in Berchtesgaden, his summer retreat, in 1934, followed by Hitler Youth leader Baldur von Schirach (left).**

1. Sports vest badge of a Nazi political leader.
2. Arm badge of the Reichsführerschule, the training school for political leaders.
3. Sports vest badge of the Hitler Youth.
4. Sleeve diamond worn by officers of the SD (Sicherheitsdienst) or Security Service of the SS, which was transferred from the Gestapo in 1936 under the leadership of Reinhard Heidrich.
5. SS Sports vest badge.
6. 1st Class Shooting Award of the SS.
7. SS fencing badge.
8. Symbol of the SS.
9. The death's head symbol of the Allgemeine SS.
10. Trumpet banner for German Young People group of the HJ.
11. Hitler Youth trumpet banner.

9

10

11

HITLER AS STATESMAN

Though the practice of foreign affairs was relatively new for Hitler he seems to have taken to it as fish to water and soon became such a practitioner as to score unexpected and unhoped for successes. Naturally even for Hitler foreign affairs were much more complicated than internal political affairs; in reality they were more complicated than he had ever imagined. After a period of germination in the interminable discussions in Munich beer cellars Hitler committed his thoughts on the subject to his *Mein Kampf* and they were there on record for all to read: Germany was to become a world power whose interests and targets lay principally in Eastern Europe and Soviet Russia. Only after this continental empire had been built, in friendship with Great Britain, or at least with Britain's benevolent neutrality, would Germany expand overseas and confront the power of the United States having absorbed colonial empires on the way. All this Hitler hoped to achieve gradually (*Stufenplan*) without a major war by means of his dominant personality and willpower.

Far left : **Hitler reviews Wehrmacht troops in 1934 with Major General Erwin Rommel on the left.**
Center left : **Hitler, Sepp Dietrich (his bodyguard) and General von Blomberg in 1934.**
Left : **Hitler speaks to one of his senior officers during the army maneuvers of 1935.**
Below : **Minister of War von Blomberg, Hitler, and Generals Beck and von Bock on maneuvers in the summer of 1935. It was already clear to the German General Staff that Hitler's grandiose schemes of conquest were unrealizable, but within two years the Wehrmacht had expanded from only 100,000 men to almost 500,000 with a large potential reserve.**

Left: **Germany's size was reduced by about 13 percent as a result of the Treaty of Versailles. The losses to Poland, especially in Upper Silesia, were especially galling, as was the cession of Danzig to the League of Nations. The myth grew that Germany had never been defeated in the field and the Germans resented being treated as the defeated by Western Europe.**
Below left: **Dr Ley and his Italian guests in Hamburg.**
Below: **King Victor Emmanuel III and Hitler visit an Italian port.**
Right: **Germany's acquisitions 1935–39 were considerable: the Saarland by League of Nations plebiscite; the Rhineland remilitarization by seizure; Austria by force; the Czech Sudetenland by default as a result of the Munich Pact; and the rest of Czechoslovakia and Memel by force. Once non-German speaking areas were taken, such as Bohemia and Moravia as protectorates, the West decided to take a firm stand.**
Below right: **Goering, Count Ciano and Foreign Minister von Neurath at the Italian Embassy.**

Although Hitler was the embodiment of the Nazi movement, different attitudes towards foreign affairs existed within the movement itself and it would be naive to brush them aside and say that Hitler managed to dominate them. Albeit he might have made use of them, all these party tendencies influenced him at different stages, and above all influenced foreign affairs independently of Hitler: thus the so-called "Brown Movement" thought foreign affairs in terms of expansion in purely military terms. The Socialist faction (Gregor Strasser) demanded colonial empires for Germany and peaceful coexistence in the East. And finally Walter Darré's ideology of blood and soil was explicitly against imperialism outside Europe. It is true that ultimately Hitler's aims and obligations would have satisfied these three tendencies; however more immediately Hitler decided on his own two-phase foreign policy which contained the elements of all tendencies, raising hopes of every one and satisfying no one. Thus in this first phase, Hitler decided on the renouncing of South Tyrol and overseas colonies in order to achieve the mastery on the European continent. The first concession was obviously aimed at Italy whose alliance Hitler needed, if the continent was to be his. The second concession was aimed at Great Britain whose friendship he likewise needed. However in phase two Hitler intended to extend the power struggle overseas and in particular challenge the United States. Ultimately the German people would be supreme all over the planet Earth.

As early as 1933 Hitler made full use of foreign policy factors at home: with the rejection of the limitations imposed on Germany at Versailles an armament boom satisfied the Army and the top capitalists who benefited most from this negative incursion into world affairs. However Hitler was determined on positive steps and sent a delegation to Geneva to attend the disarmament conference. Still France rejected Hitler's proposals and when the conference reconvened in October 1933 Germany decided not only to withdraw from the conference but also from the League of Nations. As it was Hitler wanted a bilateral agreement with Britain and to obtain it, he was prepared to withdraw into diplomatic isolation.

However Hitler was determined to use every opportunity to interfere in foreign affairs, especially to the detriment of France. Thus suddenly, and as if out of the blue, he concluded a Ten-year Non-Aggression Pact with Poland, albeit it was on the record that Poland was on his list of countries to be humbled as soon as possible. This move obviously checked France and destroyed her alliance agreements in Central Europe which was based on friendship with Poland. It also freed Hitler's hands to attend more closely to Austria and Czechoslovakia, who had always figured high in his foreign policy priorities. However in 1934 Hitler failed abysmally to tackle these two problems. In July 1934 the Austrian Nazis in a *coup de force* murdered the Austrian Chancellor, Engelbert Dollfuss, but failed to take over Austria largely thanks to the Italian dictator, Mussolini, moving Italian troops up to Austrian borders and thus intimidating them from unleashing such a reign of terror as encouraged by Hitler. Austria remained independent. Hitler had to disclaim any knowledge of the Nazi coup and as a special gesture sent his Vice-Chan-

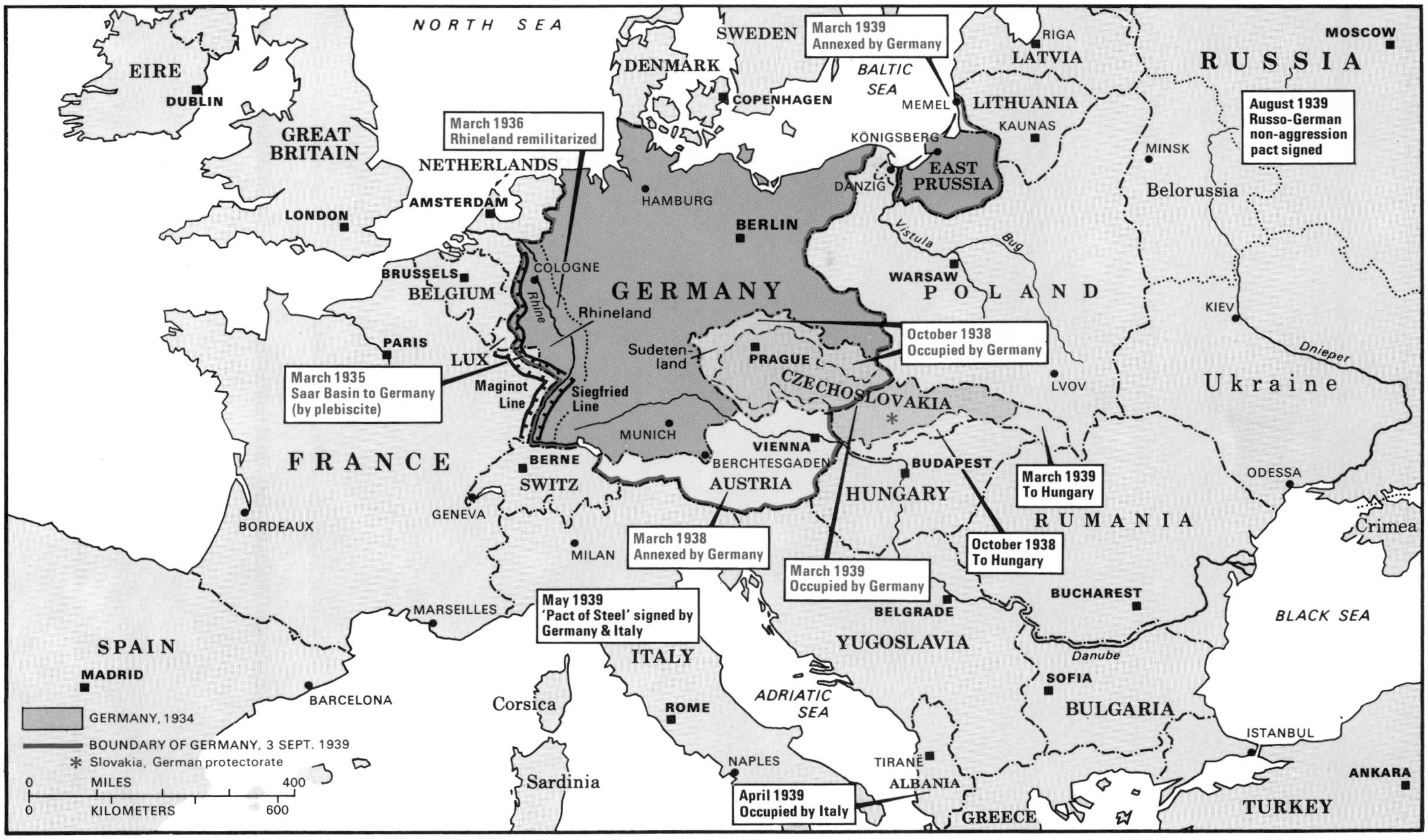

NORTH SEA
SWEDEN
March 1939
Annexed by Germany
RIGA
LATVIA
MOSCOW
RUSSIA
EIRE
DUBLIN
DENMARK
BALTIC SEA
COPENHAGEN
MEMEL
LITHUANIA
KAUNAS
August 1939
Russo-German
non-aggression
pact signed
March 1936
Rhineland remilitarized
GREAT BRITAIN
NETHERLANDS
KÖNIGSBERG
EAST PRUSSIA
MINSK
DANZIG
Belorussia
AMSTERDAM
HAMBURG
LONDON
BERLIN
Vistula
Bug
COLOGNE
BRUSSELS
BELGIUM
GERMANY
WARSAW
POLAND
KIEV
Rhine
Rhineland
PARIS
October 1938
Occupied by Germany
Dnieper
Sudeten-land
PRAGUE
LUX
CZECHOSLOVAKIA
LVOV
Ukraine
March 1935
Saar Basin to Germany
(by plebiscite)
Maginot Line
Siegfried Line
MUNICH
VIENNA
BERCHTESGADEN
BUDAPEST
March 1939
To Hungary
ODESSA
FRANCE
BERNE
SWITZ
AUSTRIA
HUNGARY
GENEVA
RUMANIA
Crimea
BORDEAUX
March 1938
Annexed by Germany
MILAN
October 1938
To Hungary
March 1939
Occupied by Germany
BUCHAREST
May 1939
'Pact of Steel' signed by
Germany & Italy
MARSEILLES
BELGRADE
BLACK SEA
SPAIN
ITALY
YUGOSLAVIA
MADRID
Danube
SOFIA
BARCELONA
Corsica
ROME
ADRIATIC SEA
BULGARIA
ISTANBUL
GERMANY, 1934
BOUNDARY OF GERMANY, 3 SEPT. 1939
* Slovakia, German protectorate
NAPLES
TIRANE
0 MILES 400
0 KILOMETERS 600
Sardinia
ALBANIA
April 1939
Occupied by Italy
GREECE
ANKARA
TURKEY

cellor, the Catholic Papen, to Catholic Austria as his special envoy.

This reverse in Austria made Hitler more determined not to be caught unprepared militarily before foreign policy moves. He ordered further extension of secret rearmament: the Army was to increase its number to 300,000 by 1 October 1934; U-Boats as well as two battle cruisers were to be built; Goering established the Luftwaffe though ostensibly for civil purposes; Krupp were developing tanks and guns, while I G Farben scientists were producing gasoline and rubber chemically from coal. By the end of 1934 some 240,000 factories were mobilized for war. With hindsight historians saw in these moves Hitler's preparation for a world war, though it is probably more correct to say that Hitler's moves were intended to strengthen his hand in international affairs.

The year 1935 proved decisive and made of Hitler a *habitué* in the game of international relations. In January France handed back to Germany the Saarland without demanding any concession; in fact in March Hitler decreed military service which brought the Army up to one million. This blatant breach of the Treaty of Versailles was countered with paper protests, but no one was willing to act, especially since Hitler made another of his frequent speeches in favor of peace. By now Hitler had dealings with Sir John

Left: **Konstantin von Neurath and Dr Meissner stand behind Hitler as he meets the Diplomatic Corps for the first time in 1933.**
Above: **Hitler congratulates Minister of State Meissner on his 60th birthday.**

Above: **Hitler discusses Franco–German relations with Ambassador François-Poncet, who feared German power throughout the 1930s.**

Simon, the British foreign secretary as well as with Anthony Eden, Minister of State, and his offer of a naval pact (fixing the ratio 35:100 in capital ships and equality of submarines) was bound to disrupt the front of Stresa, as indeed it did. In June Britain and Germany signed the naval pact without consulting their Stresa partners (France and Italy), who subsequently went their separate ways. On 3 October 1935 Mussolini attacked Ethiopia and the Locarno arrangements were overruled and defunct. The balance of power on the European continent was once again in a melting pot and new alliances would have to be forged. France rather precipitately opted for a pact of mutual assistance with the USSR thus giving Hitler an additional excuse for taking up re-armament in a big way, and this indeed was his next move. The projected Air Pact between Britain and Germany came to nothing and the Nazi foreign affairs expert, von Ribbentrop, formed the Reich Colonial Association to exert greater pressures on the colonial empires, France and Britain.

Since Hitler had so far proved successful only in a negative way, in demolishing treaties and alliances, he was growing neurotic about achieving positive results. When in February 1936 France and Soviet Russia ratified their mutual assistance pact Hitler decided on a risky initiative: with his generals dissenting and his Army quite unprepared for a major war he ordered them to occupy the neutral buffer zone of the Rhineland. This was indeed a major test case, but to every one's surprise all went according to Hitler's predictions and proved to be his greatest success. Britain, which invariably reacted sharply to German colonial and naval threats, remained quite passive. France moved thirteen divisions to the German border – General von Blomberg feared that the French would intervene and prepared the Army for retreat – but otherwise limited herself to a paper protest. Hitler's nerve carried the day and he immediately ordered the construction of fortifications, the West Wall, better known as the Siegfried Line.

Left: **Hitler surrounded by his Cabinet in 1935. Note the presence of Goering and Goebbels to the left. The swastika and Nazi paraphernalia had become emblems of government.**

As both France and Britain gave in over the Rhineland, Hitler determined to challenge them immediately in Spain. Here a civil war broke out and General Franco led the rebel Army against the left-wing forces of the Republic. In July 1936 Hitler decided to support the Army rebels, not because of ideological sympathies, though naturally Franco's ideology was nearer his own, but for strategic reasons: if Franco won the Civil War the Iberian peninsula could be used as a war base by Germany in a conflict with both France and Britain. German involvement in the Spanish Civil War also meant a rapprochement with Mussolini's Italy, which had just completed its victory in Abyssinia, was openly pro-Franco and was prepared for a deal with Germany, provided it settled its dispute with Austria. On 11 July 1936 Hitler swiftly obliged by signing an agreement with Dr Kurt von Schuschnigg and Italy and Germany signed their pact: the infamous Axis on 21 October 1936.

Hitler hoped that his involvement in the Spanish Civil War and the Axis pact would force Britain to come over to the German side and abandon the French to their Soviet ally. Ribbentrop, German Ambassador in London, however, proved completely unsuccessful in handling the British. Although the Germans increased their propaganda campaign against Bolshevism, both in the USSR and Spain, the British failed to perceive any interest from their point of view in these German initiatives, and on the contrary saw only headaches ahead arising from the German involvement in Spain. When their last chance had slipped away, Germany went all out against "Bolshevism" by concluding the Anti-Comintern Pact with Japan. By November 1936 Hitler had concluded an ideological alliance which enabled him to combat Communism in Spain and threaten the colonial empires of France and Britain at the same time. Insofar as the European continent was concerned Hitler had achieved all that he set out to do: the Versailles Treaty was dead, the Locarno pact was dead, the Little Entente had disintegrated and completely new international arrangements had come into being. While Belgium declared its neutrality, Yugoslavia and Rumania came to terms with the Axis and French and British influence on the continent were completely neutralized, thus making the Franco-Soviet pact a dead letter.

Having completed stage one Hitler was prepared for the next moves and he revealed them to his Foreign Minister, von Neurath, and Defense Minister, von Blomberg: from now on Germany would start acquiring the *Lebensraum* in the East, as he had promised in *Mein Kampf* in the 1920s. The victims were to be Austria and Czechoslovakia and they were to be acquired *even if it meant a war*. In any case Hitler believed that armed conflict between Italy, and France with Britain was inevitable and this would free Germany's hands in the East. However this straight talking was more than these conservative leaders

Left: **Colonel von Reichenau acted as Blomberg's chief of Staff in East Prussia. Hitler chose him to represent Germany on the Olympic Games Committee.**
Below: **Leni Riefenstahl directs the film** *Olympiad* **in 1936 during the Berlin Olympics.**

could stand. It is true that Blomberg issued war directives to his three service chiefs even before this interview, but these directives, Operations *Rot* and *Grün*, and *Fall Otto* (Austria) belonged to the realm of military contingency and were not really meant seriously. Even the testing of German arms and equipment in the Spanish Civil War did not convince Blomberg that his armies were ready for a war, and to his personal detriment he told Hitler. But Hitler had made up his mind in advance and throughout the year 1937 began to take minor steps towards a grand solution in 1938. In September 1937 Mussolini visited Germany and was shown armament factories and trained troops: he was so impressed by his findings that he gave in to Hitler on Austria, where henceforth he could do as he pleased. He also decided to join the Anti-Comintern pact. Internationally Hitler began to feel strong enough, but internally he still had to count on conservative opposition from both the military and foreign affairs specialists: he therefore solved the domestic problem once and for all by purging both institutions. In 1938 when it came to an armed confrontation over Austria and Czechoslovakia Defense Minister von Blomberg was no longer there; nor was the Army's Commander-in-Chief von Fritsch. Even greater changes took place in the German Foreign Ministry: Neurath was replaced by the Nazi Ambassador in London, Ribbentrop, while Papen was recalled from Vienna, Ulrich von Hassell from Rome and Herbert von Dirksen from Tokyo. In addition Dr Schacht also went because of his opposition to Goering's economic experiments. All these moves were calculated to bring about a risky international confrontation.

Hitler seems to have been obsessed with Britain all this time. Originally in the *Mein Kampf* he wanted Britain as an ally, and therefore refused to countenance any colonial aspirations. After he had taken up an interest in foreign affairs he had to depart from his initial intentions and was

forced to make "colonial" moves in order to achieve at least British neutrality on the continent. However he found it difficult to handle the British, who somehow became aware of a split in German foreign policy even before Hitler himself became conscious of it. In November 1937 the Hossbach memorandum made it clear that Hitler no longer counted on Britain as an ally: he wanted her to be neutral while he expanded in the East. By 1943–44 when Hitler thought his march in the East would come to an end, he was prepared to challenge Britain and inherit her colonial empire. When Lord Halifax, British Foreign Secretary, visited him at Berchtesgaden, he confirmed Hitler in his revised views. Britain apparently considered Germany as a bulwark against Bolshevism and her aspirations in Austria, Czechoslovakia and Danzig quite legitimate. Britain would therefore remain neutral as

Left: **Franco's uprising in Spain in 1936 was supported financially and militarily by Germany.**
Right: **Hitler greets Arthur Seyss-Inquart, the Austrian Nazi leader.**
Below: **Hitler visits his parents' grave in Leonding in March 1938.**

Above: **Hitler gazes down on Prague from the Hradčany Castle after Germany seized Bohemia and Moravia in March 1939.**

long as Hitler refrained from threatening the Empire. Henceforth Hitler began to take risks and handle the British carelessly: as it was seen he even appointed the anti-British Ribbentrop as his Foreign Minister. This was a miscalculation which ultimately led to war: the British Conservative "appeasers," among them Chamberlain and Halifax, refused to be treated in the same manner as German conservatives. However, in the short term, particularly in 1938, Hitler had it all his own way.

The year 1938 opened with Hitler's purge of the Armed Forces. Von Blomberg was suddenly struck off the Army's list for marrying a prostitute and dismissed as Minister of Defense. Von Fritsch was suspended as the Army's Commander on the completely spurious evidence of his being a homosexual; in fact the charges against him were fabricated by the SS. Dismissals and a reshuffle among the top ranking officers followed. Hitler abolished the Ministry of Defense, and assumed the office of Commander-in-Chief of the Wehrmacht (no longer the *Reichswehr*) and put General Wilhelm Keitel, an obedient tool, in charge of the *Oberkommando der Wehrmacht*, as the Defense Ministry was now called. Thus prepared militarily Hitler was ready to handle his first international crisis.

In January 1938 another anti-state plot was discovered in Austria in which the Austrian Nazis were implicated. Schuschnigg protested to Papen, but to no effect. Papen was recalled and Hitler invited Schuschnigg to visit him at Berchtesgaden, just across the Austrian border on 12 February. However Hitler's "solution" of the problems caused by the Nazis in Austria proved to be an ultimatum: Hitler gave Schuschnigg a week to fulfill the terms of the ultimatum, or else the Wehrmacht would solve Austria's problems. The ultimatum demanded that Schuschnigg commit political suicide by appointing Seyss-Inquart, the Austrian Nazi leader and plotter, as Minister of the Interior and two other Nazis to the Ministry of Finance and War. To help Schuschnigg to make up his mind the Wehrmacht staged military maneuvers. However Schuschnigg rejected the ultimatum on 24 February in his speech to the Austrian parliament: he would not agree to any more concessions *vis à vis* the Austrian Nazis. As a result demonstrations and counterdemonstrations plunged Austria into terrible chaos. Schuschnigg then sought support of the Social Democratic opposition and launched his last defiant gesture at Germany: he proposed to hold a plebiscite on whether the Austrians wanted to be annexed to Germany (as the Nazis had claimed). The day on which the plebiscite was to take place was 13 March 1938; however it came too late – Hitler decided to act on his own. The Wehrmacht was given orders to execute *Fall Otto* on that very day.

Hitler was favored by circumstances all along. In France the coalition government had fallen and the country was too busy solving its own internal crisis to bother too much about German Austria. In Britain Lord Halifax gave way to Anthony Eden and, with the spring naval maneuvers in the offing, Hitler was not quite sure how Britain would react. However Ribbentrop assured Hitler on 9 March that Britain would do nothing to help Austria. There remained the erstwhile champion of a small Austria, Italy's Mussolini, who

Below: **Hitler salutes Parading Sudeten Germans in 1938. Robert Henlein, the Sudeten leader who undermined the Czech government, is third from the left.**

had only recently frustrated Hitler's intentions. However Italy proved to be the least risky of them all: Hitler told Mussolini a somewhat fictitious story of Austria together with Czechoslovakia plotting to restore the Habsburg rule and the Italian dictator gave his Nazi friend a free hand. Hitler, aware that the plebiscite would go against him, put tremendous pressure on Schuschnigg to cancel it; in the end Schuschnigg gave in, although he knew full well that the Wehrmacht would march against Austria regardless. Hitler asked President Miklas to dismiss Schuschnigg and appoint Seyss-Inquart instead. The President refused, but Schuschnigg spoke to the nation on the radio and resigned rather than "spill German blood." Still the Nazis continued their pressures and disorders were widespread in Austria. Seyss-Inquart then sent Hitler a telegram which on 11 March 1938 was printed in the *Völkischer Beobachter*: it asked Germany and the Wehrmacht to help Austria to quell disorders and re-establish law and order.

The Wehrmacht moved into Austria the following day. Though it was in reality a joyride the occupation of Austria did uncover German unreadiness for the war which Hitler was courting in such a determined fashion. Some 70 percent of the armored vehicles employed for this joyride broke down and Hitler's entry into Vienna had to be delayed. Seyss-Inquart promulgated the *Anschluss* law on the 13 March; Hitler signed it at Linz and it was only on the next day that he triumphantly entered Vienna. As soon as he was master of the whole country Hitler put into action his old *Gleichschaltung* policy: Austria became the *Ostmark* split into *Gau*s (Tyrol, Carinthia etc). Police and civil service were purged and the Nazis set up their own organizations: Heydrich established the office for Jewish emigration in Vienna which sold permits to Austrian Jews. At Mauthausen a brand-new concentration camp was set up for the opponents of the new order. Four weeks later on 10 April, after intensive electioneering, Austria sanctioned the *Anschluss* in a plebiscite and Hitler's victory was complete. He had skillfully used political and military means to achieve his objectives in Austria without provoking a major crisis. Thus Hitler was confirmed in his intention of further expansion and immediately began his preparations.

On 21 April 1938 Hitler asked General Keitel to come and discuss with him *Fall Grün*, the liquidation of Czechoslovakia. On the surface this appeared a much bigger nut to crack peacefully, and while Keitel never blinked, the Wehrmacht as a whole began to have misgivings. Politically Hitler had his case against Czechoslovakia well worked out. Since the world economic depression the German minority in Czechoslovakia had been restless; after Hitler's ascent to power in Germany the Sudeten German Party in Czechoslovakia began to look to him for aid. He was to become a champion of the oppressed fellow Germans. Konrad Henlein, the Sudeten leader, on instructions from Hitler, Hess and Ribbentrop, whom he met on 28 March 1938, presented the Czechoslovak government with steep demands for a Sudeten autonomy and then let Hitler resolve the problem from outside even at the risk of armed conflict. Unlike Austria, Czechoslovakia was part of France's system of alliances and would undoubtedly cause a major upheaval, since this time it would be the two great powers and not Italy which would have to be placated. However even in this respect Hitler again timed his moves well, for the French international system had been disintegrating since the death of Louis Barthou, whose policy of re-arming the Little Entente and bringing into the European balance of power the USSR as a counterbalance to Germany was subtly reversed by Pierre Laval. Shortly after his assumption of office Laval wrote to Dr Beneš, the Foreign Minister of Czechoslovakia, to be more cautious towards Germany. While Beneš still hoped that France and Czechoslovakia would be able to use Soviet Russia as the stick with which to compel Germany to be amenable, the French were already pursuing different policies.

The change in French policy did not become apparent immediately. On 5 December 1934 Laval and Maxim Litvinov, Soviet Foreign Minister, signed the Geneva Protocol and it seemed that negotiations for an Eastern Pact were progressing. Beneš signed the same protocol with the Russians five days after the French. He had a long talk with Titulescu, the Rumanian Foreign Minister, before the latter's departure for France in April 1935 to find out more about French intentions. Titulescu and Beneš favored an Eastern Locarno to bilateral pacts with Russia, but the French ignored their wishes. On 5 May 1935 the Franco-Soviet Treaty was signed and as if to make his intentions clear Laval called in Berlin on his return from Moscow. Still the Czechs also signed a bilateral treaty with Soviet Russia and in June 1936 Beneš visited Moscow. So far Beneš was under the impression that he and Laval would use the Soviet stick to threaten the Germans, but he was soon undeceived. Laval in fact used the pact to achieve a *rapprochement* with Nazi Germany. Although Laval promised Beneš that Czechoslovakia would not be forgotten if France achieved a *rapprochement* with Germany, Beneš had no illusion on this account. He had tried his own initiative with Hitler and had been rudely rebuffed. All that was left for him now was periodic reminders to the French Ambassador in Prague of France's obligations to Czechoslovakia.

A short-lived but brave effort to sort out Central European problems and preempt Hitler's projects was made by the new Czechoslovak Foreign Minister, Milan Hodža, a Slovak Conservative, who replaced Beneš when the latter was elected President of Czechoslovakia. Hodža thought that a central European federation could save Czechoslovakia from being destroyed by Germany – Hitler probably used this plan as an excuse for intervening in Austria, as he told Mussolini. However Hodža's ideas never even took off the ground: the French were uninterested and since Hodža's federation hinged on French support, he resigned and handed it over to Professor Krofta, who continued the old policy of complete dependence on France and open hostility to Germany. In April 1936 Beneš saw a glimmer of hope in the new French government of the Popular Front. He sent a special envoy, Dr Ripka, to France to find out more about the new government's intentions, but he came back with a discouraging report: in foreign policy the Popular Front would follow the line of their predecessors. By now open disagreements became apparent between France and Czechoslovakia – they disagreed over Italy, Abyssinia and Civil War in Spain. In July 1936 the new Foreign Minister, Delbos, stated bluntly that France was no longer interested in the moribund Little Entente. French coolness towards Czechoslovakia became marked.

As the crisis in 1938 approached Beneš could see clearly the impasse in which Czechoslovakia found itself. He tried desperately to persuade Leon Blum to follow Barthou's old policy and come to terms with Germany by using the pact with the USSR. At first the French evinced interest and Beneš once again tried bilateral talks with Hitler: after all he had signed a pact with Germany's enemy Poland. However Hitler would not oblige and as early as July 1937 told his generals that Czechoslovakia would be destroyed. On 20 May 1938 Operation *Grün* was worked out and promptly leaked. Hitler quite rightly thought that he had the Czechs, and with them the French and the British, on the run; great was his surprise when Beneš, on hearing of Hitler's plan, took preventive measures and ordered

Above: **Mussolini meets Premier Daladier of France at the Munich Conference, 29 September 1938, as Hitler and interpreter Paul Schmidt listen to the proceedings.**

partial mobilization. Throughout this unplanned and unexpected crisis France kept aloof, while Britain, France's only remaining ally, issued paper proclamations stressing the gravity of the situation. However both allies were most unwilling to support Czechoslovakia against Germany, for they thought they would be risking a war for the wrong reason. Hitler's making use of the Sudeten German issue by claiming that Czechoslovakia was violating their self-determination, a principle over which the Great War was fought, completed Czechoslovakia's isolation.

Hitler was furious with having his timetable upset, but nevertheless told his generals that he would smash Czechoslovakia by 1 October 1938. In the meantime he issued a *dementi* of aggressive designs against Czechoslovakia and encouraged British mediation. The British Prime Minister, Neville Chamberlain, was more than willing to asume the rôle of moderator; he had received intimations from German conservative conspirators that they would get rid of Hitler if he tried to drag Germany into war against France and Britain under whatever pretext. Nonetheless Chamberlain chose to ignore this German opposition initiative and tried his own hand in international politics. Since to his mind Czechoslovakia was in the wrong, the Sudeten problem would have to be resolved to Hitler's and Germany's satisfaction. Following these concessions Chamberlain thought Hitler would be ready to accept a general peace settlement on the European continent. With hindsight we see that Chamberlain was completely wrong and that his initiative only delayed the war. As it was the British sent Lord Runciman to Czechoslovakia to try and mediate and though the Czechs were willing, Henlein, certain of Hitler's support, refused to be reasonable and British mediation failed.

Before Hitler could even begin to sort out the Sudeten German affair he had to face a minor domestic crisis. When it became clear in the Wehrmacht that Hitler in order to achieve his foreign policy target was prepared to go to war, opposition arose. General Ludwig Beck, the Army's Chief of Staff, voiced his doubts about Hitler's policy in his memorandum to the Army Commander-in-Chief, General Walther von Brauchitsch (5 May 1938): Germany was economically and militarily in a worse situation than it had been in 1917–18 and was not in a position to win the war against Western Powers. He therefore suggested that all generals resign *en masse* in July 1938 as a protest. Subsequently conservative politicians took this point up with the British, but failed to draw attention to themselves. Needless to say Hitler knew nothing of this initiative; ultimately only Beck resigned and was replaced by General Franz Halder. [Beck finally came back in 1944 when followed by many more officers than in 1938 he tried again in vain to rid Germany of Hitler with even less success.] On 18 August 1938 when Beck resigned and thus resolved the crisis for Hitler, the latter became convinced that he would destroy Czechoslovakia without having to go to war. During this month it became obvious that Lord Runciman's mission had failed and Hitler recruited another champion for frontier revision with Czechoslovakia, Colonel Jozef Beck of Poland. However the stage was now set for a peaceful *dénouement*.

On 28 August 1938 the British Prime Minister instructed his Ambassador in Berlin, Sir Nevile Henderson, to arrange a meeting with the German Chancellor, Hitler. He was determined to preserve European peace even at the price of Czechoslovakia. This policy which we subsequently called appeasement was exemplified in *The Times* leader on 7 September 1938 and Chamberlain's visit to Germany. On 12 September Hitler hysterically called for Sudeten German self-determination at the last Nuremberg Nazi rally and three days later Chamberlain was on his first visit to the Berghof. Hitler made his demands absolutely clear: if the Czechs did not agree to the secession of Sudeten Germans after a plebiscite, he would go to war. Chamberlain promised Hitler to "advocate the far-reaching German proposals." Immediately Hitler's demands were communicated to the French and on 19 September presented to the Czechoslovak government. Beneš could not possibly accept Anglo-French proposals for the secession of the Sudetenland, for the country would cease to be

physically viable. All the Czech fortifications were in that part of the territory which naturally bordered on the German Reich. However when the British and French made it quite clear that they would not support Beneš in his armed confrontation of Germany, he gave in, resigned and left the country. Throughout the crisis the USSR's position remained ambivalent despite the pact with Czechoslovakia. Beneš did not appeal to the Russians for help because he interpreted the pact as meaning that Soviet aid could only be invoked, if and after the French had been committed, and in this case France did

Left: **From left to right, Dr Schmidt, Chamberlain (partly obscured), Hitler, Mussolini, Ciano, von Ribbentrop and Daladier at Munich, 29 September 1938.** *Below:* **Von Ribbentrop, Chamberlain and Hitler at Munich.**

not want to commit herself. Still this ambivalence was later exploited by the USSR.

On 22 September, after he had obtained Czech capitulation, Chamberlain arrived at Bad Godesberg for another meeting with Hitler. He now offered Hitler his own solution of the Sudeten problem and was shocked to learn that Hitler had in the meantime changed his mind. He now wanted the Sudetenland occupied by the German Wehrmacht by 28 September 1938. The appeasers both in France and Britain surely should have their eyes opened: both the British and French Cabinets rejected these new demands and on 24 September France ordered partial mobilization. Quite unperturbed Hitler delivered his violent speech abusing President Beneš openly at the Sportpalast, Berlin and the following day gave Sir Horace Wilson, who came to Berlin to offer the supervision of the transfer of Sudeten Germans, an ultimatum: if the Czechs did not agree to the German occupation of the Sudetenland, Germany would be at war with Britain and France. Under this threat the appeasers panicked and capitulated.

Above: **Hitler discusses the technical problems of the occupation of the Sudetenland at Munich with his General Staff, from the left Generals Keitel, von Stülpnagel and Blaskowitz.**

Hitler sent Chamberlain another letter in which he defended his attitude to the Czechs and which left it to Chamberlain to mediate. The danger of war was apparently so great that Chamberlain offered Hitler a Four-Power Conference which would resolve the Czech crisis without war. Chamberlain wired Mussolini to sponsor this conference which the Italian dictator convoked at Munich. On 28 September, the date when Hitler's ultimatum expired, the French offered Hitler the surrender of a greater part of the Sudetenland without even consulting the Czechs. They also agreed to participate at the Four-Power Conference, well prepared to give in to Hitler: the only people who were not asked to attend were the representatives of Czechoslovakia itself. The Munich Conference lasted only two days, between 29–30 September, and as a result Hitler got even more than he had asked for at Bad Godesberg. For a paper concession never to go to war against France or Britain, he received not only the entire Sudetenland, but also the mixed regions, all without a plebiscite. Czechoslovakia lost not only its fortifications but also had its transport system, roads and railways, as well as telephone and telegraph disrupted. Premiers Chamberlain and Daladier thought that by means of these terrible concessions they had saved world peace and the rest of Czechoslovakia. However as soon as the conference was over Hitler told General Keitel that he would smash Czechoslovakia – meaning the pitiful remnants – despite the Munich *Diktat*: he was quite bent on a war.

Hitler was determined to bring to the logical conclusion the two projects that he set out to accomplish: swallow up the whole of Czechoslovakia and annex Danzig. In the former case he now thought that he could complete the operation by encouraging autonomist forces without a war. His first step in this direction was an agreement with France guaranteeing her existing frontiers. When, however, the Czechoslovak Foreign Minister asked for a similar guarantee, despite promises in Munich, it was not forthcoming. Instead Hitler began to think of further penetration east by means of independent Slovakia and Goering invited Slovak leaders to Berlin with this in view. Although the remnant of Czechoslovakia was in many ways "simplified" as the Nazis demanded in Munich, the country still continued more or less to function in a liberal democratic fashion. However with the increasing Nazi pressure and encouragement, President Emil Hácha, in order to avoid the break-up of the country, suspended autonomous arrangements and proclaimed emergency laws. Internally Czechoslovakia was on a brink of disaster and Hitler decided to accelerate the process. Then on 11 March 1939 Hitler became convinced that he could destroy the country with bluffing: when Monsignor Josef Tiso, the Slovak leader, arrived in Berlin, he was told to either proclaim independence or be occupied by the Wehrmacht. On 13 March Tiso proclaimed Slovakia independent. Next President Hácha was called to Berlin and after being subjected to unprecedented threats and blackmail he collapsed and signed an invitation to the Wehrmacht to occupy his country. In fact the Wehrmacht occupied part of Moravia even before Hácha's signature on the "invitation" and in any case at 0600 hours, two hours after the signature, on 15 March 1939 the Wehrmacht marched into Czechoslovakia and finally occupied the unfortunate country. Curiously Hitler's partners from Munich, who presided over Czechoslovakia's first dismemberment, failed even to speak out, albeit the French Ambassador did protest in Berlin. Formal notes went out three days later; however by this time both the British and French leaders were finally convinced that no international business could be transacted with Hitler. As if to drive this point home absolutely clearly the Wehrmacht also marched into the city of Memel which it seized from Lithuania.

Thus by the end of March 1939 the Western Allies were forced into protective actions and since the Danzig problem was unresolved Hitler's next move was obvious. In October 1938 the Poles rejected German proposals to resolve the problem "peacefully": Hitler asked the Poles to permit the free city of Danzig to revert to Germany and grant Danzig citizens extraterritorial rights in the Polish corridor separating the city from the Reich. Poland was also to join the Anti-Comintern Pact. In fact the Poles could see that although the Germans offered them peaceful solutions and participation in their expansion in the East, particularly in Lithuania, a country in which the Poles had historical interests, they were however clearly the next victim of this very same eastward expansion. When in February 1939 the Polish Foreign Minister Beck visited London and Paris he was very pessimistic and sounded alarm about German intentions. The Western Allies had their worst fears confirmed by the events in Czechoslovakia, but still did not feel strong enough to offer the Poles diplomatic and military support on their own: they wanted to have the USSR on their side and initiated talks with the USSR with this in view. The Poles felt most uncomfortable: on the one hand they were under pressure from Germany to join the Anti-Comintern Pact and have their security guaranteed. On the other hand the Western Allies offered them a similar guarantee with the USSR, whom they considered as dangerous to their security as Germany. On 31 March 1939, because of Polish opposition, Britain and France jointly undertook to guarantee the Polish frontiers leaving the USSR out of it and three days later Hitler issued the top secret directive *Fall Weiss*, signifying the invasion and destruction of Poland.

Above: **Martin Bormann (left) and Hitler greet Dr Neumann, who helped undermine the Lithuanian government's hold on Memel. Memel was taken on 22 March 1939 shortly before this photograph was taken.**

However before this could be implemented the two real antagonists,the Western Allies and Germany, had to sort out the problem of Soviet Russia. Britain and France, despite the Polish reluctance, continued their talks with the Soviets and in the teeth of Stalin's speech in March 1939, in which he criticized the Western Allies rather severely. On 28 April 1939 Hitler renounced his Non-Aggression Pact with Poland and in the same breath failed to criticize "Bolshevism" and the USSR. It was obvious that the two antagonists were both courting the USSR which was the last obstacle to an open conflict and a decisive factor in the balance of power. Both antagonists tried to tidy up their grouping: Germany reached an economic agreement with Rumania without whose oil it could not wage a war. Next Franco's Spain joined the Anti-Comintern Pact. Germany maintained good relations with Hungary, Bulgaria and Yugoslavia while it signed defense pacts with Latvia, Lithuania and Estonia. The Pact of Steel with Italy followed after Mussolini had annexed Albania. The Western Allies also signed guarantees and agreements: in April with Greece and Rumania, while President Roosevelt appealed to Hitler personally not to go to war. Still all hinged on the USSR.

In May 1939, when Foreign Minister Maxim Litvinov was replaced by Vlachislav Molotov, the Western Allies could see that they were losing out. This did not

The Munich Agreement, 29 September 1938

Germany, the United Kingdom, France and Italy, taking into consideration the agreement, which has been already reached in principle for the cession to Germany of the Sudeten German territory, have agreed on the following terms and conditions governing the said cession and the measures consequent thereon, and by this agreement they each hold themselves responsible for the steps necessary to secure its fulfilment:

1 The evacuation will begin on 1 October.

2 The United Kingdom, France and Italy agree that the evacuation of the territory shall be completed by 10 October, without any existing installations having been destroyed and that the Czechoslovak Government will be held responsible for carrying out the evacuation without damage to the said installations.

3 The conditions governing the evacuation will be laid down in detail by an international commission composed of representatives of Germany, the United Kingdom, France, Italy and Czechoslovakia.

4 The occupation by stages of the predominantly German territory by German troops will begin on 1 October. The four territories marked on the attached map will be occupied by German troops in the following order: the territory marked No 1 on 1 and 2 October, the territory marked No II on 2 and 3 October, the territory marked No III on 3, 4 and 5 October, the territory marked No IV on 6 and 7 October. The remaining territory of preponderantly German character will be ascertained by the aforesaid international commission forthwith and be occupied by German troops by 10 October.

5 The international commission referred to in paragraph 3 will determine the territories in which a plebiscite is to be held. These territories will be occupied by international bodies until the plebiscite has been completed. The same commission will fix the conditions in which the plebiscite is to be held, taking as a basis the conditions of the Saar plebiscite. The commission will also fix a date, not later than the end of November, on which the plebiscite will be held.

6 The final determination of the frontiers will be carried out by the international commission. This commission will also be entitled to recommend to the four Powers, Germany, the United Kingdom, France and Italy, in certain exceptional cases minor modifications in the strictly ethnographical determination of the zones which are to be transferred without plebiscite.

7 There will be a right of option into and out of the transferred territories, the option to be exercised within six months from the date of this agreement. A German-Czechoslovak commission shall determine the details of the option, consider ways of facilitating the transfer of population and settle questions of principle arising out of the said transfer.

8 The Czechoslovak Government will within a period of four weeks from the date of this agreement release from their military and police forces any Sudeten Germans who may wish to be released, and the Czechoslovak Government will within the same period release Sudeten German prisoners who are serving terms of imprisonment for political offences.

Munich, 29 September 1938.

ADOLF HITLER
NEVILLE CHAMBERLAIN
EDOUARD DALADIER
BENITO MUSSOLINI

Extract from *Further Documents Respecting Czechoslovakia*. Misc. No. 8 (1938) Cmd. 5848 (HMSO, London, 1938)

Above: **Prime Minister Neville Chamberlain waves the Munich Agreement triumphantly at Heston.**
Left: **The Munich Agreement.**

prevent them from trying again in July 1939 when they decided to have military talks with the USSR. These seemed the last chance to avert war, for the Western Allies now knew that throughout June 1939 the OKW (*Oberkommando der Wehrmacht*) had been planning war in the East. However these last-chance negotiations went off slowly and proceeded with great difficulties. It was realized subsequently that the Soviets were negotiating with both antagonists, hence the awkwardness. While the talks with the West dragged on, there were swift developments in negotiations with Germany. On 14 August Ribbentrop sent a long message to Molotov outlining the new Non-Aggression Pact and eight days later he flew to Moscow to sign the pact with Stalin. Britain responded with an Alliance Treaty with Poland, but by now neither Poland nor peace could be saved. Hitler had mobilized and even set a date for the attack on Poland and would accept nothing less than a complete surrender by the Poles who were also threatened from the East. Premier Chamberlain had sent Hitler a letter making Britain's position clear in case of an attack on Poland, but Hitler was beyond caring. He made his "last peaceful" effort offering to guarantee the British Empire if Britain kept out of the conflict in Eastern Europe.

While Hitler still claimed that Danzig and Polish atrocities were his reason for attacking Poland he had to stage the Gleiwitz incident to declare war on Poland. This done, on 1 September 1939, the Wehrmacht launched its *blitzkrieg* against Poland. The Western Powers offered paper threats to the invader, but when these failed Britain and France felt obliged to declare war on Germany. On 3 September 1939 Hitler suffered his first real defeat in international politics when he lost the peace. At this stage he was convinced that in fact war meant his victory, and he abandoned foreign affairs for war affairs which proved even less successful.

TOTAL WAR

BLITZKRIEG IN THE WEST

Paradoxically Hitler's war against the West started in the East with the lightning campaign (Blitzkrieg) against Poland. As has been demonstrated it was politically well prepared: Germany had a case against Poland in the form of the city of Danzig, Poland's allies were far away and could not intervene decisively and in the East, Germany obtained the USSR's neutrality at the time Hitler issued the Army with the order to march against Poland. The campaign was meticulously prepared. Curiously Hitler gave the Army a free hand – for the first and last time.

The Polish border with Germany stretched over some 3500 miles and at the best of times would have been difficult to defend; with the Danzig corridor splitting Poland, it was impossible. Moreover, because of the corridor, the Polish Army was under a constant threat of double encirclement. Field Marshal Rydz-Smigly decided to ignore these basic factors of Poland's defense, and concentrate on the defense of the industrial border areas. In July 1939 over a million Poles were mobilized and armies were disposed accordingly, in the proximity of the border. They consisted of some thirty infantry divisions of the Regular Army, while the Reserves, consisting of eleven cavalry brigades, were not yet properly organized. The Polish Army had some 500 obsolete aircraft and for its mobility it had to rely on the railways, which was its chief weakness. Army equipment also proved obsolete and given the basic foot mobility the Polish Army could not hope to defend itself in the modern way: it could not withdraw, nor bring up its reserves; neither could it re-group nor counterattack. All it could do was to stay put and fight to the death – and this it did in several instances – or to fragment under the impact of German attack, get enveloped and surrender, which was its actual fate. However even then the Germans did not have it all their own way; although they tried hard to seize the Dirschau bridge over the Vistula, the Poles succeeded in blowing it up in the last moment.

Below: **SA Chief of Staff Victor Lutze addresses his men at the outbreak of the war. By 1936 the SA's military role in the Third Reich had lapsed. It remained as an ineffective counter to the SS.**

Hitler ordered the OKW to prepare *Fall Weiss* long before the actual attack and on 25 March 1939 warned the soldiers most solemnly, fixing the attack for 26 August 1939. Still it appears that Hitler quite unreasonably expected to avoid a large-scale war, especially after he had succeeded in procuring Soviet neutrality. The Wehrmacht prepared to launch the attack with some 59 divisions, fourteen of which were mechanized, supported by some 1600 Luftwaffe aircraft. The armies were grouped in the north under General Fedor von Bock (Third Army under General Georg Küchler and Fourth under General Günther von Kluge) and in the south under General Gerd von Rundstedt (with the Eighth Army commanded by General Johannes von Blaskowitz and the Fourteenth by General Wilhelm von List). The Tenth Army under General Walther von Reichenau occupied a western position in between the Army groups and was to strike directly against Warsaw. The tactical plan envisaged the Fourth Army striking from Pomerania into the Polish corridor, while the Third Army struck at the corridor from East Prussia. Then the two armies would combine in their drive on Warsaw. In the south the Eighth and Fourteenth Armies were striking north-east from Silesia and Slovakia to meet with all the other armies outside Warsaw. German superiority in men and equipment was so clear that Poland's Allies thought that Germany would be overwhelmingly successful; still no one expected that the German Blitzkrieg would only take three weeks to accomplish the destruction of Poland.

On the eve of the invasion Hitler told

Above: **Generals Paulus, von Brauchitsch and Keitel go over the map of eastern Poland during the month-long Polish campaign of September 1939.**
Right: **The Molotov-Ribbentrop Pact of August 1939.**

The Non-Aggression Pact between Germany and the USSR, 23 August 1939

Guided by the desire to strengthen the cause of peace between Germany and the Union of Socialist Soviet Republics, and basing themselves on the fundamental stipulations of the Neutrality Agreement concluded between Germany and the Union of Socialist Soviet Republics in April, 1926, the German Government and the Government of the Union of Socialist Soviet Republics have come to the following agreement.

Article 1 The two contracting parties undertake to refrain from any act of force, any aggressive act, and any attacks against each other undertaken either singly or in conjunction with any other Powers.

Article 2 If one of the contracting parties should become the object of war-like action on the part of a third Power, the other contracting party will in no way support the third Power.

Article 3 The Governments of the two contracting parties will in future remain in consultation with one another in order to inform each other about questions which touch their common interests.

Article 4 Neither of the two contracting parties will join any group of Powers which is directed, mediately or immediately, against the other party.

Article 5 In case disputes or conflicts on questions of any kind should arise between the two contracting parties, the two partners will solve these disputes or conflicts exclusively by friendly exchange of views or if necessary by arbitration commissions.

Article 6 The present agreement is concluded for the duration of ten years with the stipulation that unless one of the contracting partners denounces it one year before its expiration, it will automatically be prolonged by five years.

Article 7 The present agreement shall be retified in the shortest possible time. The instruments of ratification are to be exchanged in Berlin. The treaty comes into force immediately it has been signed.

Done in two original documents in the German and Russian languages, respectively.

MOSCOW, 23 August, 1939. For the German Government
RIBBENTROP

As plenipotentiary of the Government of the Union of Socialist Soviet Republics
MOLOTOV

Extract from German Library of Information's *Documents on the Events Preceding The Outbreak of the War* New York, 1940)

his generals about a new type of warfare in which he was engaging: the war objective was not only the destruction of the Polish Armies but the destruction of the Polish nation, a task which would be accomplished by handpicked SS troops (*Einsatztruppen*) who would be operating alongside the advancing armies. He did not specify these special task duties, but all the assembled generals guessed what Hitler was talking about; they all felt uneasy, for this type of warfare was indeed an innovation. None, however, felt strong enough to refuse permission to the SS troops to operate in their military zones. Neither did any one of them resign in protest as they were all totally absorbed with the execution of the invasion.

On 1 September 1939 the German Armies and Luftwaffe attacked Poland and the latter destroyed Polish aircraft on the ground and completely disrupted the railways. In the south there was some

Right: **Hitler flanked by Martin Bormann and Gauleiter Forster on the Long Bridge in Danzig after the city was taken on the first day of World War II.**

Left: **Junkers Ju 52 transport over Poland.**
Right: **A squadron of Stukas which were assigned to bombing airfields behind the Polish lines. Stukas also pounded key road and rail points, which threw the retreating Polish Army into confusion.**

stubborn fighting, but by 4 September the German Armies had broken through the Polish lines and began to roll and march on Warsaw, often by-passing large pockets of Polish forces. In the south some six or seven Polish divisions succeeded in withdrawing but were caught up and encircled south of Warsaw in the second week of the campaign. In the northwest large undefeated Polish forces attempted a breakthrough to Warsaw, but were encircled and surrendered. General Heinz Guderian's Panzers struck out of East Prussia, east of Warsaw taking Brest-Litovsk on 17 September; in the south Lvov held out until 21 September. Hitler wanted to take Warsaw before his Soviet ally, who now expressed its desire to join in rather than remain neutral, could launch attacks against the hapless Poles from the east. The city was subjected to intensive air and artillery bombardment and after 56 hours of resistance the Polish Army surrendered. On 17 September the Soviet armies joined the war and a week later Hitler and Stalin divided Poland between themselves even before actual fighting ceased. Hitler controlled the provinces of Warsaw and Lub-

Directive No 1 for the Conduct of the War

1 Since the situation on Germany's Eastern frontier has become intolerable and all political possibilities of peaceful settlement have been exhausted, I have decided upon a *solution by force*.

2 The attack on Poland will be undertaken in accordance with the preparations made for 'Case White,' with such variations as may be necessitated by the build up of the Army which is now virtually complete.

The allocation of tanks and the purpose of the operation remain unchanged.

Date of attack 1 September 1939.

This time also applies to operations at Gdynia, in the Bay of Danzig, and at the Dirschau bridge.

3 In the *West* it is important to leave the responsibility for opening hostilities unmistakably to England and France. Minor violations of the frontier will be dealt with, for the time being, purely as local incidents.

The assurances of neutrality given by us to Holland, Belgium, Luxembourg, and Switzerland are to be meticulously observed.

The Western frontier of Germany will not be crossed *by land* at any point without my explicit orders.

This applies also to all acts of warfare *at sea* or to acts which might be regarded as such.

The defensive activity of the *Air Force* will be *restricted* for the time being to the firm repulse of enemy air attacks on the frontiers of the Reich. In taking action against individual aircraft or small formations, care will be taken to respect the frontiers of neutral countries as far as possible. Only if considerable forces of French or British bombers are employed against German territory across neutral areas will the Air Force be permitted to go into defensive action over neutral soil.

It is particularly important that any infringement of the neutrality of other states by our Western enemies be immediately reported to the High Command of the Armed Forces.

4 Should England and France open hostilities against Germany, it will be the duty of the Armed Forces operating in the West, while conserving their strength as much as possible, to maintain conditions for the successful conclusion of operations against Poland. Within these limits enemy forces and war potential will be damaged as much as possible. The right to order *offensive* operations is reserved absolutely to me.

The *Army* will occupy the West Wall and will take steps to secure it from being outflanked in the north, through the violation by the Western powers of Belgian or Dutch territory. Should French forces invade Luxembourg the bridges on the frontier may be blown up.

The *Navy* will operate against merchant shipping, with England as the focal point. In order to increase the effect, the declaration of danger zones may be expected. The Naval High Command will report on the areas which it is desirable to classify as danger zones and on their extent. The text of a public declaration in this matter is to be drawn up in collaboration with the Foreign Office and to be submitted to me for approval through the High Command of the Armed Forces.

The Baltic Sea is to be secured against enemy intrusion. Commander in Chief Navy will decide whether the entrances to the Baltic should be mined for this purpose.

The *Air Force* is, first of all, to prevent action by the French and English Air Forces against the Germany Army and German territory.

In operations against England the task of the Air Force is to take measures to dislocate English imports, the armaments industry, and the transport of troops to France. Any favorable opportunity of an effective attack on concentrated units of the English Navy, particularly on battleships or aircraft carriers, will be exploited. The decision regarding attacks on London is reserved to me.

Attacks on the English homeland are to be prepared, bearing in mind that inconclusive results with insufficient forces are to be avoided in all circumstances.

Signed: ADOLF HITLER

Extract from H R Trevor-Roper *Hitler's War Directives, 1939-1945* (London, 1964). Quoted by permission of Sidgwick & Jackson Limited.

Left: **Hitler's First Directive at the outbreak of fighting in 1939.**
Below: **Hermann Goering observes aircraft on a Polish airfield used to bomb Warsaw in late September 1939.**

Above: **Hitler driven by his aide Kempka with General Keitel and another aide Schmundt in the rear somewhere near the fighting outside Warsaw.**

lin right up to the river Bug while Stalin swallowed up the Polish east including Lithuania. Before all resistance stopped on 5 October Poland, divided between its two neighbors, ceased to exist as a state; its government, administration and part of its armed forces withdrew from the country and through Rumania and Hungary found refuge in France. In the meantime the Soviets and Germans took over the administration of the defeated Poland.

Below: **Axmann, General von Falkenhorst and Vidkun Quisling, whose name has been synonymous with treason since 1940.**

The stories of atrocities during the campaign were confirmed by eye witnesses, among them the American journalist, William Shirer, but this was only a beginning. Even the most appalling massacre of some 50 Jews by SS artillery men paled into insignificance after the arrival of Reinhard Heydrich, Himmler's deputy, to execute Hitler's ideas of genocide. On 21 September 1939 Heydrich produced his plan for the "housecleaning of Jews, intelligentsia, clergy and the nobility in Poland," which again appalled the Army, but which was nevertheless carried out by the newly appointed Governor General of the remnants of the Polish state. Within a year over 1,200,000 Poles were deported from the newly annexed German provinces eastward, while Governor Hans Frank boasted of summary sentences on two batches of Polish intellectuals, some 2500 and 3500 each. Hitler's Germany demonstrated in the case of Poland, how it would launch wars, carry them out and what consequences it would have in store for the defeated country.

In the meantime, while all this was going on in Poland, Hitler made his "last effort" to re-establish peace. On 7 October 1939 in a speech in the Reichstag Hitler offered a comprehensive peace settlement to France and Britain, which was turned down, for the Western Allies by now fully realized what the *pax germanica* had meant in Poland. Hitler, therefore, turned his mind to the conquest in the West. The Polish campaign which he left almost entirely to his generals to plan and execute, nevertheless confirmed him in his opinion that he possessed extraordinary strategic and tactical instincts, and he now proceeded with the planning of the war in the West. On 9 October 1939 he issued a memorandum justifying his policies and at the same time issued directives for the *Fall Gelb*, the conquest of France and Britain via Holland and Belgium. While he wanted to "start this war to end the war" as soon as possible it had to be postponed again and again, for the weather and the Western Allies offered him important distractions which he could not ignore.

While the Eastern Campaign secured him oil supplies in Rumania and the Soviet Union, it also exposed his only supply of iron ore from Sweden to new dangers. For, while the "Phony War" on land continued unabated, real war was being waged at sea. As early as 3 September the *U.30* sank the liner *Athenia* with the loss of 112 lives, many of them American. British merchant shipping losses amounted to ten per week. Moreover the aircraft carrier, *Courageous*, was sunk by *U.29*, while the battleship *Royal Oak* sunk at anchor at Scapa Flow. However Admiral Raeder only had a small naval force at his disposal and soon the British fleet began to assert itself in the North Sea. For two months it chased the two German pocket battleships to no avail, but it did prove to Hitler that it could cut his vital shipping line from Sweden via Narvik. Then the Soviet–Finnish war broke out, and it made Scandinavian public opinion not only sharply anti-Soviet, but also anti-German. Hitler began to fear that the Swedes might terminate iron ore deliveries, especially if the Norwegians decided to loan Narvik as a supply base to the Western Allies for their aid to Finland. On 14 December 1939, in this atmosphere of tensions, the

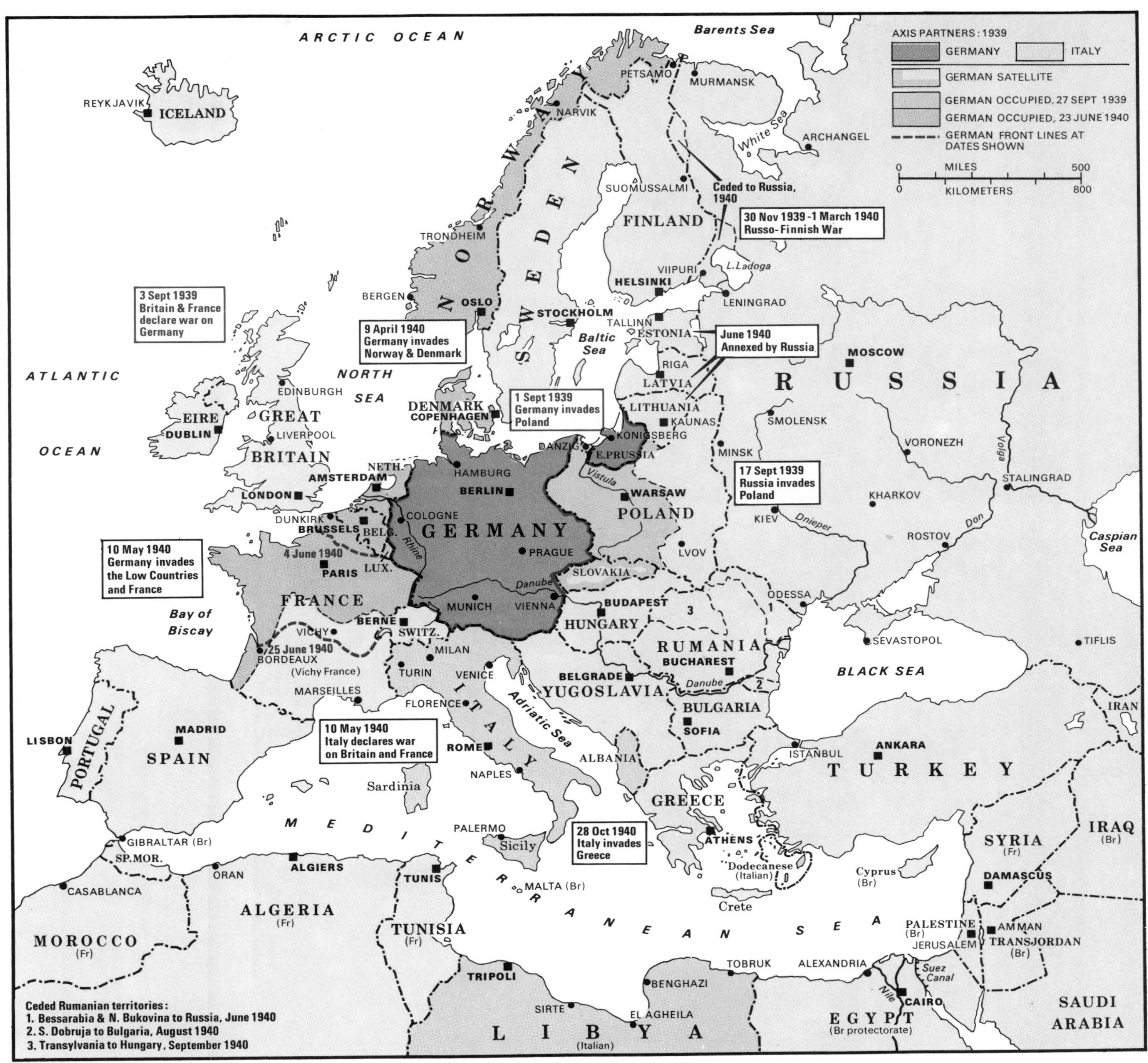

Norwegian fascist leader, Quisling, met Hitler and invited him to make sure of Norway by occupying it. Though Hitler seemed busy with the preparations for war in the West, he immediately ordered the *Oberkommando der Wehrmacht* (OKW) to investigate this possibility, but what finally decided him to have another dress rehearsal campaign before attacking France was the incident with the *Altmark*, which Allied warships cornered in a Norwegian fjord relieving it of its cargo of Allied POWs. In February 1940 he told General Falkenhorst exactly what he wanted in Norway and ordered him to plan and subsequently command the expedition.

Albeit the reasons for the occupation of Denmark and Norway were largely economic and naval; Hitler still wanted to confirm the efficacy of his blitzkrieg tactics in these more difficult conditions than in Poland. Once again surprise, speed and concentration were to achieve victory. Integration of all arms was indispensable and the command itself had to be restructured so that more initiative could be left to those lower down executing the general plan. This made leadership on all levels more dynamic; excellent communications and co-ordination were essential. In these conditions Hitler determined what tasks the Armed Forces were to perform and when, and victory seemed assured both in Scandinavia and France. The Allies in fact hesitated so long that Hitler set operations in motion a day before the Allies started to mine the seas off Norway in order to threaten Germany's supply line. On 7 April 1940 two groups of German warships sailed for Norway.

The operation was perfectly integrated and the Germans achieved their objectives with token forces only. Copenhagen and Denmark were occupied on the way, and the Germans gained advanced airfields as well as sheltered sea corridors for further journeys to Norway. When the forces reached Norway, coastal batteries caused limited damage to German shipping, but their integrated operations were too much for the Norwegians: one parachute bat-

Left: **Wehrmacht troops advance during the Norwegian campaign, in which the Germans ran into stiff opposition.**

talion seized two airfields and henceforth the Luftwaffe's intervention became decisive. There was a bit of fighting at Trondheim and Bergen, but none at Oslo. After the initial resistance to the landing itself, the King and the government had time to slip away into exile. Only after 14 April did British and French troops begin to arrive. First of all they tried to recapture Trondheim, but were beaten off, because they lacked air support. Allied intervention north of Oslo proved equally indecisive and after a week of confused fighting the troops were withdrawn. The face-saving operation against Narvik soon ran into difficulty. The tiny German garrison was only dislodged on 27 May, when France was on the point of collapse. Ten days later

Right: **Trucks are unloaded on a Norwegian dock to support the German invasion.**

the troops were ordered out of Norway having only achieved the destruction of the port of Narvik and its ore-handling installations. However before this diversionary blitzkrieg came to an end, Hitler had launched his drive against France and Britain.

In the West it was obvious that operations could not be launched before the winter was out; nevertheless Hitler fixed a firm date for 17 January 1940. Fortunately for the Allies, German plans of this attack fell into their hands a week before its execution; still the weather postponed operations. By then the Allies knew that the attack would be delivered from the Netherlands and they evolved Plan D which meant that they would move into Belgium.

Below: **Wehrmacht troops watch a supply ship arrive in a Norwegian fjord.**

Left: **Dutch artillery was of little use against the might of the German Army during the five-day conquest of Holland in May 1940.**
Right: **Dutch citizens watch the burning city of Rotterdam.**
Far right: **German soldiers watch a ship of the Holland–America line steam out of Rotterdam after its occupation.**

Apart from this planning innovation they failed to make use of the respite: their troop movements were slow and disposition of tanks unimaginative. Though they were inferior to the Germans in anti-aircraft and anti-tank weapons, they were superior to them in men (four million to two million), aircraft and tanks. However their strategic concepts were static and defensive, while Hitler was improving his dynamic strategy all the time. Earlier he had accepted General Manstein's plan for the annihilation of the enemy north of the river Somme. Then he decided on the main thrust via Sedan and for this purpose transferred practically all the Panzer force from Army Group B (Belgium) to Army Group A (Sedan); 44 divisions, of these seven armored ones, were going to break through and drive to the Channel under General von Rundstedt.

On 10 May 1940 Hitler finally launched his operations in the West. On that day Ribbentrop summoned the Belgian and Dutch ambassadors to tell them that German troops would invade their respective countries in order to prevent the Western Allies from occupying them. Although the previous night Colonel Sas, the Dutch military attaché in Berlin, had been warned of the impending attacks by General Oster, and passed on the information both to Brussels and The Hague, the invasion, spearheaded by dive bombers, the *Stukas*, created indescribable chaos and panic. Rather belatedly both the Belgian and Dutch governments sent frantic appeals to the French and British Allies for help. However Plan D was ready and the whole of the BEF as well as the bulk of the French Army in the north moved up into Belgium to help the Low Countries. However far from saving these countries the Anglo-French armies walked into a trap. It took the Germans five days to smash the Dutch armies. On 10 May German paratroopers landed near Rotterdam and the Hague capturing bridges and airfields. General Küchler's Eighteenth Army then attacked on a broad front and forced the Dutch Army as well as the French who had rushed up to Breda to fall back. When on 13 May a German armored division effected a junction with the paratroops near Rotterdam, Queen Wilhelmina and her government left the country for England. On 14 May the Germans issued an ultimatum to the Dutch to surrender or they would flatten Dutch cities with their *Stukas*; then, possibly by mistake, they actually did smash the business center of Rotterdam to smithereens causing some 1000 civilian casualties. Late on that day General Winckelman surrendered and the elements of the Eighteenth Army poured down south towards Antwerp to aid General von Reichenau and his Sixth Army. The irony of this most successful military operation was that it was quite unnecessary: it was only included in *Fall Gelb* on the Luftwaffe's request for its future operations against Britain.

It was thought that the Belgian Army, which consisted of some fifteen divisions, would hold up the invading Germans longer than it did. It was not because the Belgians fought badly but Reichenau's troops were magnificently prepared and fought like lions. Specially trained paratroopers were landed beyond Belgian lines and seized the three important bridges before the Belgians guarding them could blow them up. The impregnable Fort Eben

Left: **Wehrmacht anti-aircraft in Holland destroy the few planes which attacked their position near The Hague.**

VEENDAM-HOLLAND

Emael with its garrison of 1200 men surrendered after a surprise attack by eighty German paratroopers: they used special explosives to blow holes in its roof and then kept the garrison helpless for thirty hours. These feats of valor as well as the sustained pressure of Reichenau's Sixth Army supported by General Erich Höpner's XVI Panzer Corps forced the Belgians to fall back steadily though more rapidly than was calculated. When the Dutch surrendered no one had the slightest idea that the Belgians would entertain the same idea; after all, under the steady pressure of the invading armies all the Allied Armies were retreating. Then suddenly, out of the blue, the Belgian Army surrendered unconditionally leaving a huge gap in the right wing of the Allied Front.

During the early fighting much confusion was caused by the implementation of Plan D which made General Henri Giraud's 7th Army dash up to Holland and the BEF under Lord Gort to Belgium. Holland's collapse increased the mobility of Allied forces and not much time was left for co-ordination and consultation. The King of the Belgians as Commander-in-Chief of the Belgian Army was tactfully left to his own devices and was told nothing of Allied intentions. He had witnessed the surrender of Holland and heard about the breakthrough in the Ardennes area; on 24 May he heard that Calais had been

Below : **A damaged ship of the Holland–America Line in Rotterdam after the air attack.**
Right : **Luftwaffe paratroops get ready for the aerial assault on Holland the night before the invasion of 10 May 1940.**
Below left : **The nose of a Ju 88 bomber.**

Above : **German troops construct some new signs in The Hague after the fall of Holland.**

Above : **General Kurt Student inspects paratroops before their assault on Fort Eben Emael in Belgium.**
Above right : **Marshal Philippe Pétain, who took over the French government after the debacle in May–June 1940.**
Above far right : **Pierre Laval, Pétain's Premier, meets Hitler after the fall of France.**
Right : **From left to right General Keitel, Hitler, General Jodl and Martin Bormann at the Führer's headquarters on the Western Front in Belgium in June 1940.**

surrounded by German troops and that made him panic. The following day he held a meeting with his government and told them about his intention to sue for peace. The government unanimously rejected the proposal and constitutionally the King should have abdicated or gone into total exile. Instead he dispatched General Derousseaux to the Germans, who brought back Hitler's conditions for a cease-fire. Early in the morning of 28 May hostilities between the Belgian and German Armies ceased, for the King had accepted Hitler's conditions. He thought that the Allied cause was lost and that he had saved Belgium, but was wrong on both counts: the Allies certainly lost the Battle of France, but not the war. As for Belgium itself Leopold's government condemned him and went into exile, while the Belgians had to suffer the indignities of German occupation for the rest of the war.

With the Dutch and Belgian disasters the Anglo-French Allies began to sense that an even greater one was in the offing. As in the case of the German military leaders, the French and British generals had only paid scanty attention to the area round Sedan which was outside the Maginot defensive perimeter and in unsuitable terrain for large-scale offensive actions, especially by tanks. It was precisely for this reason that General von Manstein suggested that the Wehrmacht should concentrate its armor there, break through the hills and then cut across the plains to the Channel splitting Allied defenses in two. While the Wehrmacht in the person of the Chief of Staff, General Franz Halder, disliked this "eccentric" plan, Hitler immediately fell for it, and in time came to believe that it was in fact he who thought of it first. In any case he gave personal orders to concentrate General Hermann Hoth's XV Panzer Corps, General Reinhardt's XLI Panzer Corps and General Guderian's XIX Panzer Corps in this sector. All these Panzer forces, under General Ewald von Kleist's command, would carry out Hitler's "breakthrough plan." It so happened that this devastating attack fell on the weakest elements of the feeble 2nd Army (General Huntziger) and the 9th Army (General Corap); moreover the Generalissimo Gamelin had no strategic reserves in this area and only had cavalry formations to slow down German armor. By nightfall on 11 May Guderian's XIX Panzer Corps was in the vicinity of Sedan and two days later General Rommel's 7th Panzer Division controlled a bridgehead across the Meuse. Although Huntziger counterattacked with cavalry the following day and despite the Royal Air Force bombers bombing the vital bridge, all these efforts failed to halt or even slow down the Germans. Guderian's and Reinhardt's offensive punched a hole some 50 miles wide in the Allied Front. The German invaders were formidable; they used the *Stukas* instead of heavy artillery, but also had self-propelled guns; mechanized infantry followed the armored formations and engineers used rubber boats to cross rivers throwing up pontoon bridges. By 17 May the three armored columns which broke through the French front were halfway to the Channel and for the first time they had to face a serious counterattack. The newly promoted General Charles de Gaulle assembled a newly created armored division north of Laôn and advanced against the southern flank of the armored thrust. Since de Gaulle remained unsupported he soon had to break off the engagement, and the German armor could pour on.

Curiously and certainly not as a result of de Gaulle's counterattack, Hitler himself lost his nerve, and ordered the armor to halt. Both he and Rundstedt who was in overall command of this Army Group expected a massive French counterattack with the aim of cutting through the thin line of German armor. For two days Hitler held up his armored force, albeit their advance really continued under the guise of a "reconnaissance in force." What probably confused the Führer was General Maurice Gamelin's plan of an offensive from both north and south to prevent the Germans splitting the front into two. However on 19 May General Gamelin was relieved of command and his

Right: **A turret of the Maginot Line, which proved no adequate defense for France. It was outflanked.**
Far right: **The triumphal parade staged by the Nazis after their seizure of Paris on 14 June 1940. They moved up the Avenue Foch, shown here, and down the Champs Elysées.**

successor, General Maxime Weygand, cancelled the combined counteroffensive. On 20 May, when Hitler gave his Armies the green light to roll on again, the 2nd Panzer Division reported that it had reached Abbeville thus cutting the armies in the north from the south. On 21 May Lord Gort and the French 1st Army made a last attempt at breaking south near Arras, but when this last attempt failed, all dissolved in chaos.

Whether the Germans were also affected by the general chaos of the fighting is still unclear and disputed. By 24 May Guderian's tanks had captured Boulogne, bypassed Calais and were within sight of Dunkirk, when they were again halted on Hitler's personal orders. In the north the Belgians were about to surrender, while the French 1st Army was holding a salient southeast of Lille. General Gamelin's orders for re-grouping and counterattack certainly made sense, but they served only to disorganize still further the demoralized French and British troops and command. The newly appointed Commander-in-Chief not only cancelled the counteroffensive, but also failed to restore morale in the north; despite his seeing King Leopold (or perhaps because of it) the Belgians surrendered. General Billotte would probably not have restored French morale in any case after his talk with Weygand; mercifully he was killed in a car accident before he could even start. Weygand did not find Lord Gort, the commander of the BEF, and it is not clear whether Gort would have obeyed French orders anyway. As it was he was ordered by Premier Churchill to "save" the BEF by evacuating it from the only remaining port, Dunkirk. Thus the combination of Allied chaos and Hitler's momentary hesitation produced the miracle of Dunkirk.

While General Weygand was roving in Northern France in search of his ally, Lord Gort had decided to cut his losses and withdraw to England. He warned London of his intentions a week in advance and when on 25 May he actually gave orders to start evacuation, the Navy had the situa-

Above right: **A German soldier observes a burning village in northern France in June 1940.**
Right: **A wrecked British ship left at Dunkirk after its capture. By the time it was taken almost 350,000 Allied troops had been evacuated.**

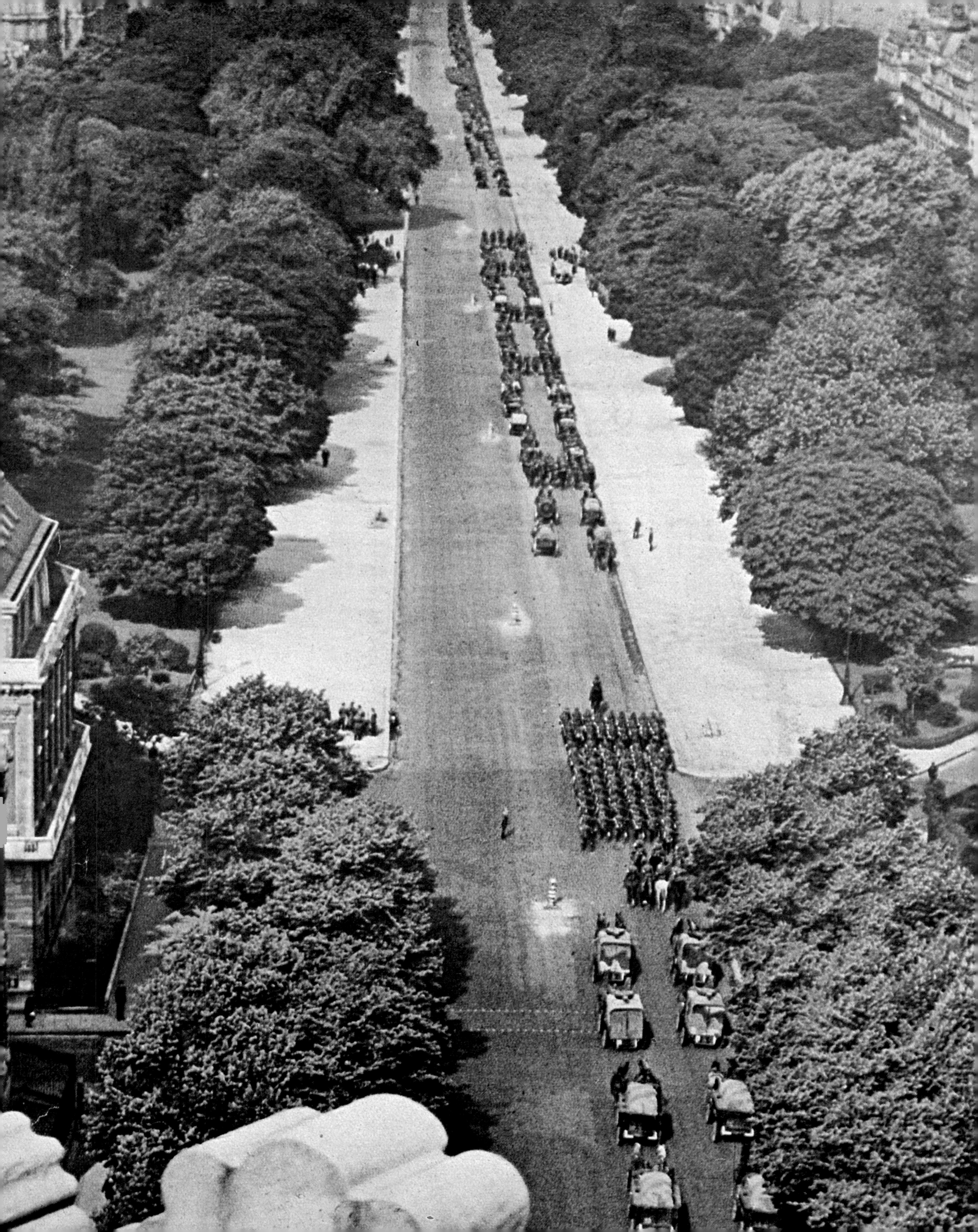

Above: **General Friedrich Fromm, who was awarded the Knight's Cross during the Battle of France.**
Below: **British troops huddled on the Dunkirk shore await evacuation.**

tion more or less under control. Everything seemed to have worked in Gort's favor: the sea was calm; there were clouds about which prevented the Luftwaffe from attacking Dunkirk; Hitler had halted the armor. By 31 May 126,000 troops had been evacuated. The 1st French Army fought the rearguard actions to enable the BEF to withdraw taking with them numerous French troops. On 1 June 1940 only some 4000 British troops were left at Dunkirk; however 95,000 mainly French troops left behind had to surrender. By 4 June 1940 while Dunkirk was still defended by some 40,000 French troops, the Navy was able to evacuate about 338,226 British and French soldiers. Naturally the BEF lost all its equipment and while the evacuation was a miracle, it was also a heavy military and political defeat.

Still the main reason for the miracle was obviously Hitler's decision to halt the advance of his armor. Hitler must have been influenced by serious military factors which were subsequently disputed by his generals: (a) the unsuitability of the terrain and potential losses; (b) plentiful infantry in General von Bock's Armies coming south from Belgium; (c) Marshal Goering's intervention on behalf of the Luftwaffe. Probably all these factors influenced Hitler's decision and he had two additional political reasons to let the BEF escape from the Dunkirk trap. He did not want to fight a major battle in Flanders which he considered as pro-Nazi, deserving an independent Flemish state, and he wanted to defeat the French first, offer them an equitable peace, and then come to terms with Britain.

However, even after this Allied disaster, the decisive battle with the French Armies was still to come and Hitler concentrated von Bock's and von Rundstedt's Army

Groups, together with all the armor, against the new French front line running from the Somme to the Aisne. General Weygand managed to amass 62 French and three British divisions which were to block the way of the 143 German divisions which Hitler had at his disposal. Although the ten Panzer divisions had facing them four armored divisions and three light cavalry divisions the French gave no thought to checking the Panzers with their own medicine and continued to use their armored formations instead of infantry. Moreover General Weygand did not believe in orderly retreat and he therefore ordered his troops to hold on to their defense line at all cost. Still his defense line was riddled with gaps and not properly covered with artillery; neither had it protective minefields. Mostly it lacked mobile formations which could search for dead ground and seal enemy penetrations.

Above: **An abandoned British truck and the burning town of Dunkirk after its seizure by the Germans.**
Bottom: **British Tommies use their rifles against attacking German aircraft which tried to impede the evacuation.**

Above: **Thousands of British and French troops line up to await evacuation from Dunkirk by the armada of "little ships" which were to take most of them back to England.**
Below: **Some of the last little ships crossing the Channel with their precious human cargo.**

On 5 June von Bock's armies went onto the offensive and after three days of fighting they managed to break through the improvised line on the Somme. On 9 June they crossed the Seine and at the same time Rundstedt unleashed his offensive in the Champagne region. For three days he made no progress until the French were forced back by their exposed left flank, caused by the collapse in the northwest. On 11 June von Kleist's armor crossed the Marne at Château-Thierry and raced on to Besançon to trap the 17 French divisions on the Maginot line. France's fate was sealed: Küchler's Eighteenth Army converged on Paris and took the city without firing a shot. To complete the humiliation of France *Il Duce* now decided to join the Führer and Italy entered the war. The military confusion after the breakthrough in Picardy and Champagne was even worse than previously in the north. Even German units became bewildered by their rapid advance, often crossing their own line, sometimes getting in each other's way. Politically the disaster was absolute.

The French government left its capital on 10 June and repaired to Bordeaux. Two days later General Weygand declared the military situation hopeless and requested his government to sue for an armistice. Premier Paul Reynaud resisted these defeatist moves as long as he could, but on

Left : **Poster advertising the German Navy, which was unable to stop the Dunkirk evacuation or transport Wehrmacht troops to England in the projected invasion, Operation Sea Lion.**

16 June, after his cabinet had rejected Churchill's offer of a Franco–British Union, he resigned and was replaced by Marshal Philippe Pétain. On the next day the aged *Maréchal de France*, defender of Verdun, applied for armistice terms through the Spanish ambassador. Hitler first declared that he had to consult Mussolini and requested the French to send a delegation to hear his conditions at Compiègne, the same spot on which the Germans signed the armistice in November 1918.

On 21 June 1940 Hitler and his entourage arrived first and installed themselves in the railway car in which Marshal Foch presided over the signature of the armistice. The French armistice delegation, led by General Huntziger, was visibly shaken by this circumstance, but bore itself with great dignity even when General Wilhelm Keitel had read to them Hitler's conditions, which were tough and made even more humiliating by being made contingent on an armistice with Italy. Then Huntziger revealed that he was not authorized to sign them on the spot, but had to have his government's consent. To the great annoyance of the German generals – Hitler left with Goering and Hess after the preamble – telephone communications had to be established with Bordeaux and Huntziger transmitted the terms to General

Weygand. The French particularly objected to the surrender of the anti-Nazi refugees to the Germans, but Hitler gave orders that nothing could be modified in his *Diktat*: French ships had to be disarmed and placed under German supervision in French ports; some 1,500,000 soldiers had to lay down their arms and go into captivity (until a peace treaty was signed which meant for the duration of the war); and France was to be divided into two with only the southern zone to be left under Marshal Pétain's administration. Still the French objected and bickered, until Keitel had to issue an ultimatum. Then on 22 June, on orders from his government, Huntziger signed the humiliating armistice conditions which made France a vassal of Germany. The armistice with Italy was signed in Rome and was much more bearable – thus on 24 June France was pacified by the conquering Germans and Hitler was master of the European continent, with the exception of the USSR in the east and Great Britain in the west. All this was accomplished at the cost of some 156,000 men (including 27,000 killed and 18,000 missing); Hitler's belief in his military genius was confirmed and he was most impressed with his instrument, the Wehrmacht, which implemented his inspiration and plans. Even as he gloated over his achievements – the exiled Kaiser congratulated him – he was thinking of the last obstacle to a complete victory, Britain.

Britain had always puzzled Hitler and he professed a soft spot for her. However this time he committed military and political miscalculations *vis à vis* that mysterious Albion. Politically he was quite convinced that after the beating the British received in Norway and in France, particularly after Dunkirk, they would sue for peace. The armistice terms which he imposed on the French were also not as severe as he, the victorious Führer, would have wished, because he thought that Britain would be moved by them to apply for terms. At the same time, the Pope and the King of Sweden were instigating peace initiatives which would result in a peace settlement between Germany and Britain. Even in the United States peace moves were afoot and isolationists exerted great pressure on President Roosevelt and his government. Hitler was so convinced that he would have peace without further fighting that he failed to issue orders to his Wehrmacht to plan a campaign against Britain itself. Only on 16 July, when it became clear to everyone that Churchill would never sue for peace, did Hitler issue Directive 16 for Operation Sea Lion, the invasion of England; still he was not sure whether it would ever be carried out; no date was fixed – plans were to be ready in mid-August.

Still planning had to start in earnest and the Army obliged first. The newly created Field Marshal von Rundstedt was to command the main action against Britain,

Below: **Submarine Spitfires of No 610 Squadron of the RAF.**
Right: **Roof spotters watch the fires in London from Northcliffe House during the Blitz.**

Right: **Holborn Circus under fire during the German bombing of London.**
Below right: **Firefighters are unable to stop the collapse of a building in London bombed by the Luftwaffe.**

UNSERE

Luftwaffe

Above left: **Top, front, bottom and side views of the Messerschmitt Bf 109, the principal fighter aircraft of the Luftwaffe used to protect bombers during the Battle of Britain.**
Left: **An Me 109 over England. Their short range prevented them from remaining in the battle zone for much more than ten minutes.**
Top: **A Heinkel 111 takes on fuel.**
Above: **Me 110 and its crew during a briefing session in France before a mission over England.**
Above right: **Recruitment poster for the Luftwaffe.**
Right: **A squadron of Focke-Wulf 200 Condor bombers shortly before take-off.**

a thrust from the Pas de Calais into Kent. Six infantry divisions of General Busch's Sixteenth Army were to execute this thrust. Four divisions of General Strauss's Ninth Army were to strike Brighton from Le Havre, while three divisions of Field Marshal (also very recently created) von Reichenau's Sixth Army were to deliver their blow against Weymouth from Cherbourg. All these forces and additional ones (six Panzer divisions, two airborne divisions) were to land in three waves and achieve three objectives: (1) move from the bridgeheads to the line between Gravesend to Southampton; (2) then from the Thames estuary to the Severn estuary; and (3) surround London and continue the drive north. Field Marshal von Brauchitsch told Admiral Raeder that the operations would take about a month to complete, that is provided the Navy got the Army across the Channel and the Luftwaffe knocked out the Royal Air Force. Both these provisos were formidable and nothing could be done about any of these plans until 15 September 1940, when the Navy would have assembled enough boats for the shipping of the invading armies. Although in July Hitler reminded his soldiers and sailors several times (21 July, 31 July) at conferences and in Directives 17 and 18 that Britain had to be finished off quickly, no one, not even Hitler, exerted himself to the utmost to bring this about. They all seem to have concentrated on vague political hopes and on carrying out the threefold tasks which General Alfried Jodl proposed to Hitler back in June: (a) intensification of the German air and sea war against British shipping, storage depots, factories and the Royal Air Force, (b) terror attacks against the centers of population, (c) culminating in a landing of troops with the objective of occupying England. Jodl also suggested that the protectorates and outlying colonies of the British Empire should be attacked in conjunction with Italy, Japan, Spain

Left : **Part of the extent of the damage near the Cathedral in Coventry, which was almost totally wiped out by the Luftwaffe during the Battle of Britain.** *Above :* **Cockney humor carries on in London's East End during the height of the Blitz in September 1940.**

and Soviet Russia, in order to subdue the incorrigible British indirectly.

While waiting for the Navy to get ready, the newly created Reichsmarschall Goering, Commander-in-Chief of the Luftwaffe, proposed to Hitler to drive the RAF out of the sky, thus launching what later became the Battle of Britain. It started on 10 August and was to be concluded in two to four weeks. With hindsight Hitler committed his first strategic error by allowing his political confederate, Goering, to assume leadership of the struggle against Britain. The poor (fat) *Reichsmarschall* not only failed to inspire his airmen as Hitler had done with the army, but also had his judgments proved wrong: he could not destroy the RAF by switching air attacks from the fighter airfields to London and other cities, and above all, by failing to concentrate on knocking out radar stations, he was reponsible for losing the Battle. Otherwise he had clear air superiority: two air fleets with 875 high level bombers and 316 dive bombers protected by some 929 fighters were opposed by only 650 fighters of the RAF. Moreover Britain was short of pilots and as the battle intensified the casualties were that much harder to replace. German pilots though more plentiful had to go on escort duties which affected their morale and thus cancelled their numerical superiority. Also they were handicapped technically, their aircraft being of a limited range and their radio equipment truly primitive. As a consequence of the fighter shortcomings bomber crews suffered heavy losses and in time their morale declined as well. Above all the Luftwaffe suffered from poor intelligence: it practically ignored radar installations and took little notice of the British weather. Still despite these weaknesses, when the two Air Forces finally joined battle, the issue was largely undecided and could have easily gone either way.

For three days, between 13 and 15 August, the Luftwaffe delivered softening-up blows. First it bombed radar stations, knocking out only one of them. Next it attacked fighter airfields damaging them only slightly but sustaining relatively heavy losses (between 34 which the Germans admitted were lost and 47 aircraft which the British claimed had been shot down). On 15 August the first large-scale air battle took place: in the north of England Air Fleet 5 coming from Scandinavia suffered unexpected losses which knocked it out of further fighting, while in the south, Croydon and its aircraft factories were damaged as well as several fighter airfields. But again German losses were relatively high – some 75 planes – which greatly boosted British morale. Up to 19 August when the weather prevented either side from flying, the British inflicted heavy casualties on the Germans, especially on the *Stuka* bombers, which were withdrawn from the Battle.

On 24 August the Battle was resumed and this time the Luftwaffe was better prepared: forward airfields were attacked more efficiently and many more were seriously damaged. Also the communication system was damaged and the RAF began to feel its numerical inferiority. Goering then decided to increase the number of bombers to 1000 per day to wear the British out. However these massive bomber formations, intended to bomb airfields, got lost and unloaded their bombs on London. This led to reprisal raids on Berlin and counter-raids on London thus diverting the Luftwaffe from its original purpose, the destruction of the RAF. While during August the British

Above: **A British transport sinking after an attack by a Ju 88. The Ju 88 still ranks as one of the most effective bombers.**
Left: **Luftwaffe ground mechanic with his ammunition belt.**

lost 338 Hurricanes and Spitfires and were very much on the way to destruction, in September the Luftwaffe suddenly switched to bombing aircraft factories thus giving the pilots a chance to recover. On 7 September there was a daylight raid on London, in which the East End suffered particularly; but two days later a similar raid failed due to the interception of the bombers by British fighters. On 15 September the German raiders suffered very heavy losses and failed to reach their targets. This was probably the main reason why Hitler decided to postpone the invasion of England and subsequently postpone it indefinitely, when it transpired that neither the Luftwaffe nor the Navy was capable of achieving its primary objectives: destroy the RAF or transport the Army safely across the Channel.

The air battles went on though no one knew why. Hitler stressed that the "pressures" on Britain had to continue, but he was already exploring the "indirect" alternatives. From 9 September London was attacked by 160 bombers for 57 nights without interruption. On 14 November 1940 a night raid destroyed Coventry and gave the British ideas for retaliatory raids in the future. Still Hitler wondered why Britain would not submit and with the dropping of Operation Sea Lion he turned seriously to the Mediterranean alternative; with the aid of his allies he would seize Gibraltar and North Africa, especially Egypt, and thus humble the invincible British enemy. Quite unwittingly Hitler began the geographical dissipation of the Wehrmacht, which in the end would prove fatal. First he consulted his allies but was quickly disappointed. The recently victorious Generalissimo Franco of Spain demanded too high a price for helping him to conquer Gibraltar, while Pétain did not want to help at all with his North African designs although he did sign a paper declaration. Only Mussolini was willing, but he was an unpredictable ally: on 28 October, without the slightest consultation, Mussolini invaded Greece and achieved nothing for his trouble. On 20

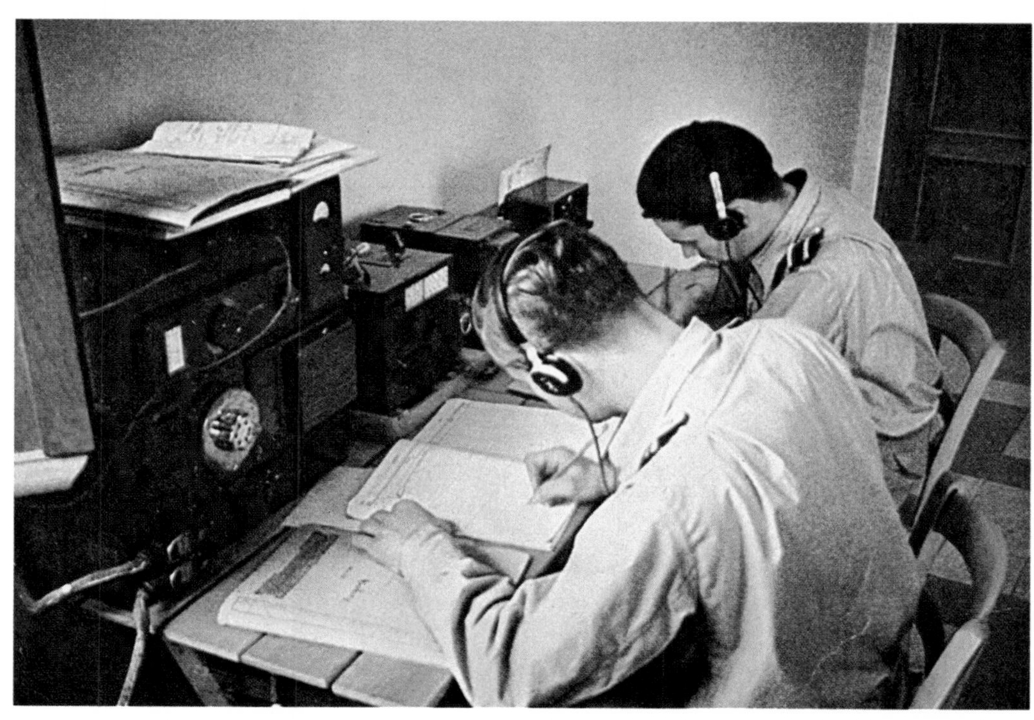

January 1941 Hitler and Mussolini conferred in the Berghof to sort out their alliance problems, for Italy by now was committed everywhere in the Mediterranean and was obviously unable to cope. Hitler seemed in perfect strategic control and told Mussolini that by 15 May 1941 all would be solved, even his conflict in Libya and Greece.

After the abandonment of the invasion of Britain, Premier Churchill had nothing left but to challenge Germany and her allies in North Africa and the Middle East. He therefore planned a war of attrition in this area as a preliminary to the assault on Fortress Europe, which was now firmly in Hitler's hands. The bulk of the fighting

Left: **A field radio station in Norway. The Luftwaffe briefly used Norwegian bases for attacks on Britain, but most airfields were in France.**
Below: **An Me 110 which was sent to the North African campaign in 1941.**

Above : **British tanks in action in Libya during the first stages of the North African campaign.**
Right : **Germans pause to get their bearings as the Afrika Korps moved along the coast in Libya in 1941.**

was done in northern Africa, and started as soon as Italy declared war on the Western Allies. Under Field Marshal Graziani the Italian Army advanced into Egypt, but was halted because of heavy losses. The British under General O'Connor counterattacked in December 1940 and successes followed in quick succession: Bardia, Tobruk and Benghazi were captured and some 130,000 POWs taken. This was, however, the limit for O'Connor's Army of some 31,000, for reinforcements were now directed to Crete and Greece, which were threatened by both Italy and Germany. However Hitler decided to lend a hand to Mussolini and on 5 February 1941 the Afrika Korps, under the command of Lieutenant General Rommel, made its appearance in Libya to prop up its Italian ally. Early in March Rommel, contrary to all expectation, launched a major offensive which wiped out all British gains and was a major disaster for

Below: **Panzer Mark IV, the most modern German tank in 1942, one of the few available for the defense of Tunisia after Alamein.**

Top : **The Germans outside Tobruk, whose siege slowed their advance to Egypt.**
Above left : **An Me 109 in the Western Desert.**
Above : **German paratroops in rocky North African terrain.**

the British Army in North Africa. The Germans supported by the Italians very quickly recaptured Benghazi, inflicted heavy casualties on the British and came to a halt at the El Gazala–Bir Hacheim line when they ran out of steam overextending their lines of communications. Still this was a tremendous success, quite unhoped for, as Hitler intended to concentrate on clearing his flank in the Balkans for a much grander battle, the invasion and destruction of the USSR.

There were so many diversions and obstacles before Hitler could embark on Operation *Barbarossa*, that his actions in the Balkans seemed savage. As soon as the weather permitted, and after failing to win over Yugoslavia politically, Hitler launched a devastating attack against that country and on 17 April she capitulated. A week later Greece was captured after some spirited fighting, but Hitler once again overreached himself dissipating his Wehrmacht forces unnecessarily. As a preventative move he wanted to take Crete from the British and did so in Operation Mercury; the island was seized on 20 May by a paratroop force brought to Crete in gliders and transport aircraft. However casualties were heavy: some 6000 elite troops killed and 400 aircraft either damaged or destroyed. This diversion, as well as the imbroglios in North Africa, Yugoslavia and Greece was to upset his timetable for *Barbarossa*: the dissipation of resources delayed the execution of *Barbarossa*, an operation directed against a one-time ally, but now mighty enemy, the USSR.

Left: **The port of Tobruk after an aerial attack.**
Below: **Antiquated aircraft of the Italian Air Force.**

1

2

1. The personal standard of Adolf Hitler.
2. 3. 4. 5. Hitler's standard in use.

3

4

5

ON THE EASTERN FRONT

Above: **The famous Russian T-34/85 medium tank which devastated early German tank models on the Eastern Front.**

Above: **The antiquated T-26 light tank was phased out by the Russians.**
Below: **Sleds carrying German equipment trudge through the bleak Russian snows.**
Right: **Soviet poster showing a stake being driven into the German tiger.**
Far right: **Nazi poster showing the Wehrmacht slaying the Soviet dragon on behalf of "Europe's Freedom."**

The alliance with the USSR, concluded in August 1939, was always considered by the Germans and especially by Hitler to be purely tactical and thus short term. Hitler was on record that Germany's vital *Lebensraum* interests lay in the East, and throughout the years of alliance the two "incompatible" allies had looked at each other's moves and actions with suspicion. In April 1940, when the Germans moved against Denmark and Norway, the Soviets approved the operation as being forced on Germany, albeit Germany had never approved the Soviet war against the Finns in the same fashion. Again in May Molotov approved the "defensive" attack on France and her allies, but this time the USSR wanted something more than approval in return. While the German armies were busy humbling the West, the Soviets were on a rampage in the East; to preempt British and French intrigues in the Baltic states, in order to sow discord between Germany and the USSR, the Soviets decided to annex them. On 14 June Lithuania was sent an unacceptable ultimatum and on the following day the Red Army occupied the country, even though its government complied with the ultimatum. Immediately afterwards the same technique was applied to Latvia and Estonia and both countries were occupied by the Red Army. In all three countries the Soviets "organized" elections and the new parliaments applied to join the Soviet Union to which they were admitted in August 1940.

Hitler was extremely annoyed with these *faits accomplis*. However they did not mark the end of Soviet ambition. Molotov immediately raised with the Germans the old problems with Rumania, the question of Bessarabia and Bukhovina. While the former had been a Russian province before 1918, and as such was part of the Soviet sphere of influence, Bukhovina had never been discussed. Still the real inconvenience for Germany stemmed from the fact that both provinces were part of Rumania and Rumania was their only source of oil. If the Soviets occupied that country as well, without the Rumanian oil fields the

БЕЙ НЕМЕЦКИХ ЗВЕРЕЙ!
УНИЧТОЖИТЬ ГИТЛЕРОВСКУЮ АРМИЮ—МОЖНО И ДОЛЖНО.

Deutschlands Sieg
EUROPAS FREIHEIT

Directive No 21 Case Barbarossa

The German Armed Forces must be prepared, even before the conclusion of the war against England, *to crush Soviet Russia in a rapid campaign* (Case Barbarossa).

The *Army* will have to employ all available formations to this end, with the reservation that occupied territories must be insured against surprise attacks.

The *Air Force* will have to make available for this Eastern campaign supporting forces of such strength that the Army will be able to bring land operations to a speedy conclusion and that Eastern Germany will be as little damaged as possible by enemy air attack. This build up of a focal point in the East will be limited only by the need to protect from air attack the whole combat and arsenal area which we control, and to ensure that attacks on England, and especially upon her imports, are not allowed to lapse.

The main efforts of the *Navy* will continue to be directed against *England* even during the Eastern campaign.

In certain circumstances I shall issue orders for the *deployment* against Soviet Russia eight weeks before the operation is timed to begin.

Preparations which require more time than this will be put in hand now, in so far as this has not already been done, and will be concluded by 15 May 1941.

It is of decisive importance that our intention to attack should not be known.

The preparations of the High Commands will be made on the following basis:

I General Intention

The bulk of the Russian Army stationed in Western Russia will be destroyed by daring operations led by deeply penetrating armored spearheads. Russian forces still capable of giving battle will be prevented from withdrawing into the depths of Russia.

The enemy will then be energetically pursued and a line will be reached from which the Russian Air Force can no longer attack German territory. The final objective of the operation is to erect a barrier against Asiatic Russia on the general line Volga-Archangel. The last surviving industrial area of Russia in the Urals can then, if necessary, be eliminated by the Air Force.

In the course of these operations the Russian *Baltic Fleet* will quickly lose its bases and will then no longer be capable of action.

The effective operation of the Russian *Air Force* is to be prevented from the beginning of the attack by powerful blows.

II Probable Allies and their Tasks

1 On the flanks of our operations we can count on the active support of *Rumania* and *Finland* in the war against Soviet Russia.

The High Command of the Armed Forces will decide and lay down in due time the manner in which the forces of these two countries will be brought under German command.

2 It will be the task of *Rumania* to support the attack of the German southern flank, at least at the outset, with its best troops; to hold down the enemy where German forces are not engaged; and to provide auxiliary services in the rear areas.

3 *Finland* will cover the advance of the *Northern Group* of German forces moving from Norway (detachments of Group XXI) and will operate in conjunction with them. Finland will also be responsible for eliminating Hangö.

4 It is possible that *Swedish* railways and roads may be available for the movement of the German Northern Group, by the beginning of the operation at the latest.

III Conduct of Operations

A *Army* (in accordance with plans submitted to me):

In the theater of operations, which is divided by the Pripet Marshes into a Southern and a Northern sector, the main weight of attack will be delivered in the *Northern* area. Two Army Groups will be employed here.

The more southerly of these two Army Groups (in the center of the whole front) will have the task of advancing with powerful armored and motorized formations from the area about and north of Warsaw, and routing the enemy forces in White Russia. This will make it possible for strong mobile forces to advance northwards and, in conjunction with the Northern Army Group operating out of East Prussia in the general direction of Leningrad, to destroy the enemy forces operating in the Baltic area. Only after the fulfilment of this first essential task, which must include the occupation of Leningrad and Kronstadt, will the attack be continued with the intention of occupying Moscow, an important centre of communications and of the armaments industry.

Only a surprisingly rapid collapse of Russian resistance could justify the simultaneous pursuit of both objectives.

The most important task of Group XXI, even during these Eastern operations, remains the protection of Norway. Any forces available after carrying out this task will be employed in the North (Mountain Corps), at first to protect the Petsamo area and its iron ore mines and the Arctic highway, then to advance with Finnish forces against the Murmansk railway and thus prevent the passage of supplies to Murmansk by land.

The question whether an operation of this kind can be carried out with *stronger* German forces (two or three divisions) from the Rovaniemi area and south of it will depend on the willingness of Sweden to make its railways available for troop transport.

It will be the duty of the main body of the Finnish Army, in conjunction with the advance of the German North flank, to hold down the strongest possible Russian forces by an attack to the West, or on both sides of Lake Ladoga, and to occupy Hangö.

The Army Group operating *South* of the Pripet Marshes will also seek, in a concentric operation with strong forces on either flank, to destroy all Russian forces west of the Dnieper in the Ukraine. The *main attack* will be carried out from the Lublin area in the general direction of Kiev, while forces in Rumania will carry out a wide enclosing movement across the lower Pruth. It will be the task of the Rumanian Army to hold down Russian forces in the intervening area.

When the battles north and south of the Pripet Marshes are ended the pursuit of the enemy will have the following aims:

In the *South* the early capture of the Donets Basin, important for war industry.

In the *North* a quick advance to Moscow. The capture of this city would represent a decisive political and economic success and would also bring about the capture of the most important railway junctions.

B *Air Force*

It will be the duty of the Air Force to paralyse and eliminate the effectiveness of the Russian Air Force as far as possible. It will also support the main operations of the Army, that is those of the central Army Group and of the vital flank of the Southern Army Group. Russian railways will either be destroyed or, in accordance with operational requirements, captured at their most important points (river crossings) by the bold employment of parachute and airborne troops.

In order that we may concentrate all our strength against the enemy Air Force and for the immediate support of land operations, the Russiam armaments industry will not be attacked during the main operations. Such attacks will be made only after the conclusion of mobile warfare, and they will be concentrated first on the Urals area.

C *Navy*

It will be the duty of the Navy during the attack on Soviet Russia to protect our own coasts and to prevent the breakout of enemy naval units from the Baltic. As the Russian Baltic fleet will, with the capture of Leningrad, lose its last base and will then be in a hopeless position, major naval action will be avoided until this occurs.

After the elimination of the Russian fleet the duty of the Navy will be to protect the entire maritime traffic in the Baltic and the transport of supplies by sea to the Northern flank (clearing of minefields!).

IV. All steps taken by Commanders in Chief on the basis of this directive must be phrased on the unambiguous assumption that they are *precautionary measures* undertaken in case Russia should alter its present attitude towards us. The number of officers employed on preliminary preparations will be kept as small as possible and further staffs will be designated as late as possible and only to the extent required for the duties of each individual. Otherwise there is a danger that premature knowledge of our preparations, whose execution cannot yet be timed with any certainty, might entail the gravest political and military disadvantages.

V I await submission of the plans of Commanders in Chief on the basis of this directive.

The preparations made by all branches of the Armed Forces, together with timetables, are to be reported to me through the High Command of the Armed Forces.

signed: ADOLF HITLER

Extract from H R Trevor-Roper *Hitler's War Directives, 1939-1945* (London, 1964). Quoted by permission of Sidgwick & Jackson Limited.

January 1941 – November 1942

German war machine would have been in real trouble. Thus to save the oil fields Rumanians were told to cede to the Soviets the two provinces which the Red Army immediately occupied. Excited by these developments in the East Hitler told his generals about his intentions to sort out the USSR as soon as he finished the war in the West. However the first concrete step in this direction was taken on 21 July 1940, when Hitler ordered Brauchitsch to plan the invasion of Soviet Russia.

The Army had made a technical study of such an invasion, but it was rather limited. The campaign against the USSR, whose aim was to defeat the Soviet armies, was to take four to six weeks and be carried out by 80 to 100 German divisions. Hitler had in mind something more grandiose and informed his generals on 31 July when they all gathered in the Berghof. The invasion of Russia (and he persisted in calling the USSR by its old name) was to have as its aim the smashing of the Russian nation, the destruction of the Russian state (*schwer zerschlagen*), and its division into many parts: the Ukraine, White Russia, the Baltic states. Although this was a conceptual conference at which he tried out strategic terms Hitler also gave his generals a military framework within which to work and also set a deadline: May 1941. He visualized some 120 divisions invading Russia in two thrusts: one in the north, through the Baltic states whose goal was Moscow; the other through the Ukraine to Kiev and the Dniepr, after which a special operation would be mounted to secure Baku and its oil fields. It would all be finished by the winter. This then was Hitler's decision on European hegemony, the solution of his *Lebensraum* problem and the first and last step towards German mastery of the European continent economically sustained by the conquered Slavs (Himmler's *führerloses Arbeitsvolk*). The following day the German General Staff began to fill in these strategic concepts with real military meat, and no one thought of inquiring about, not to mention protest against, the

new type of warfare that Hitler envisaged.

On 12 November 1940 Hitler issued a comprehensive directive about his military plans in Europe. Concerning Soviet Russia Hitler said that he wanted to eliminate this last remaining enemy on the continent because of its ambitions in the Balkans. He was obviously reacting in anger to Molotov's recent demands in that area [Bulgaria and the Straits], because no further planning talks took place until March 1941. Early in that month Hitler convoked top party and military leaders to a conference in which he further described the type of fighting he had in mind to pursue in Russia and further clarified his ultimate "ends." More than the armies had to be destroyed: the state itself was to be obliterated and the succession "states" would conclude peace with Germany. He then proposed to liquidate "the Jewish-Bolshevik intelligentsia which had so far oppressed the nation" with brutal violence (*brutalste Gewalt*). The state would be destroyed by wholesale liquidation of its officials (*Funktionäre*). He considered these tasks so hard that he told the gathering that not even the Army could be told. This was the type of clash of *Weltanschauungen* that Hitler had in mind, when he first considered the Bolshevik problem in 1940. He returned to the same theme on 30 March, when he discussed Soviet Russia with the top Wehrmacht generals: "*wir müssen von dem Standpunkt des soldatischen Kameradentums abrücken . . .*

Left: **A German mobile column on the long road east into the Soviet Union during Operation** ***Barbarossa.***
Below: **A German Mark IV tank in Russian snows in 1942.**

wir führen nicht Krieg, um den Feind zu konservieren . . ." (no feeling of soldierly comradeship must be left . . . the war is not fought to preserve the enemy). Hitler seems to have been obsessed with the annihilations in the East; he thought that 75 percent of the Slavonic population would be deported to Siberia and the remaining Slavs would be reduced to the status of helots (slaves). Since he did not think he had enough Germans to settle the conquered *Lebensraum* he hoped to settle Norwegians, Swedes, Danes and Dutchmen there. All these deliberations finally led Hitler to issue concrete orders on the conduct of the war in the East.

Directive 21, *Fall Barbarossa*, was issued on 18 December 1940 and made Hitler's ruminations lethal. The Army, as bidden in the directive, got down to military planning, but at the same time had to deal with Hitler's extra-military ideas. On 3 March 1941 General Jodl, Chief of Staff of the OKW, tried to get out of Hitler's terroristic plans much too neatly: he proposed that the Army would concern itself with military operations only, while the *Reichskomissariat* would look after the administration of the conquered territory

Above: **Panzergrenadiers follow closely behind their tank during the German drive into the Caucasus in the summer of 1942.**
Below: **A Russian village ablaze during the German onslaught.**

and Himmler's SS and SD after "security" matters. The OKW discussed these ideas and ten days later Field Marshal Keitel issued them as a directive to the Armed Forces. However the Army would not get out of the responsibility for the proposed war crimes so easily. On 26 March the Army agreed to give a free hand to the SS *Einsatzgruppen* in their zones of operations to avoid using terror on the population. It was hoped that in any case terror would be used *after* the conquest, as had happened before in Poland.

While the generals discussed these matters and probably quite genuinely tried to avoid carrying them out, Hitler was more than determined to have everybody involved in his terroristic orders and their application in Russia. The Army's order on the discipline during the *Barbarossa* operation was countered by Hitler's order of 15 May 1941: all court-martials were canceled during the operations; troops were permitted to execute partisans (*Freischärler*), and even civilians who attacked them, on the spot without fear of judicial action; even collective measures against places (for example, villages) from which anti-German attacks were launched, were covered by this order. Thus the Army had a free hand to behave in the East like the medieval marauding hordes of the Mongols or Tartars; in addition it had to co-operate in carrying out the notorious *Kommissar Ordnung* issued by Hitler in March 1941. On 6 June the OKW issued the so-called guidance (*Richtlinien*) for carrying out this order by the troops. Only top Army and Air Force personnel were issued with this order in writing (and they were ordered to destroy it afterwards) subordinate commanders received the order by word of mouth: they were bidden to execute fighting *Kommissars* immediately, while the non-combatant *Kommissars* were to be handed over to the SS *Einsatzkommandos*.

The preoccupation of Hitler and the German Army with these measures for genocide betrayed not only the uncivilized character of their warfare in the East, but also their abysmal ignorance of the East. Apart from the ideological point which described the coming struggle as the rooting out of a rival *Weltanschauung*, Hitler was quite wrong on all counts which he used to justify his terrorist policies in the East. He considered that since the USSR was not a signatory to the Hague and Geneva Conventions it would treat German prisoners inhumanly and he therefore thought it right to retaliate. Moreover, his definition of a *Kommissar* was extremely naive: the nine points of the definition covered anyone in the USSR who could read and write. Nonetheless the Soviets made efforts to come to an agreement with the Germans, but instead were ignored. In July 1941 they told the Germans through Sweden that they recognized the 4th Hague Convention, naturally on a mutual basis, and in August 1941 they informed the Red Cross in Geneva that they would retaliate against German barbarism and were again ignored. This did not prevent the USSR from coming to an agreement with the satellites, Finland, Italy, Slovakia and Rumania, for proper behavior in war and treatment of both combatants and non-combatants. Ultimately it was the German armies who suffered most from Hitler's criminal orders, for Russian retaliation proved much more consistent, methodical and widespread than the German. Still even the limited application of these orders, especially by the armies, revolted even such a hardened man as the *Reichskommissar*, Alfred Rosenberg, who pleaded with the soldiers to treat Russian prisoners of war within the laws of humanity.

This obsession with genocide probably obscured for Hitler and the Army the real military problems of the coming invasion; thus apart from humanitarian mistakes, the Germans began to make strategic and tactical errors even before the invasion. The Army worked out two strategic concepts for the operation: the first was orthodox and envisaged the destruction of enemy armies in short, sharp battles of encirclement at not great distances from the border; the second, favored by the tank men, envisaged deep thrusts by tank forces, encirclement and destruction of the enemy by the motorized infantry with the armor continuing its thrusts to the nerve centers of the Soviet Union (Moscow, Leningrad). Hitler, who in the past always favored the more adventurous plans, plumped this time for orthodoxy and practically lost the war before it had even started. He had not interfered in the Polish *Blitzkrieg* in the least and it ran its course as he predicted; in the West he actively intervened in the operations, usually against his generals' wishes, and on the whole his intervention insured the ultimate success. Now he decided to intervene overwhelmingly, and

Below : **A German Panzer Mark IV from a Waffen-SS division and some wrecked T-34s which were its victims.**
Above : **A Soviet SU-122 self-propelled gun, equipped with a 122mm howitzer on a T-34 tank body.**
Above left : **Captured officer of the Red Army is transported into captivity on a motorcycle of the Waffen-SS.**

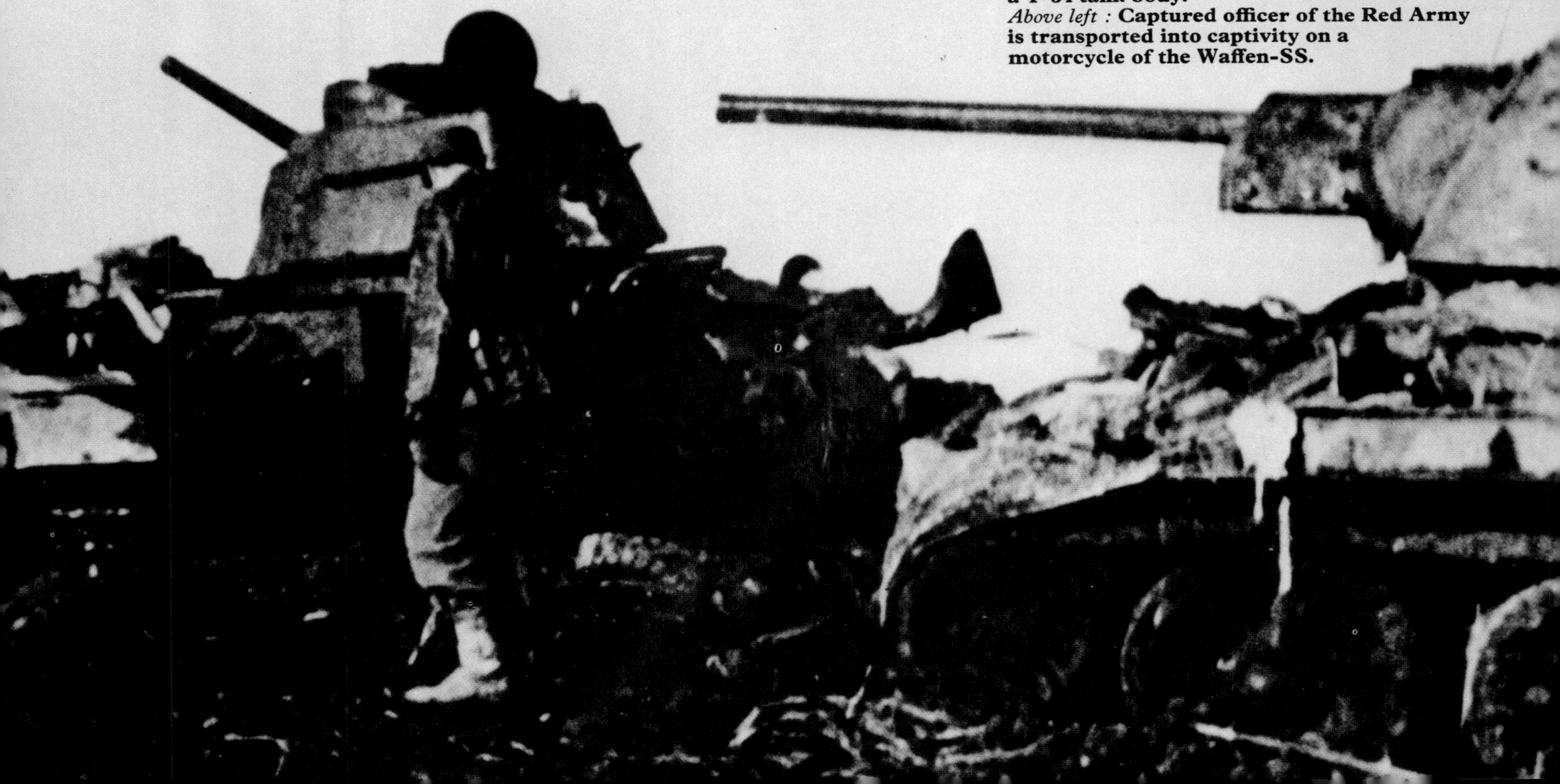

ultimately ruined everything. This only became obvious later, though it was inevitable from the very beginning.

As in the past the success of the *Barbarossa* operation depended on the mechanized forces, especially the tanks; their mobility was to play the vital role in the destruction of the Soviet armies, as it had played the same role in France. However two miscalculations affected the vital role of the tanks in Russia. Firstly, the Germans fielded 19 Panzer divisions which were almost twice as many as in France; however in absolute terms they only had some 800 tanks more than in France and that was clearly insufficient for a decisive campaign of this magnitude. Secondly, this disadvantage could have been recouped if the motorized divisions had been really mobile, but since they were transported on wheels, given the Russian road conditions, they were doomed to delays and disruption of operations. However with the initial impact on the Soviet forces the Germans hoped that somehow both strategic and tactical miscalculations would cancel themselves out; instead, after two years of hard fighting, they rebounded with a vengeance.

Early in the morning on Sunday 22 June 1941, the German Army, well poised and concentrated in the proximity of the Soviet border, fell on the unsuspecting enemy to execute Operation *Barbarossa*. Three mighty thrusts were planned. In eastern Prussia, Army Group North

under the command of Field Marshal Wilhelm Ritter von Leeb, struck with its 600 tanks (4th Panzer Group under General Erich Höpner) against the Baltic states and on to Leningrad. In the west, the largest of the armies, Army Group Center, under Field Marshal Fedor von Bock, with two Panzer armies (2nd Panzer Group under General Heinz Guderian and 3rd Panzer Group under General Hermann Hoth) was to deliver the heaviest blow ultimately taking the capital. In the south Field Marshal Gerd von Rundstedt was in command of Army Group South which with its 1st Panzer Group under General, later Field Marshal Ewald von Kleist, was to conquer the Ukraine.

The surprise factor was supreme; while

Above left: **Wehrmacht cavalry pause during the German drive into the USSR in the summer of 1941.**
Above right: **The Wehrmacht during street fighting in Zhitomir, a town in the Ukraine near Kiev which was taken in late summer 1941.**

Left: **A Focke-Wulf 200 Condor bomber, used on both Eastern and Western Fronts during the war.**

Above: **Russian KV tanks begin their encirclement of Stalingrad in the late autumn of 1942, isolating the German Sixth Army.**
Left: **Field Marshal von Kleist wearing his Iron Cross.**

the Soviet Commanders asked Moscow for orders and were at a loss as to what they should do, the German Luftwaffe attacked and destroyed airfields and aircraft thereon, while the army seized important bridges which enabled the Panzers to pour into Russia. Within two days the Russian front was in pieces and the Panzers wheeled round to perform encirclement movements. However the first two cauldrons, *Kessel*, as the Germans called them, were only partially successful. When the Panzers closed the ring around the Bialystok salient the Fourth Army and the Ninth Army were too slow in coming up to destroy the enemy, which largely managed to break through and retreat. From the very beginning, and quite contrary to their experience in the West, the Germans found out that Soviet armies and even leaderless groups of soldiers resisted to the last, thus holding back the infantry which was so necessary for the destruction of the enemy in the massive armor encirclements. Thus the fortress of Brest held out for a week; some 100,000 men of the elite border troops, Soviet security forces, put up hard fights, and even when defeated, tended to carry on fighting as roving partisan bands delaying the progress of German infantry still further. The second cauldron in the Minsk-Bobruysk area also proved unsatisfactory; the infantry was delayed by tough fighting and rain, and most of the trapped enemy managed to escape. Of the planned encirclements only the Smolensk one lived up to the expectations. After hard fighting the Germans captured some 300,000 Russians, among them Stalin's son, but were far from the initial objective of destroying the Soviet Armed Forces. After Smolensk the Panzers of the Center Group were diverted south to help Rundstedt in his encirclement of the

Soviet southwestern armies. Although this proved to be the largest cauldron ever with some 500,000 prisoners taken, it finally dislocated German strategic and tactical plans. Without decisively destroying the Soviet armies the encirclements proved to be much deeper into Russia than was ever envisaged. Operations were hopelessly and irretrievably behind the planned schedule.

It is obvious that Hitler and the German High Command committed a number of mistakes which threw the planned operations badly out of gear. For example, Halder admitted that he underestimated Russian resources: instead of the estimated 200 divisions he found 360 divisions fighting hard despite defeat. The unexpected, suicidal resistance also upset German planning and schedules and was entirely due to the criminal orders which Hitler had issued before the campaign. As their application quickly spread, Russian soldiers preferred to die fighting and by so doing successfully harassed the numerically weak German infantry; even the Panzers began to suffer heavily, becoming technically immobilized, because the Russian partisans refused to surrender. It was quickly noted that Russian resistance was toughest in the operational zones of the 3rd and 4th Panzer Groups, who seem to have applied the *Kommissar* order most consistently. By 8 July these Panzer armies executed 101 and 170 *kommissars* respectively. Soon Soviet soldiers began to retaliate and the German Army became unnerved when it discovered mass evidence of these retaliations.

However the greatest havoc on both sides was caused by the activity of the SS *Einsatzkommandos*: the scale of their operations confirmed the masses of demoralized Russian soldiers in their resistance and retaliation. With typical German bureaucratic thoroughness the *Einsatzgruppen* were organized in four sections. Group A under the command of SS *Brigadeführer* Dr Stahlecker operated in the Baltic states and the Russian North. By 15 October 1941 it succeeded in massacring some 125,000 Jews and 5000 others. Group B under SS Oberführer Dr Naumann operated in the area of Army Group Center and by 14 November reported some 45,000 executions. Group C under the command of Dr Braune and Dr Thomas operated in the Ukraine and in the first three months managed to massacre 75,000 Jews and 5000 others. In the South SS Brigadeführer Dr Ohlendorf operated with his Group D and they *only* liquidated some 55,000 human souls. All the *Einsatzgruppen* operated in military zones and the impact of their activity on both German and Soviet soldiers can be imagined, though not properly evaluated; for example, at Mogilev 337 Jewish women were publicly executed. Moreover other SS groups operated in POW camps and at Borisov they executed 41,752 *kommissars* and 41,357 Jewish POWs. At Borisov also the first 24 Soviet partisans were publicly executed. *Einsatzkommando* 5, which operated deep in the Ukraine, reported 15,110 executions on 20 October, and at the same time the Gestapo became active on the POWs and quickly eliminated them all. On 5 December 1941 Gestapo chief Müller, reported that after screening 22,000 POWs he liquidated 16,000 of them. Altogether 1,030,157 POWs were

Above: **Field Marshal von Kluge issues his orders. Von Kluge was one of Hitler's most competent generals and was known as *Kluger Hans*, Clever John.**

Above: **Russian forces in the trenches surrounding Leningrad at the start of the 900-day siege of the former Czarist capital.**

Right: **Soviet partisans prepare to blow up a railway track behind German lines in the winter of 1942–43.**
Overleaf: **German field artillery is moved up to the front.**

Right : **The T-32 medium tank, a prototype for the famous T-34.**
Far right : **Stalin and Marshal Voroshilov.**
Below : **Soviet boats continue the trickle of supplies across Lake Ladoga which kept Leningrad alive during its long siege.**

liquidated by the SD or shot while trying to escape, which in time proved a more convenient type of execution. At the end of the war only some 1,000,000 POWs survived out of the 5,700,000 captured.

The short-term effect of these atrocities was catastrophic from the German point of view: German soldiers were paralyzed by fear, fought only in close formations refusing to comb large, conquered areas, thus abandoned to the partisans. Long before Hitler and the High Command realized, the common German soldier and his officer felt that they were being trapped in the open spaces of Russia and that they would only come out alive with luck. However their leaders, encouraged by the vast encirclement successes, were determined to drive the Army on, deeper into Russia. On 21 August 1941 Hitler issued an order in which priorities were modified: Moscow was no longer top priority – Hitler, facing opposition from his generals, whom he declared economic ignoramuses, ordered

Above: **Field Marshal von Manstein studies his plan of attack.**
Above right: **German mountain troops engage a distant enemy with their MG42 machine gun.**

Below: **"War Until Victory" was the slogan used on this "Freedom Loan" Soviet poster.**

the conquest of the Crimea, the industrial Donets basin and the cutting off from Russia of the oil supplies in the Caucasus. Although he permitted further attacks on Leningrad, the northern Group soon became stuck and spectacular advances were only noticeable in the south.

It was only in October 1941 that the offensive against Moscow, Operation Typhoon, was resumed. The Panzer formations besieging Leningrad, were transferred to Army Group Center for this offensive, thus saving that city from German occupation. In launching this offensive the German High Command thought that it would end the war. The Germans attacked on a broad front north of Smolensk with Guderian's tanks striking against Bryansk and Hoth's against Vyazma. After a breakthrough they both wheeled round and netted some 500,000 prisoners, thus destroying Stalin's strategic reserves, many brought in from the Far East. Although the infantry again found it difficult to keep up with the tanks, Moscow was unprotected and within easy reach of the armor and infantry. However the Germans began to encounter difficulty they had never even dreamt about: on 7 October the first snow fell and many vehicles broke down as a result. Still they broke through in the northern sector of the front and the town of Kalinin was taken. This provoked panic in Moscow itself and government offices began to be evacuated to Kyubyshev on the Volga. Although defense positions and trenches were being built, the panic affected not only the population but also political leaders who fled from the city. Widespread looting was reported and Stalin, the lonely dictator, who had not panicked, proclaimed martial law in the city and NKVD troops restored order. As for the Germans their advance in the center had been slowed down, while in the south, where Guderian's breakthrough would have sealed Moscow's fate, desperate Russian counterattacks virtually destroyed Guderian's Panzers. Throughout November 1941 the Russians were forced to retreat, sometimes fast, sometimes slowly, but always fighting hard; they harried the advancing Germans using Katyusha mortars against them and even the Red Air Force revived. Still on 12 November the High Command instead of abandoning the offensive because of supply problems, decided to press on despite mud, cold, snow and general exhaustion.

During November 1941 Stalin reorganized the defenses of Moscow. General Georgi Zhukov was appointed Commander to save the capital after all the other generals had failed. Zhukov was reinforced by troops from the Far East and got some 1700 tanks and 1500 aircraft for his counteroffensive, which Stalin approved on 30 November. By now the ground was hard and the fields and swamps were iced over. Still the Germans kept advancing. Hoth's Panzers had taken Klin and a week later reached the Moscow–Volga canal. However, when Guderian tried to advance in the south, he was heavily mauled by the newly arrived Siberian reinforcements. He tried to have the objectives changed, as he could not carry out his tasks, but both Field Marshals Brauchitsch and Bock were ill, and in any case they refused to change their orders. On Hitler's personal order Field Marshal Günther von Kluge's Fourth Army set out to attack Moscow directly without armored envelopments. It reached the suburbs of the city, but then the Russians finally counterattacked and smashed the attacking German armies to pieces. Throughout 4 and 5 December a snow blizzard raged round the capital; the well-equipped and seasoned Siberian troops tore the exhausted Germans, suffering from cold and dysentery, into shreds. Fragmented as they were, in order not to be completely wiped out, the Germans had to retreat. Seeing the disaster the ailing Field Marshals asked for permission to retreat to a line of defense which was not prepared and when Hitler refused, they resigned. Hitler then took over personally as Commander-in-Chief of the armies and ordered no retreat anywhere.

There is no doubt that Hitler's "take-over and no retreat" order saved the German armies from a rout in December 1941. It is also obvious that the Germans found themselves in a most perilous situation as a result of Hitler's miscalculations and changes of mind. However the collapse of the German Army in the winter conditions in Russia, which had not been taken into account at all by Hitler or the planners, was general and total. Field Marshal von Leeb also resigned when Hitler refused him permission for a tactical retreat on the Leningrad front. In the south Rundstedt's armies conquered the Crimea, Donets and reached Rostov, but were completely exhausted on reaching that city; when the Russians counterattacked, General Höpner ordered withdrawal and abandoned the city. For this he was cashiered and dismissed from the Army. Field Marshal von Rundstedt requested Hitler's permission to withdraw to the river Mius, where he wanted to take a

Below: **Wehrmacht troops construct a temporary bridge over the Velikaya on the road to Leningrad as reinforcements arrived to continue the siege. The siege lasted 890 days.**

stand and halt the Russian counter-offensive. When the permission was not granted, he also resigned. Ultimately Hitler's no retreat orders were obeyed after such energetic actions and the fronts were stabilized. But at a terrible price, for the SS Reich Panzer Division was virtually wiped out. The fighting continued throughout the winter months finally petering out in February 1942 when both armies were totally exhausted. The stalemate in the north and center would last for two years and large-scale offensive operations would never be resumed there.

Throughout the winter Hitler went on with the reorganization of his forces in Russia. Even General Guderian was dismissed and many other less important commanders were changed. Field Marshal von Kluge succeeded Bock; Field Marshal Walther von Reichenau, who had taken over from Rundstedt, had a heart attack and died in February 1942. General Ernst Udet of the Luftwaffe committed suicide in November 1941. Hitler had no one else to replace the dead Reichenau so he had to turn to von Bock who had recovered from his illness. Obviously nothing would be the same as far as Hitler's generals were concerned, even though they were still replaceable. Hitler found it much harder to replace the 1,005,636 casualties, which the German armies incurred by February 1942. However he optimistically managed to collect some 52 satellite divisions: 27 Rumanian, 13 Hungarian, nine Italian, two Slovak and one Spanish, and thus raise the 800,000 men, which he required for the offensive he planned in the spring. In the end, over one million foreign soldiers fought for Germany in Russia. But to replace his German grenadiers he had to juggle with the numerical strength of the German divisions raising them at least on paper. Thus henceforth infantry divisions consisted of seven instead of nine battalions; companies contained 80 men instead of 180. The same was done with the armor that he needed for the offensive: two new armored divisions were formed, but only ten of the twenty existing armored divisions were brought up to strength. Once again the campaign was badly prepared: German armies were drawing on untried satellite troops for numerical strength, no margins were left for losses and there were no increases in air and tank power, the two factors upon which the successful outcome of the offensive depended, even more so now than in June 1941.

Strategic planning was also questionable. Hitler no longer relied on the advice of his senior generals for they all wanted to withdraw either to the original Polish line or not so far. He therefore dismissed

them all and began to listen to his economic experts. Consequently the planned offensive had as its objective economic gains, the oil, ores and wheat of the Caucasus. While leaving the north and center inactive the southern front was reorganized and was to carry out the offensive. Army Group B under Field Marshal von Bock was to break through the Soviet line, turn south and on meeting Army Group A under Field Marshal Wilhelm von List, turn east and take Stalingrad on the Volga. List was going to continue south, take Rostov and then press on with a two-pronged thrust deep into the Caucasus until Batumi on the Black Sea and Baku on the Caspian were reached. This was indeed bold strategic planning which had one vital flaw in it: it left some 400 miles of the left flank insufficiently protected. Combined with the fictional strength of the attacking armies this strategic flaw made the whole operation highly risky and dangerous. In addition by spring 1942 Hitler also lost the political battle in the Soviet Union.

Above : **Petlyakov Pe 2 Russian aircraft under construction in the Urals out of the range of German fire. Altogether 11,427 Pe 2s were completed during the war.**
Left : **Russian tanks roll off the assembly line across the Volga into the fight around Stalingrad in the fall of 1942.**

Before he invaded Soviet Russia Hitler prepared policies which he would apply in the conquered territory: his *Ostpolitik* consisted of the *Untermensch* theory which claimed that all the Slavs were inferior to the Teutons and therefore subject to economic exploitation and ultimately to slavery. As his *Kommissar* order showed, he also thought in terms of extermination. But Hitler formulated only the basic principles for a policy and left his subordinates to apply it; henceforth he kept aloof from the policy and the problems that its application created, only occasionally upholding it when he thought it was applied wrongly. Most of the time he ignored it and busied himself with military matters. Thus in the initial period between June and December 1941, when the conquered populations in the East responded in a most friendly fashion to the invading Germans, they were totally disregarded. *Einsatzgruppen* spread terror almost indiscriminately and Russian prisoners were being exterminated on an enormous scale. On the surface it seemed that Hitler's basic policy was carried out systematically without deviation: in fact there were several policies in operation, though the official *Ostpolitik* gave them all its fatal seal.

Obviously the invading army, while also subscribing to Hitler's basic policy, though not as absolutely as the SS, did not apply that policy as effectively as the latter. It certainly shifted the emphasis from extermination to exploitation, especially where men, particularly combatants, were concerned. Even before the invasion the Army was interested in anti-Russian nationalities, and since Hitler also evinced theoretical interest in these nationalities, the Army took them up seriously, organized them, trained them and used them against the Soviet enemy. This was particularly true of the Ukrainians whose two leaders, Colonel Melnyk and Bandera, were chosen by the Wehrmacht to command the special regiments, Nightingale and Roland, which were to operate in the Lvov and Vinnitsa, and Jassy and Odessa areas respectively. The Abwehr chief, Admiral Wilhelm Canaris, even told these foreign mercenaries the date of the *Barbarossa* Operation thus making sure that it was reported to Soviet intelligence, for all these emigré movements were thoroughly penetrated by the NKVD, Soviet security. Subsequently at Lvov, the Ukrainians organized an uprising, even before the Wehrmacht reached the city, but they were easily suppressed by the Soviet security forces which anticipated it. However, when Bandera's Nightingale force arrived it massacred so indiscriminately all the Russians, Poles, Jews and Ukrainians not of its political persuasion, that even the German Wehrmacht was appalled. When in addition to these massacres Bandera proclaimed a Ukrainian state after a rally, and made Stetsko the Prime Minister, the Wehrmacht dropped him and in July 1941 Stetsko's government was dispersed by the SD and Bandera imprisoned in Berlin.

Above : **Wehrmacht troops stealthily move through a Ukrainian wheat field in the summer of 1942 as supply lines were extended to the breaking point.**
Above center : **German corporal carefully moves a mine forward.**
Agove right : **German flame thrower in action to storm a Russian barricade.**
Right : **A German infantry squad gather around their 37mm PAK36 anti-tank gun.**
Below : **A Panzer Mark IV moves across Ukrainian snows in the winter of 1942–43.**

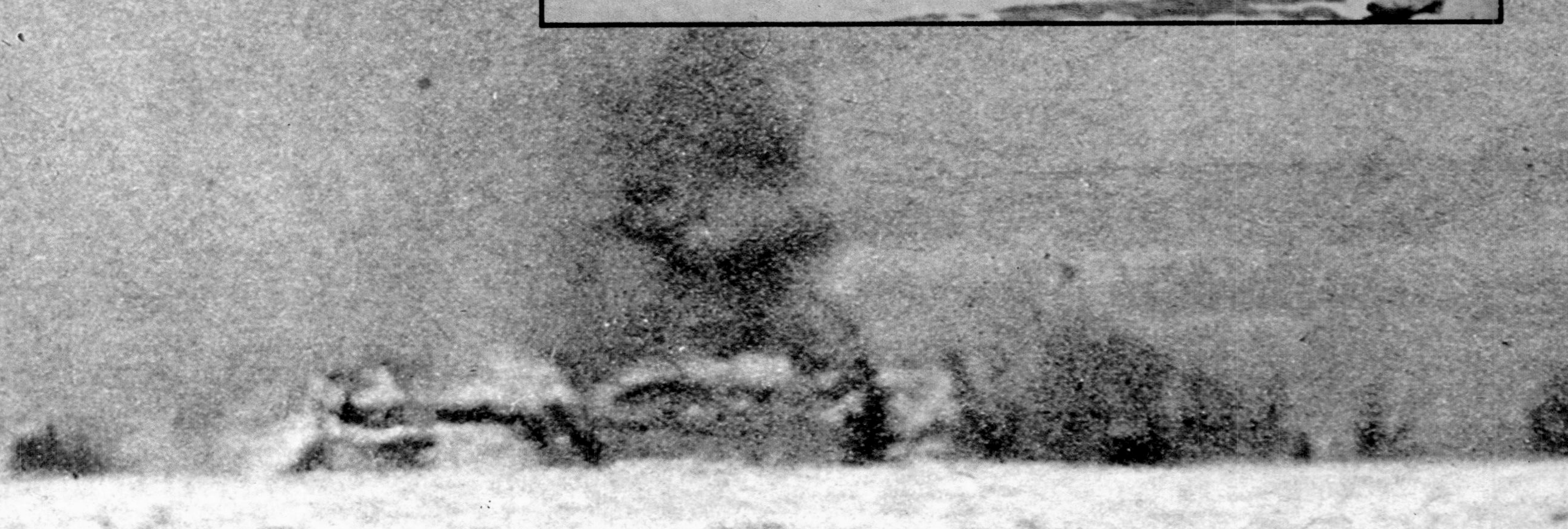

However the two regiments continued their operations of terror all over the Ukraine, leaving in their trail many a mass grave. Apart from these concrete military measures the Wehrmacht also experimented in psychological warfare which had political undertones, contradicting Hitler's basic principles. Between June and December 1941 some 400 million leaflets were dropped over Soviet lines promising immunity to soldiers who surrendered and liberation to the population with such privileges as self-government and private agriculture. However the surrender offer soon proved to be a lie, and in any case before the Wehrmacht's propaganda could discredit itself, Hitler put a stop to it. In October 1941, when he thought that he had won the war, he explicitly forbade such sophisticated propaganda in the East.

Though rudely checked, the Wehrmacht was far from giving up and instead turned to other agencies to use them as cover for their own *Ostpolitik*. Foreign Minister Joachim von Ribbentrop had always been considered pro-Soviet; on the urgings of his last ambassador in Moscow, Count Friedrich von der Schulenberg, he began to show active interest in the Soviet Union and the application of the *Ostpolitik*. Encouraged by the Wehrmacht, Ribbentrop even went as far as to organize a conference on the independence of small nations in the USSR: Count Bagration and Said Shamil took part in it. However Ribbentrop never thought his interest in the USSR was vital, and when in May 1942 Hitler told him to leave the USSR alone, he immediately complied and the Wehrmacht had to go to the hornets' nest itself for support. In July 1941 Hitler set up the *Reichsministerium für die besetzten Ostgebiete* whose head, Alfred Rosenberg, had been collecting staff for this overlord ministry since April 1941. Though a Nazi ideologist Rosenberg was far less extreme in his views on Russia than Himmler and his SS – perhaps as a Russian emigré (of German descent) he had a special instinct for Soviet problems which even his ideological prejudice could not blunt. On 29 June Rosenberg publicly told the peoples of the USSR that National Socialists welcomed all those who wanted to fight with them against Judeo-Bolshevism. This undoubtedly attracted the Wehrmacht's attention to this supposedly supreme agency in the East. After being rebuffed by Hitler, the Wehrmacht, rather naively, turned to his satrap, Rosenberg. Although he never personally committed himself Rosenberg allowed his subordinate, Dr Georg Leibbrant, to deal with the Wehrmacht in order to prepare a *new* policy *vis à vis* the USSR. By the time they got together in December 1942, it was already impossible to forge such a policy, which would have enabled the Wehrmacht to replace the 2,500,000 troops it needed by members of the various dissatisfied nationalities in the USSR. It is curious to observe that among the army officers involved in this enterprise, were so many future resistance leaders such as General Eduard Wagner, Count Claus von Stauffenberg, Colonel Fabian von Schlabrendorff and others. Despite the dire necessity for the new policy Hitler once again vetoed this effort and the Wehrmacht had to continue unofficially using non-German troops (*Hilfswillige*), especially in auxiliary capacities.

However by the spring of 1942 no policy, however generous, would put right the damage done to Germany's relations with the conquered Eastern peoples by the two *Reichskommissars*, Heinrich Lohse and Erich Koch, who began to administer the occupied territories. In theory all the Nazis were one in their contempt for the Slavonic peoples in the East and their ultimate fate as subhuman slaves of the German *Herrenvolk*. Even Goering, who was only involved in the Eastern problems indirectly, did not sound particularly cynical, when he declared that the best solution for the Ukraine would be if all the men over 15 years of age were killed and SS "stallions" were let loose afterwards. Though on paper the various Nazis differed as to which methods should be used to achieve the ultimate objectives in the East, in the actual application of these policies both Lohse and Koch stuck to the following precepts: firstly, the German people is the *Herrenvolk*; secondly, the Eastern peoples, Ukrainians and all the others, are destined to serve their natural masters; thirdly, it is Germany's right and duty to exploit the East; and lastly, complete control of the conquered territory requires the destruction of the native intelligentsia and of all elements – Russian, Ukrainian, Jewish and others – who might potentially constitute a threat to Germany. The incredible way in which Lohse and Koch chose to carry out these precepts completely alienated the populations which in many cases welcomed the Germans and in almost all cases were prepared to collaborate with them either to achieve their national liberation from the Russians or in the case of the Russians, to rid themselves of the Stalinist régime.

Koch and his behavior in the Ukraine were particularly blamed for turning the Ukrainians against the Germans; however Lohse's milder rule achieved exactly the same results, even in the non-Slavic Baltic provinces, and it is therefore clear that Hitler's *Ostpolitik* as a whole was to blame. In any case Hitler positively encouraged Koch's public behavior and utterances. For example Koch once claimed that the Ukrainians as colonial people must be handled with the whip like the Negroes and must be kept as dumb as can be. Koch's subordinates actually indulged in public whipping of the population and he had to forbid it, although he had initially provoked it. As Koch's superior,

Rosenberg quickly predicted that the rule of National Socialism was more brutal than Bolshevik policy: the inevitable consequences were to be acts of sabotage and the formation of the partisans.

Despite this warning Koch ruthlessly set out to gather some three million tons of wheat in order to increase bread rations in Germany. Without the slightest regard for the well-being of the Ukrainians he demanded that they devote eight out of their ten working hours to Germany; he ordered the rounding up of population and had them shipped to Germany to work as slaves in industry and agriculture. At the

Left : **Finnish Field Marshal Mannerheim (left) is visited on his 75th birthday by Hitler in 1942.**
Below : **Moscow's defenders throw up makeshift anti-tank defenses in the winter of 1941–42 with German soldiers less than 25 miles away.**

slightest sign of reluctance or hesitation the whips were out for public punishment; he felt free to insult them even without reason – he thrust aside a Ukrainian welcoming party offering him traditional salt and bread. Apart from gratuitous insults Koch offered the Ukrainians nothing in return for their sweat and blood – since he was dealing with inferiors there could be no contacts with the Ukrainian population. Social contacts were not permitted and sexual intercourse severely punished. They had no say in the administration above the *raion* level (basic district administration) and no political promises to raise their hopes at least. No wonder this policy had an immediate and devastating effect: rather than be slaves in Germany men and women flocked into forests and steppes to swell the ranks of Nationalist, Soviet, non-Nationalist and other partisan groups who

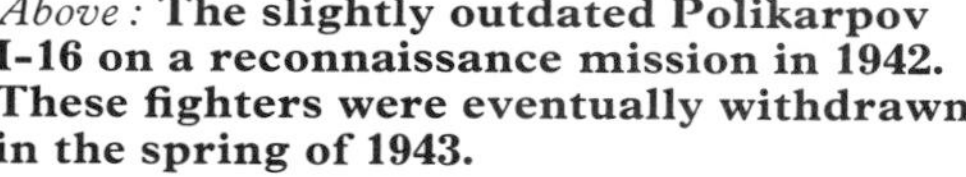

Above: **The slightly outdated Polikarpov I-16 on a reconnaissance mission in 1942. These fighters were eventually withdrawn in the spring of 1943.**

Above: **General Zeitzler was named head of the German General Staff after Halder quit in a huff after the Stalingrad debacle. Zeitzler held this position until 1944.**

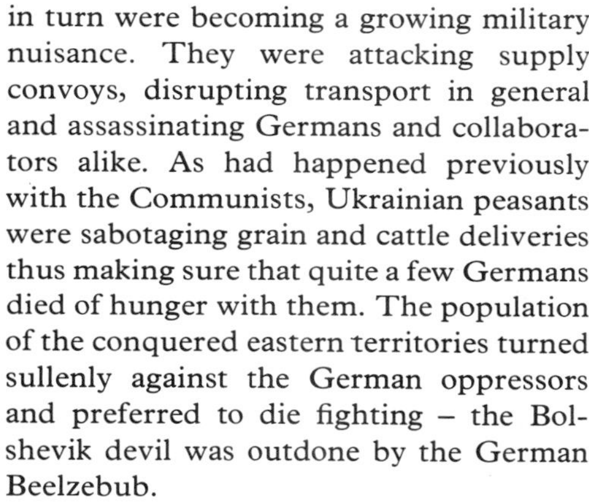

in turn were becoming a growing military nuisance. They were attacking supply convoys, disrupting transport in general and assassinating Germans and collaborators alike. As had happened previously with the Communists, Ukrainian peasants were sabotaging grain and cattle deliveries thus making sure that quite a few Germans died of hunger with them. The population of the conquered eastern territories turned sullenly against the German oppressors and preferred to die fighting – the Bolshevik devil was outdone by the German Beelzebub.

Thus badly prepared militarily, with the political situation verging on the ruinous and strategic planning doubtful, Hitler launched his second large-scale offensive in Russia. As a preliminary, Manstein's Eleventh Army attacked the Crimea in order to clear that peninsula of Russians and prepare it as a springboard for the invasion of the Kuban area in the northern Caucasus. As it happened Manstein ran into a Soviet offensive which he easily defeated, and took Kerch, but was only able to take Sevastopol on 4 July. Quite unwittingly Stalin's plans for a three-pronged offensive in the Crimea, Leningrad and Kharkov were upset and the Crimean reverse cost the Soviets some 200 tanks and 100,000 prisoners. The Leningrad offensive never got off the ground, but it did nullify German intentions in that sector: Hitler could not hope to take the city, and his offensive in the Kharkov area now hinged on beating off Timoshenko's offensive.

As it was, Army Group B under Bock completed its preparations for the offensive when Timoshenko unexpectedly launched his own offensive south and north of Kharkov with the obvious aim of taking the city. Although German intelligence, *Fremde Heere Ost* under Colonel (later General) Gehlen predicted this offensive, Hitler never fully believed the prediction. This was Stalin's first strategic offensive launched a week earlier than planned and against the advice of the generals and politruks, as Nikita Khrushchev claimed later. Although the attacking Russians penetrated the German lines round Kharkov, they never reached the city. However they did not manage to destroy the German enemy and they opened themselves to a deadly counterattack by Paulus's Sixth Army and Kleist's First Panzer Army, defending the north and south of Kharkov respectively. On 17 May, a week after Timoshenko, Paulus and Kleist counterattacked and by 26 May they completed their pincers round Timoshenko's armies capturing 241,000 prisoners. This was an unexpectedly bloody defeat for Stalin, but for Hitler an incredible piece of luck as the Soviet reserves had been spent in the attack thus enabling the insufficiently strong German armies to carry out the grandiose offensive which Hitler had planned so carelessly.

Finally on 28 June the two Army Groups South went forward for the last time achieving their intermediate objectives with gusto: the Second Army and the Fourth Panzer Army broke through at Kursk, took Voronezh and then swung south to Rossosh, where they were joined

Above: **Soviet T-34 tanks captured by German arms in the spring of 1943.**
Left: **Aerial view of a German armored offensive near Kursk in the late spring of 1943.**
Below: **German tanks move up to the Kursk front for their last major offensive of the Russian campaign in June 1943.**
Right: **Panzergrenadiers clear the way for their stalled Panzer Mark IV in the winter of 1942–43.**

by the Sixth Army driving east from Belgorod. The Sixth Army then continued on its fateful drive to Stalingrad, while Hoth's Fourth Panzers pushed on south to the Don to help the First Panzers of Kleist. Subsequently Hoth turned north and via Kotelnikovo tried to help the Sixth Army take Stalingrad. The First Panzer Army struck from Izyum to Chertkovo and then turned south to divide and capture Rostov on the Don, while its other drive aided by the Fourth Panzers crossed the Don to take Proletarskaya to open the way to the Caucasus. Both Panzer armies were too slow in executing their tasks; moreover Kleist came to a halt on the Manych river delaying his drive deep into the Caucasus still further.

Throughout the offensive both infantry and armor seemed to have no speed at all; the armor in particular failed to trap any large-scale Russian formations. After all it was a limited blitzkrieg; the German armor crossed empty spaces which on the map looked like considerable territorial gains. However the disorganized and shattered Russian armies were not even rounded up but allowed to filter back to their lines. In their hurry to attain objectives the German Army was not prepared to be held back by prisoners of war and these were exterminated in hundreds of thousands. Important partisan units also began to disturb German supply lines for the first time and large SS formations had to deal with them. While the first large-scale action against the partisans in the area of Osipovichi took place in February and March 1942 (that is before the offensive), the center of partisan activity shifted to the areas near Dorogobush and Osova and the Dniepr River as soon as the offensive started. While at Osipovichi only the 1st SS Infantry Brigade dealt with the partisans; in July the 221st and 286th Security Divisions together with detached army units had to clear the rear areas of partisans who were seriously disrupting supplies to the front thus slowing down German offensive still more.

Throughout July and August 1942 German successes flowed in thick and fast

Left : **Il-2 Shturmoviks on the assembly line east of the Urals.**
Right : **General Heinz Guderian was relieved of command after his plan for decisive armored thrusts against the Soviets was scrapped by Hitler.**
Below : **Soviet cavalry in 1942–43.**

to Hitler's GHQ situated at Vinnitsa, but he seemed to be perturbed by the slowness of his armies. Soon after the first victories Hitler convinced himself that the Soviet armies were decisively beaten, in fact finished, and Goering confirmed this conviction after receiving air intelligence reports. Notwithstanding he was warned by his intelligence (General Gehlen's *Fremde Heere Ost*) that the enemy had substantial reserves (some 70 rifle divisions and over 80 armor formations) which he again chose to ignore. Neither would he understand that the advance on Stalingrad was slowed down because of his useless diversion of the Fourth Panzers to the Don, and heavy fighting which the Sixth Army had to undergo to reach Kalach on the Don. Their combined onslaught on Stalingrad only started on 23 August by which time Russian resistance also considerably stiffened. As for Army Group A it progressed slowly for more complicated reasons: after Rostov and Manych the Seventeenth Army and the First Panzers continued slowly because they had insufficient air cover, the Panzers lacked gasoline supplies and the infantry had difficulties with the railways which it had to re-lay practically the whole way to the Caucasian mountains. However the Seventeenth Army took Krasnodar and struck down to Novorossiysk, but before it could achieve its tactical objective, Tuapse, the elite paratroop division was withdrawn and rushed to Smolensk. The infantry was then halted by the mountains. Eventually even Kleist's armor was stopped, after it had overrun Stavropol, Maykop with its oil derricks and Pyatigorsk in the foothills of the Caucasian mountain range. Throughout the crossing of the north Caucasian plains Kleist was attacked in the flanks by Russian cavalry and checked by Russian aircraft since he had no Luftwaffe cover. As a result Hitler once again began to bicker with his generals who in any case did not really believe in this offensive.

Since Hitler more or less assumed personal control of field operations and subsequently took the blame for the Stalingrad catastrophe, German generals have since blamed him for all the failures, especially the one at Stalingrad. After the return of the captured German documents from the USA, researchers have discovered evidence which indicates that too much blame had been apportioned to Hitler. However it appears that this atmosphere of bickering and mutual mistrust, in which Hitler refused to take his generals seriously and vice versa was largely responsible for the failure. Thus for example, the tactical dangers on the Stalingrad front were fully realized by Hitler on 16 August 1942. At his GHQ at Vinnitsa he was given a captured document in which the Red Army's breakthrough on the Don had compelled the Whites to run away from Stalingrad (then Tsaritsyn) rather than be encircled and cut off in 1919. The map of the operation seems to have impressed Hitler particularly deeply, for the situation of his Sixth Army was almost identical with that of General Denikin's armies. To the north, on the left flank of some 400 miles, he only had satellite Hungarians, Italians and Rumanians, while on the right, south of the city, some 80 miles were held by weak Rumanian forces. Furthermore, if the Red Army broke through this time and then took Rostov, it would not only encircle the Sixth Army, but cut off three more armies in the Caucasus. From that day Hitler insisted on securing the flank of the Don, but seemed strangely isolated. Gehlen offered seven other points for offensive (*Schwerpunkte*) apart from Stalingrad and subsequently settled for Smolensk as the most likely point where the main Soviet attack would come. Since German intelligence failed to detect strong armored forces in and around Stalingrad, General Halder treated Hitler's fears and instinctive strategy with caution bordering on contempt. A few days after the discovery of the Stalingrad dangers, Hitler ordered Halder to transfer heavy artillery and anti-aircraft guns behind the Hungarian sector of the Stalingrad front, but Halder carried out the order only weeks later and with insufficient forces. Almost at the same time Hitler wanted to transfer the 22nd Panzer Division to the Italian sector, but Halder failed to record the wish. This division and two others were finally transferred to the Italian sector in mid-September, after Halder's dismissal. However even then the generals did not take Hitler's fears seriously and Gehlen predicted a large-scale offensive in the Orel area, while forecasting that only on the Don would probing attacks occur. Hitler alone continued to issue orders to check the expected counteroffensive. On 2 November he ordered the Luftwaffe to bomb the Don bridges and troop concentrations, and even ordered the transfer

Below: **A bridge and motorized transport wrecked by heavy aerial and artillery bombardment west of Moscow.**
Right: **Much of German transport was not motorized, and everything from motorcycles to horses were used to bring troops and supplies up to the front. Fuel supplies were running short as well.**

from the West of the 6th Panzer and two infantry divisions to stiffen the front held by the Third Rumanian and Eighth Italian Armies.

German intelligence kept assuring Hitler that the main Russian attack would come in the area of Army Group Center, while he sensed that it would be the Don. These premonitions, however, did not prevent him from leaving the fronts and delivering a speech in a Munich beer cellar on the eve of 9 November. This behavior seemed to indicate that he was completely confused and certainly acted irresponsibly by going to Munich at such a critical point. Two days later German intelligence captured the Red Army's battle orders and discovered that the 5th Tank Army, which was last located near Orel, was in fact in battle positions on the Don. As Hitler had done previously, Gehlen's intelligence refused to believe that the elite 5th Tank Army with its 376 T-34 tanks could have been moved without being detected. This time Gehlen was wrong and did not redeem himself even with the intelligence appreciation of 12 November, a week before the Soviet breakthrough, in which he deemed it probable that a major operation would take place on the Stalingrad front against the Italians and Rumanians. He certainly failed to detect (until too late) this large Russian counteroffensive carried out by eleven armies, 13,500 pieces of artillery, 900 tanks and 1414 aircraft. Long before this blow came, Hitler lost patience with his generals and since he could not shuffle his armies around, shuffled his generals instead.

Left : **SS Chief Heinrich Himmler salutes the grave of his murdered subordinate Reinhard Heydrich in Bohemia in 1942.**
Below : **General Höpner and Field Marshal von Leeb check a map in 1941. Both were replaced after arguments with the Führer.**

Above : **General Dietl and Schörner discuss plans for the Kursk offensive in May 1943.**

Early in September 1942 Hitler summoned Field Marshal von List to Vinnitsa, to explain the lack of progress of his Army Group A; when he could not, Hitler dismissed him and assumed command in person. Almost at the same time General Halder was sent off to restore his nerves and was replaced by General Kurt Zeitzler. All these changes failed to remedy any weaknesses in German positions, but it seemed to restore Hitler's nerves. Under his pressure Kleist was forced to launch his probing attack in the Caucasus in order to reach the Caspian Sea and oil at Grozny and Baku. Since Hitler was apparently fully aware of the dangers of the Soviet breakthrough on the Stalingrad front, it seemed frivolous to drive Kleist and his First Panzers and Seventeenth Armies deeper into the Caucasus. However even these operations, initially successful, failed to reach their objectives, Grozny and Ordjonikidze, and before another offensive could be launched the long expected breakthrough did occur and Kleist had to dash back to Rostov to escape being cut off and captured.

Thus the fate of the Third Reich was decided at Stalingrad, which as a strategic target was completely useless for Hitler and the Germans. Nonetheless Hitler was attracted to the city, which bore his adversary's name, like a magnet. Despite forebodings he kept sending more and more troops to take Stalingrad, the city which ate up all his reserves and he had to be on the defensive everywhere else as a result. His grandiose summer offensive of 1942 came to grief there and the German armies never recovered the initiative on the battlefield. This indeed was Hitler's turning point, and probably the decisive point of the war.

THE END OF THE REICH

THE EMPIRE'S LIMITS

The road to Stalingrad was long and painful for the Germans and the Wehrmacht; still the same was true for the Russians, who, however, seemed to have read the danger signs much earlier than the Germans. In contrast, Soviet decisions were instinctive or vague; because the Southeastern and Southern Fronts, for all practical purposes, had collapsed, Stalin decided to set up a new, separate, Stalingrad Front as early as 12 July 1942. The senior Marshal, Semyon Timoshenko, was put in command of this new front, with Nikita Sergeyevich Khrushchev as Commissar, and Lieutenant General Bodin as Chief of Staff, to help him. Apart from the retreating and demoralized troops Stalin put at Timoshenko's disposal his strategic reserve armies: the 62nd Army (Major General Kolpakchi), the 63rd (General Vasily Kuznetsov) and the 64th (General Gordov). At this stage these reserves were still on trains in the north, far from Stalingrad, and while moving towards the city no one as yet knew where they would be deployed when they finally arrived.

During the 1941–42 winter fighting on all fronts, the Germans provided the Russians with examples of a new type of mobile defense which the Russians were now to employ themselves. Like Hitler, Stalin however had had no better idea than to re-organize his armies by reshuffling his generals, but he also had recourse to another totalitarian expedient – mass political indoctrination. He observed that his chief politruk, Leonid Mekhlis, was largely responsible for the defeats in the south and he therefore dismissed him, appointed Shcherbakov instead and strengthened the political leadership of the armed forces with senior party leaders, Zhdanov, Manuilsky, Yaroslavsky, Rogov and Aleksandrov. They then worked out a system for the restoration of morale by means of special agitator groups which lectured to the troops and bombarded them with

Below: **Soviet troops pass German dead which were unable to break out of the Caucasus.**

patriotic leaflets and books. The stress on patriotism certainly must have worked, but what made it really work was the observed fact that the Communist party itself took these matters seriously and acted on them.

At Stalingrad Stalin ordered the First Secretary of the Stalingrad *oblast* (district), Chuyanov, to set up the City Defense Committee, and take care of the auxiliary tasks. On 20 July Chuyanov, a member of the party's Central Committee, reported to Stalin that he had improved anti-aircraft defenses, and had some 180,000 men build rough defenses round the city which he wanted to convert into a fortress. In turn Stalin sent army and civilian engineers to the city who improved its defenses: stores and industrial equipment were shipped to the other side of the Volga, anti-paratroop battalions were formed and barricades were set up to block the streets. The Sixth Army had no idea of the formidable trap into which it was about to fall.

Stalin also reshuffled the command. First he sent his trusted Chief of Staff, Colonel General Aleksandr Vasilievsky,

Left: **Fighting around the Krasny Oktyobr factory in Stalingrad was fierce as the ring closed around Paulus's Sixth Army.**
Below: **Russian field artillery in action around a wrecked factory in Stalingrad in January 1943.**

down to Stalingrad to supervise everything on the spot and then he dismissed Marshal Timoshenko. His successor was Gordov who was replaced as Commander of the 64th Army by General Vasiliy Chuikov. But despite these preparations and changes the Sixth Army broke through the line of the 62nd Army at Kamensk and threatened to encircle it. Two days after this breakthrough, on 25 July 1942, Chuikov's 64th Army came under heavy attacks. The junction between the 62nd and 64th Armies was under attack and the Russian armies faced constant bombardments by the Luftwaffe whose 4th Fleet Hitler transferred from the Caucasus to Stalingrad. The bridges across the Don had to be destroyed to prevent Chuikov's troops from panicking and running away. The general had to restore the dangerous situation personally which he did in an exemplary fashion.

But to relieve the 62nd and 64th Armies the Russians had to counterattack. They hardly had any forces left for this counteroffensive which, General Vasilievsky decided, would be carried out by the 1st and 4th Tank Armies and General Danilov's 21st Army. Chuikov and Kolpakchi were also given specific tasks to support this counterstroke, but no one on the Soviet side was adequately prepared to conduct such complicated operations which in any case were observed by enemy aircraft able to count the numbers of tanks deployed. As the Soviet tanks waded across the Don to attack, they were harassed by the Luftwaffe, which on 27 and 28 July flew more than 1000 sorties against Moskalenko's 1st Tanks alone. General Fedor Tolbukhin's 57th Army, another strategic reserve, was brought to the southern wing to prevent a German breakthrough there. However despite the counterattack and feverish maneuvering the Soviet armies were mercilessly pushed from their position on the bend of the river Don; still Paulus's Sixth Army was obviously insufficiently strong to destroy them. Finally on 31 July the Fourth Panzer Army reappeared and crushed the 51st Soviet Army taking Kotelnikovo. Stalingrad was now under pressure from both north and south, German advance could be resumed and the Russians had some re-organization to do.

Stalin as usual did all this in far away Moscow. General Vasilievsky returned to Moscow and told Colonel General Andrey Yeremenko that he would command a front at Stalingrad. Between 2–4 August Stalin could not decide how to organize the front: in the end he split it into two, under Gordov and Yeremenko, the dividing line running through the center of the city. This meant duplication of staff and effort, but Yeremenko said nothing. When he arrived at Stalingrad in an American aircraft, Gordov, who was on the spot, launched another ill-prepared counterattack to save the 62nd Army from annihilation. Paulus's XXIV and XVI Panzer Corps broke through the Russian line and encircled most of the 62nd Army. On hearing of this disaster Stalin changed his mind about the arrangements at Stalin-

Right: **Motor and wing of a Junkers Ju 52 transport.**
Far right: **The Ju 52 in Russian snows. Called "Tante" or "Auntie," it was the workhorse of the Luftwaffe. It was introduced in the early 1930s but played an important part in World War II.**

Below: **The He 111 bomber was utilized against Britain as well as on the Eastern Front.**
Right: **Sorrow: a Russian peasant searches among the dead outside Stalingrad for the body of her son. Soviet casualties were immeasurable.**

Far left: **A Soviet defender of Stalingrad in his factory.**
Left: **House-to-house fighting was the loathsome characteristic of the Battle of Stalingrad.**

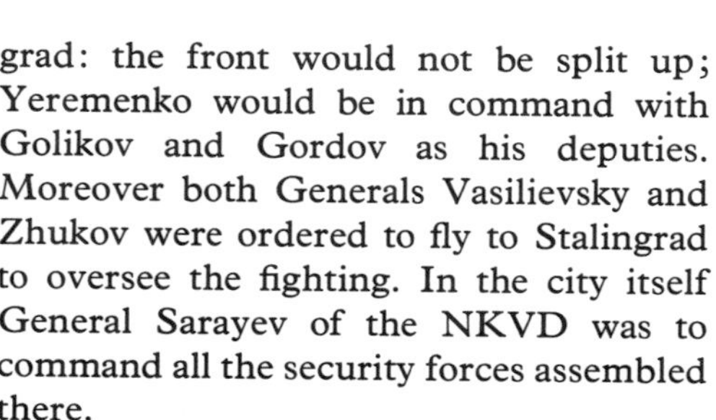

grad: the front would not be split up; Yeremenko would be in command with Golikov and Gordov as his deputies. Moreover both Generals Vasilievsky and Zhukov were ordered to fly to Stalingrad to oversee the fighting. In the city itself General Sarayev of the NKVD was to command all the security forces assembled there.

The German armies had reached the outer defenses of the city and on 15 August launched a concentric assault; Gordov who took personal command could not hold back the Sixth Army, while Chuikov, in command of the southern sector, succeeded in holding off the Fourth Panzers. The XIV Panzer Corps of Paulus's Sixth Army made its way to the northern suburbs which it reached on 22 August. However in the south the Panzer break-through failed and the Luftwaffe was called in instead to soften up the city. The 8th Air Fleet flattened the city in massive raids: residential as well as administrative parts of the city were burned down with incendiaries while storage tanks, containing oil supplies, were set on fire. On 23 August 79th Panzer Grenadier Regiment radioed its headquarters that it was at Spartanovka, the northern suburb, on the Volga, looking at the city further south.

Stalin was furious with his commanders for the German breakthrough, for like his adversary Hitler, he was determined to keep the city. He had personal knowledge of the area and during the days of crisis, between 23–25 August he more or less commanded field operations in person. Vasilievsky and Zhukov reported back as to how his orders were carried out. Although he had collected reserves on the other side of the Volga, it was obvious that he would have to ferry them across the Volga into the city, if the German attack was to be stemmed. However the Luftwaffe was equally determined not to allow the boats to cross the river. Nonetheless the Russians succeeded in transporting fresh forces into the besieged city who immediately participated in a new type of street fighting. Stalin also forbade the evacuation and destruction of industrial plant and machinery to signify clearly that there would be no surrender this time. He issued his famous order, *Not a Step Back*, and poured all the available resources into Stalingrad. And these resources were by now far from mean: in the first half of 1942 the Soviet factories produced 9600 planes, 11,000 tanks and 14,000 pieces of heavy artillery, the greater parts of which went to the fateful city on the Volga.

The battle now raged for the city itself. More than 1000 armed workers were helping the army in defense of their districts; tanks were moving in and out of the town with Luftwaffe planes relentlessly bombing it. However each block and factory was turned into a fortress while the bulk of the Sixth Army was arriving at the inner defenses. On 27 August Stalin decided to reinforce the Front by sending in three more armies, the 24th, 1st Guard and 66th, to attack the Germans on the northern flank, "else we may lose the city." As soon as Zhukov got to Stalingrad, where he met Vasilievsky as well as Khrushchev, Malenkov and Malyshev, he could see that the armies which were supposed to deliver the northern strike were not ready, and

Below: **Russian troops beat back the Germans as Stalingrad was surrounded. The remains of the once-proud Sixth Army were starving and helpless. Tens of thousands of men died or starved to death before the battle was over.**

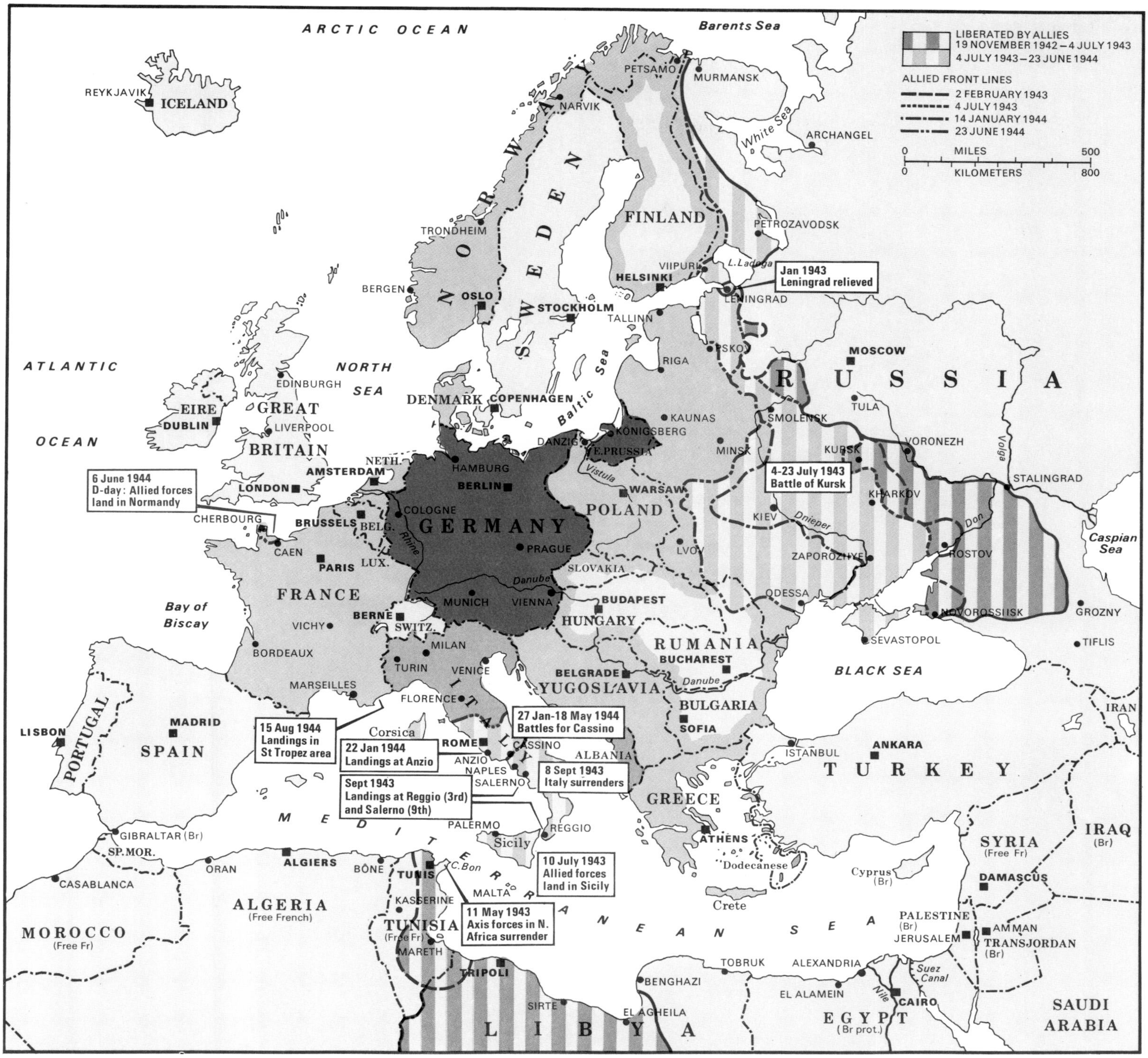
ARCTIC OCEAN
Barents Sea
LIBERATED BY ALLIES
19 NOVEMBER 1942 – 4 JULY 1943
4 JULY 1943 – 23 JUNE 1944
ALLIED FRONT LINES
2 FEBRUARY 1943
4 JULY 1943
14 JANUARY 1944
23 JUNE 1944
MILES
0
500
KILOMETERS
0
800
REYKJAVIK
ICELAND
PETSAMO
MURMANSK
NARVIK
White Sea
ARCHANGEL
NORWAY
SWEDEN
FINLAND
PETROZAVODSK
TRONDHEIM
VIIPURI
L. Ladoga
Jan 1943
Leningrad relieved
HELSINKI
LENINGRAD
BERGEN
OSLO
STOCKHOLM
TALLINN
PSKOV
MOSCOW
ATLANTIC
OCEAN
NORTH
SEA
RIGA
RUSSIA
EDINBURGH
Baltic Sea
TULA
EIRE
DUBLIN
GREAT
BRITAIN
DENMARK
COPENHAGEN
KAUNAS
SMOLENSK
LIVERPOOL
KONIGSBERG
E. PRUSSIA
DANZIG
MINSK
KURSK
VORONEZH
Volga
NETH.
AMSTERDAM
HAMBURG
BERLIN
Vistula
4-23 July 1943
Battle of Kursk
STALINGRAD
6 June 1944
D-day: Allied forces
land in Normandy
LONDON
WARSAW
KHARKOV
CHERBOURG
BRUSSELS
BELG.
COLOGNE
GERMANY
POLAND
KIEV
Dnieper
Don
Caspian
Sea
CAEN
Rhine
PRAGUE
LVOV
ROSTOV
PARIS
LUX.
SLOVAKIA
ZAPOROZHYE
Danube
FRANCE
MUNICH
VIENNA
ODESSA
Bay of
Biscay
BERNE
BUDAPEST
NOVOROSSIISK
GROZNY
VICHY
SWITZ.
HUNGARY
MILAN
RUMANIA
SEVASTOPOL
TIFLIS
BORDEAUX
TURIN
VENICE
BELGRADE
BUCHAREST
BLACK SEA
MARSEILLES
YUGOSLAVIA
Danube
FLORENCE
BULGARIA
IRAN
PORTUGAL
MADRID
15 Aug 1944
Landings in
St Tropez area
Corsica
27 Jan-18 May 1944
Battles for Cassino
SOFIA
LISBON
SPAIN
ITALY
ROME
CASSINO
ALBANIA
ISTANBUL
ANKARA
22 Jan 1944
Landings at Anzio
ANZIO
NAPLES
SALERNO
8 Sept 1943
Italy surrenders
TURKEY
Sept 1943
Landings at Reggio (3rd)
and Salerno (9th)
GREECE
MEDITERRANEAN SEA
PALERMO
REGGIO
GIBRALTAR (Br)
Sicily
ATHENS
SYRIA
(Free Fr)
IRAQ
(Br)
SP. MOR.
10 July 1943
Allied forces
land in Sicily
Dodecanese
ORAN
ALGIERS
BÔNE
TUNIS
C. Bon
Cyprus
(Br)
DAMASCUS
CASABLANCA
MALTA
KASSERINE
Crete
ALGERIA
(Free French)
11 May 1943
Axis forces in N.
Africa surrender
PALESTINE
(Br)
AMMAN
MOROCCO
(Free Fr)
TUNISIA
(Free Fr)
JERUSALEM
TRANSJORDAN
(Br)
MARETH
TOBRUK
ALEXANDRIA
Suez
Canal
TRIPOLI
BENGHAZI
EL ALAMEIN
Nile
CAIRO
SIRTE
EL AGHEILA
SAUDI
ARABIA
LIBYA
EGYPT
(Br prot.)

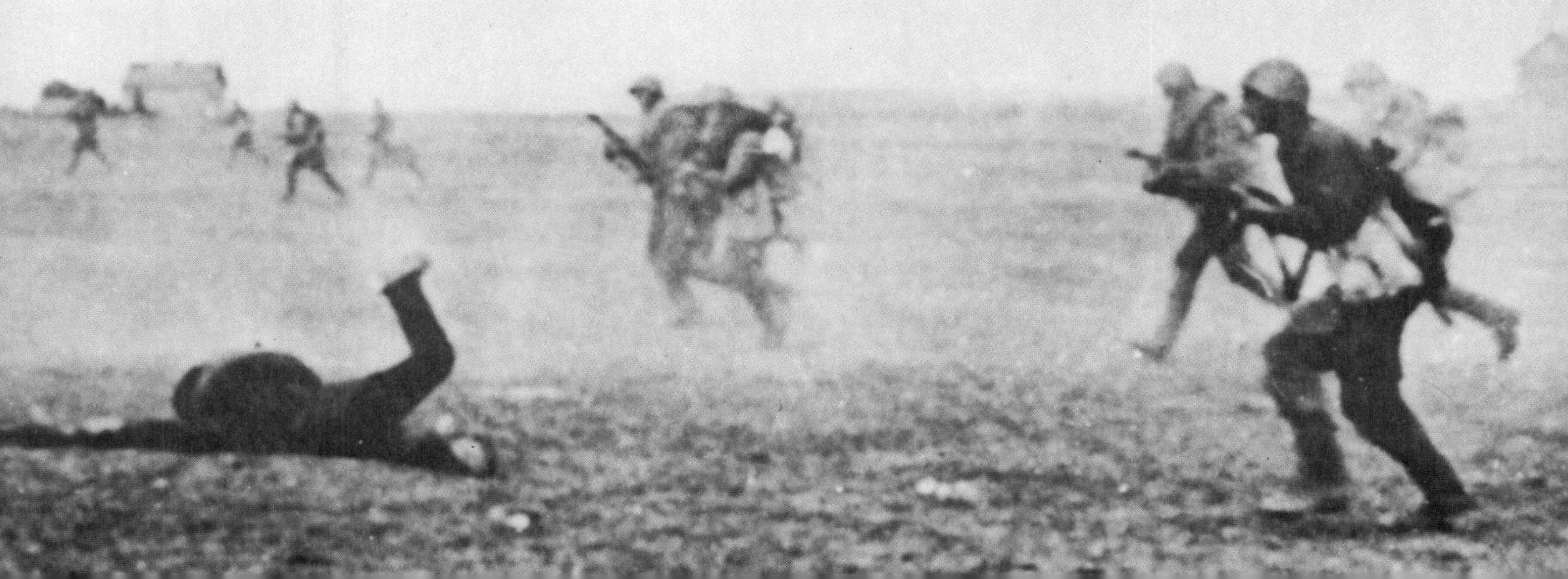

that their counterattacks would not work. On 3 September the 1st Guard Army under General Moskalenko did attack, but after advancing a few hundred meters, was beaten back. Stalin told Zhukov to go on attacking and to throw in these attacks all he had, else the city would fall. Two days later the 1st Guards were beaten off again though they retained a few hundred meters of their gain; the 24th Army which by now was also attacking, was, however, beaten to its starting line.

On that very day the Soviets finally noticed that the Germans began to withdraw forces from the central sector where the city was most threatened, transferring them to the north. Zhukov decided to deploy everything he had, from heavy artillery and rockets to aircraft. General Aleksandr Golovanov's long range bombers were sent out every night to bomb German supply bases and lines. General Aleksandr Novikov arrived as Stalin's special air representative together with the 16th Air Army under General Rudenko. Fighter regiments commanded by Generals Khryukin and Stepanov went into action together. After a week of heavy fighting Zhukov reported to Stalin that his forces could not break through in the northern sector and was in turn asked by Stalin to fly to Moscow and report in person. Hitler seems to have had the same idea and Paulus also had to fly to Vinnitsa headquarters. After their departures offensive probings continued; however the Germans succeeded in launching theirs more effectively.

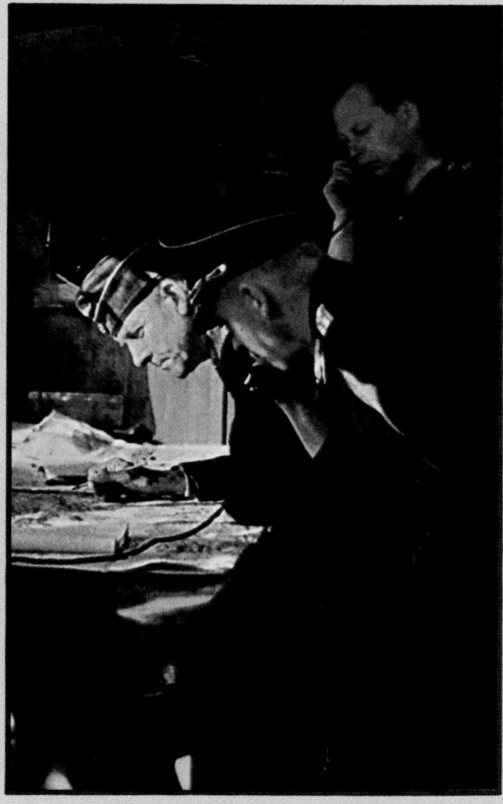

On 12 September the Germans threw into the battle against Stalingrad 11 infantry and three Panzer divisions. Hoth's tanks had broken into the southern suburb, Kuporosnoye, thus dividing the two Russian armies. They also took the Mamaya Kurgan, a height overlooking the city and penetrated into the city itself. All through the night that followed the Russians were ferrying General Rodimtsev's 13th Guards Division across the Volga to stem the German breakthrough. At daybreak the following day, the Germans resumed their two-pronged assault of the city: first, 295th, 71st and 94th Infantry Divisions supported by the XXIV Panzer Corps and second, 20th Motorized Division supported by the XIV Panzer Corps. Although many units and even regiments of the 62nd Army, whose commanding general Lopatin

Above left: **Mussolini says good-bye to Field Marshal Keitel after visiting the Führer in the Wolf's Lair, Hitler's headquarters in East Prussia.**
Above: **A Luftwaffe command post on the Eastern Front.**
Below: **Soviet General Rokossovsky at his command post.**

was sacked the previous day and replaced by Chuikov, were wiped out, it nevertheless contained the breakthrough and held the attack. On 14 September Chuikov tried to stage counterattacks, but his troops could not make much progress after being pinned down by German artillery fire and Stuka bombardment. The fresh 13th Guards, despite aerial bombardment, retook the principal German gains in the central town sector: in hand-to-hand fighting they drove the 71st Division from the main railway station and the 29th Division from the hillock, Mamaya Kurgan.

After this bloody rebuff General Paulus regrouped his forces dividing them into two attacking groups in the center and north. For the center attack he picked the crack 71st Division and the 100th Jäger Division with orders to retake the Mamaya Kurgan, and the station. The bloody fighting continued until 21 September: Mamaya Kurgan was not retaken by the Germans, but the hillock was never covered by snow or anything except shells and fresh earth craters. The station changed hands fifteen times before the 13th Guards consolidated their hold. The diversionary northern attacks were beaten off and Chuikov's counterattacks failed to drive the Germans out of town. This onslaught petered out when both sides became exhausted: but the Germans regrouped and were ready to strike again.

Once again the Russians managed to ferry reinforcements into the city: the fresh Siberian (284th) rifle division with which Chuikov tried a spoiling attack to dislocate German preparations. After a Stuka bombardment on 27 September the Germans resumed their assault, gained over one kilometer of bombed-out ruins, lost some 2000 men and 50 tanks, and came to a standstill exhausted. At night the Russians counterattacked and re-took German gains. By 29 September Paulus committed the regiments of 16th Panzers, 60th Motorized Division and 389th and 100th Infantry Divisions, and switched his efforts to Orlovka where heavy fighting continued.

Above : **Soviet troops advance briskly in the winter of 1942–43.**
Below : **A makeshift German airfield under Soviet aerial attack somewhere west of the Don River in early 1943. Goering's promise of adequate supply lines being maintained to the Sixth Army proved false.**

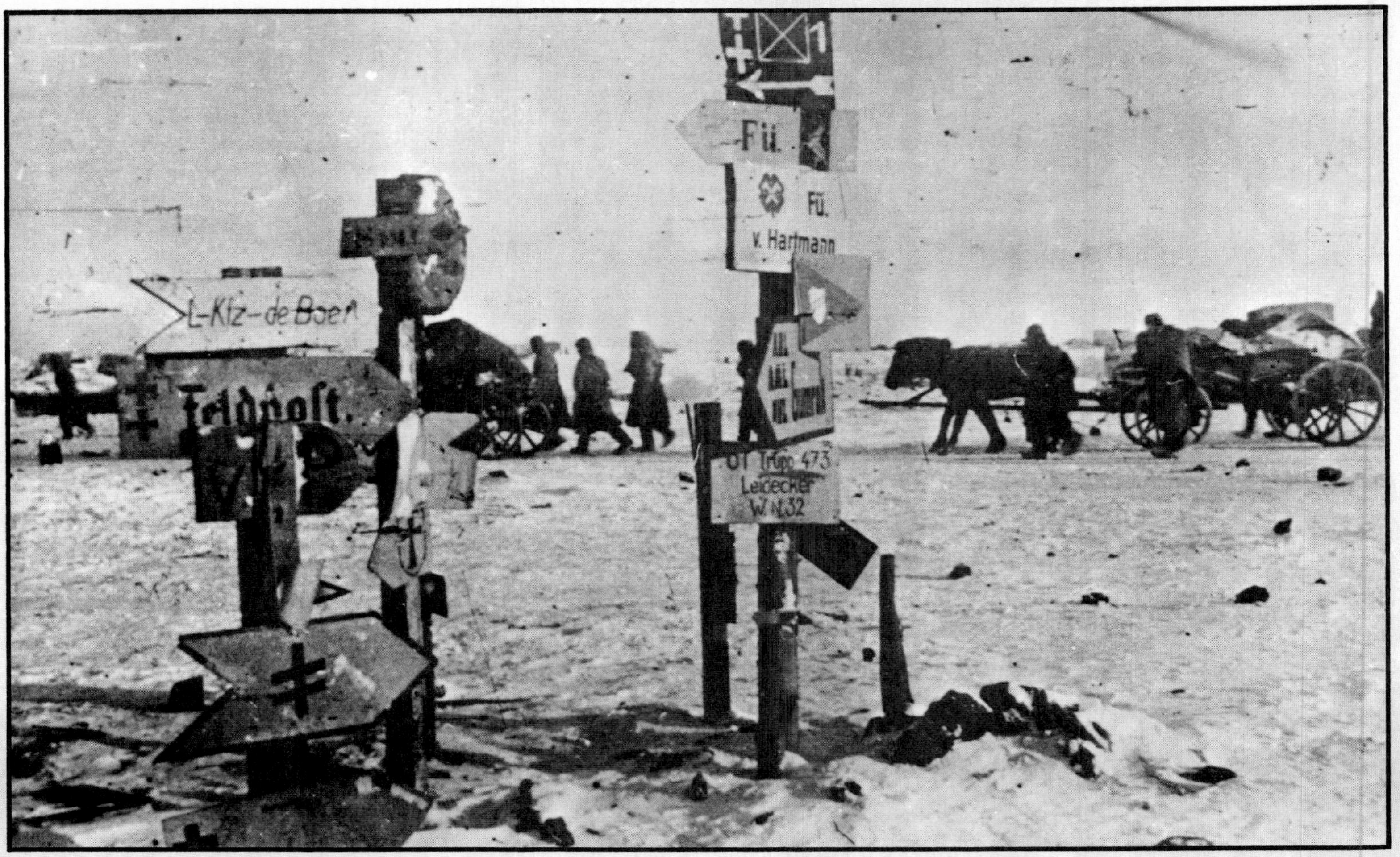
L-Kfz-de Boer
Feldpost.
Fü.
Fü.
v. Hartmann
Leidecker
W.N.32

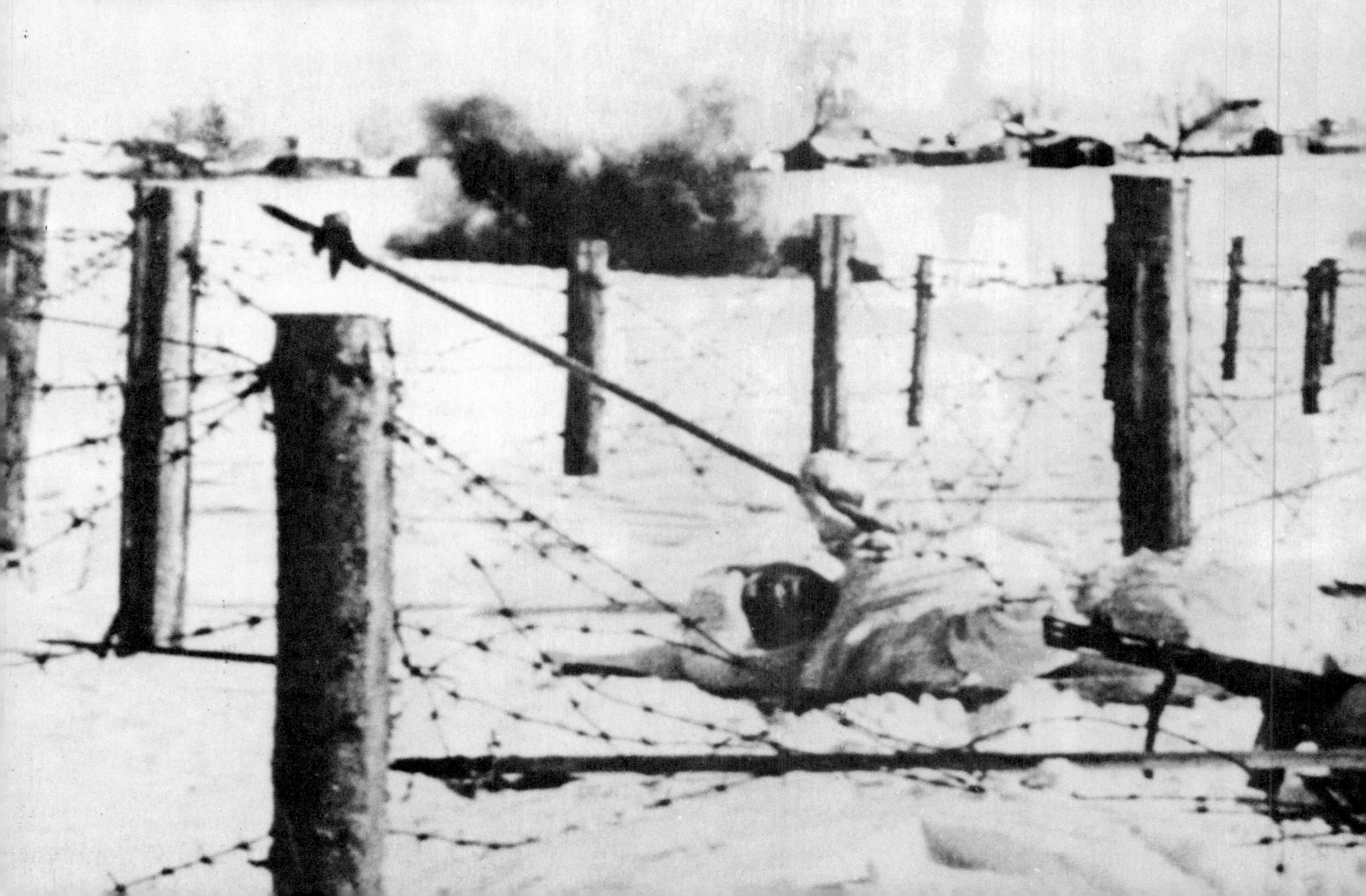

Left: **Russian forces pass abandoned German road signs during their counteroffensive in early 1943.**
Below: **German sappers cut Russian barbed wire in their attempt to re-establish a front west of Stalingrad in March 1943.**

At one stage some 300 men of the 295th Infantry Division raided the Russian rear on the Volga by crawling through a sewer pipe, but were wiped out. On 29 October Chuikov's headquarters was bombed and burning oil spilled over it; still all escaped from this blazing inferno alive. On 5 October Stalin ordered Yeremenko to keep Stalingrad at all costs, while Chuikov found a new headquarters, evacuated by the NKVD 10th Division which was withdrawn from the fighting after being decimated.

On 7 October Chuikov's planned counterattack never got off the ground, for two German divisions launched their own assault. In the heavy fighting which ensued the Germans lost some four battalions of dead and scores of tanks were wiped out. General Paulus ordered these suicidal attacks, as he was told by General Schmundt that a Field Marshal's baton was at the end of Stalingrad fighting. Paulus seemed quite ruthless about getting his baton – when fellow commanders objected to his way of handling the operations, they were dismissed: General von Wietersheim of the XV Panzer Corps and General von Schwendler of the IV Panzer Corps. Between 9 and 13 October a sort of lull settled over Stalingrad; fighting continued, but there were no large-scale attacks while the Wehrmacht regrouped and prepared for the final assault.

On Monday 14 October at 0800 hours three infantry divisions (94th, 389th and 100th) and two Panzer divisions (14th and 24th) hurled themselves onto the central sector of the town, surrounded the Tractor Factory and reached the Volga splitting Chuikov's army into two. Overnight Chuikov received reinforcements (138th Regiment), but even the fresh troops could not stop the German battering ram. On the following day the Germans overran the height, Mamaya Kurgan, and they penetrated the improvized Russian fortresses, the Krasny Oktyabr and Barrikady plants on the Volga itself. Only on 24 October could the Russians counterattack, skillfully using their artillery from the other side of the Volga, make any impact. The 45th Division was ferried over and it finally cleared the Germans from the Volga; by 29 October the Germans spent themselves and on the following day there were no attacks. All this time both in the south and north, Generals Shumilov's and Rokossovsky's relief attacks were beaten back and subdued.

Once again an uneasy lull settled over the city while street fighting continued

unabated. The Russians continued to ferry over fresh troops to replace casualties, while the Germans were running their men into the ground. On 11 November, after an artillery and Stuka bombardment, the Germans launched their last attack in the city. Casualties were high on both sides, but the Germans once again reached the Volga splitting Chuikov's forces for the third time. The city was in danger of falling into German hands, for by now Chuikov could not get any more reinforcements, as they were required elsewhere. In fact this German attack caused a crisis in Moscow at the Stavka (Supreme HQ), whose strategic offensive, planned and prepared throughout October, was now only a week from being launched. Chuikov had to survive a week without relief; by 20 November all offensive activity by the Wehrmacht in Stalingrad ceased. The Germans had to face the consequences of the Soviet strategic counteroffensive, Uranus.

As we have seen Hitler realized the dangers of a strategic offensive in the Don area in mid-August. Still by October he seemed to have forgotten these dangers and on 14 October issued his *Operationsbefehl No 1* in which he ordered all the offensive activity, except in Stalingrad and in the Caucasus, to cease, while the Wehrmacht prepared for winter defense; he promised to destroy the Red Army in 1943. The thinking behind this order is best exemplified in General Zeitzler's commentary in which it was claimed that no major Russian offensive was possible so late in 1942. In fact they were both wrong, for the Russians, ever since 12 September, when Generals Zhukov and Vasilievsky first spoke to Stalin about the "other solution," as distinct from the diversionary attacks north and south of Stalingrad, went ahead with their planning of a strategic offensive. Needless to say the operation was a top secret, which Stalin did not divulge even to Churchill, whom he entertained in Moscow late in August 1942. Even Russian commanders, among them General Yeremenko, were told nothing of the planning, so that Yeremenko later mistakenly claimed that he planned the counteroffensive, at least in his southern sector.

Zhukov and Vasilievsky worked out two plans of the strategic offensive: the one codenamed Saturn, which was the major breakthrough to Milerovo–Rostov feared so much by Hitler, and the other code-

Below: **A street in Kursk is cleared of rubble after the Russians retook the city and created a salient which the Germans attacked in June 1943.**

207

Left : **Russian paratroops provide the backdrop for a self-propelled gun west of Moscow during the 1943 Soviet offensive.** *Above :* **A Nazi soldier leaps from his burning tank as the Soviets close the trap.**

Above : **Germans had orders not to retreat and fear was used to insure that the German soldiers did not abandon their positions.**

named Uranus, which aimed at simultaneous breakthroughs in the north and south some 60 miles west of Stalingrad trapping the German armies on the Volga. It was the second variant which was adopted and planned to be launched on 9 November, possibly to coincide with Operation Torch, Allied landings in North Africa. Logistic problems delayed the offensive for a week but it was an extremely well planned and executed offensive. As early as September, when the fronts to carry out this offensive were formed, both Zhukov and Vasilievsky personally studied the terrain and the troops. On 22 October the newly established three fronts were finally told of Uranus. In the north the offensive would be carried out by the Southwestern Front under General Vatutin, who would have at his disposal the 1st Guards and 21st Armies, 5th Tank Army and would be covered by General Krasovsky's 17th Air Army. Vatutin would attack in conjunction with the newly formed Don Front under General Rokossovsky whose 24th, 65th and 66th Armies were to be covered by General Rudenko's 16th Air Army. In the south General Yeremenko's Stalingrad Front, also newly formed, would break through with 51st, 57th and 64th Armies spearheaded by General Volsky's IV Mechanized Corps. The two armies would close their pincers in the Kalach area. Zhukov and Vasilievsky went through the offensive tasks of all the fronts and armies in person with all the commanders, and still did not convince them that the offensive would be a success. On 17 November, rather late in the day, General Volsky felt it his duty as a party member to warn Stalin that his offensive in the south, in which he played a vital role, would fail. Stalin was most perturbed and asked his two commanders, Zhukov and Vasilievsky, to explain Volsky's complaint: when they could not, Stalin telephoned Volsky to go into the offensive despite his lack of conviction, for it could not be called off or postponed. For Operation Uranus the Russians amassed some 1,000,500 men, 13,541 guns, 894 tanks and 1115 aircraft, in order to break the two flanks held by badly equipped Rumanians, 3rd Army and VI Corps respectively. Given the wrong intelligence evaluation and bad meteorological conditions which prevented the Luftwaffe from reconnoitering, Uranus was the greatest surprise attack ever to hit the Wehrmacht.

On 19 November at midnight snow clouds arrived over the northern sector and freezing fog enveloped all. Still the artillery barrage started as planned at 0730 hours. At 0850 hours the infantry and tanks went into action and soon began to overwhelm the Rumanians who were fighting most valiantly. Hitler in his HQ at Vinnitsa, which was in even greater darkness than the battlefield, ordered General Heim's XLVIII Panzer Corps to counterattack

Left : **Soviet planes and tanks press forward repelling an attack of the Waffen-SS during the Battle of Kursk.**

Above: **Peasant girl gives Soviet soldiers some liquid encouragement during their drive westwards.**
Left: **Soviet T-34s roll off the assembly line as Russian tank production outstripped German armored production by the end of 1943.**
Below left: **Soviet infantry drive forward during the long German retreat.**

towards Kletskaya, but the Russian tanks were not there. Heim had to turn to face General Romanenko's 5th Tank Army which emerged from the snowy darkness pulverizing all in its path. General Radu's 1st Rumanian Armored Division, without communication with HQ, was lost in the snow and drove to its doom without realizing it. After this catastrophe Romanenko's tanks caused panic among the Rumanian infantry. The breakthrough was achieved and the tanks began to pour south leaving the infantry to do the mopping up and secure the flanks. Late that day Hitler ordered Paulus to break off attacks in Stalingrad and plug the hole in his northern flank. He had no idea that another hole would be punched in the German southern flank.

On 20 November fog delayed Yeremenko's offensive only slightly: the barrage started at 1000 hours and forty minutes later the tanks and infantry went into action. When the tanks caught up with them the VI Rumanian Corps surrendered and the Fourth Panzers had to withdraw in a hurry to avoid encirclement. Two days later Volsky's advance reached Sovetsky and forced the German headquarters to disperse: Hitler ordered Paulus to fly back to his headquarters at Gumrak-Stalingrad thus sealing the fate of the General and his armies. On 23 November at 1400 hours the two Russian pincers linked and Hitler proclaimed the encircled Sixth Army and Fourth Panzer Army as *Festung* Stalingrad, a fortress, rather than permit the armies to break out of the encirclement, which at this stage would have been possible. However when Reichsmarschall Goering assured Hitler that the Luftwaffe could supply the encircled armies, he decided that Paulus should hold out until relief operations could be organized. Some 270,000 men were in the trap and the Russians almost immediately launched their "chop up operation" against them.

Hitler also initiated the relief action almost immediately, but there would be another surprise in store for him, when the Russians launched Operation (Little) Saturn. Field Marshal von Manstein was called from Vitebsk to the Don and given the task of organizing a new relief army. On 24 November, when he arrived at Starobelsk he found the railway system disorganized and often unusable due to partisan activity, with no forces to form the new army and counsels divided: both Paulus and the Army Group B wanted to break out from the encirclement. However Hitler overruled them and Manstein decided to relieve Stalingrad from the southwest with the invigorated Fourth Panzer Army. However General Balck's 11th Panzers who were coming up from Rostov to the Chir, where the breakthrough was to start, ran into Russian tanks and had to fight in order to advance to the starting line. Blizzards raged over the Don area, men and vehicles were lost; snow delayed the 57th Panzers, too. On 12 December Manstein launched his relief operation with insufficient forces and badly prepared. Russian diversionary attacks soon slowed down his progress and he sent Major Eismann to Paulus to ask him to break through in order to help the relieving force. However both Paulus and Hitler refused to break out and Manstein inevitably ran out of steam. He lost most of his armor and in the subsequent retreat most of his infantry. All this time Hitler had at his disposal large forces in the Crimea and even in the Caucasus where the offensive was also stuck and could not be resumed. Then on 16 December General Golikov's Voronezh Front smashed the Eighth Italian Army thus setting into motion Operation Saturn. If Milerovo and Rostov were reached as a result of this breakthrough, the disaster on the Eastern front in 1942 would be complete.

Nothing could save Paulus at Stalingrad. On 8 January 1943 General Rokossovsky demanded Paulus's surrender, but it was refused because the men were convinced that the Russians would not stick to the honorable treatment they promised. Four days later Rokossovsky launched a concentric assault on the city, gained some five miles of the perimeter and more significantly took the airfield at Pitomnik through which most German supplies trickled in. Paulus, who was made Field Marshal in his defeat, contained the attack, but the Russians renewed it and on 23 January the last airstrip at Gumrak was under Russian control. The Germans were driven into the ruins of the town, where they surrendered after another week of desperate fighting; with Paulus, 24 generals and some 92,000 men went into captivity. Ironically hardly any of them survived, not because the Russians practiced on them the *Einsatzgruppen* techniques, but because of their generally weak condition which coupled with the inhospitable climate and disease wiped out most of the men, though not their officers.

While Manstein failed to save Paulus and Stalingrad, he did save the Caucasian Front armies. In January 1943 when Hitler finally gave orders to withdraw from the Caucasus, it was rather late and the Russians began to converge on Rostov from two directions. If they could reach Rostov, General von Kleist, who succeeded Field Marshal List, would have been cut off and his First Panzer Army and the Seventeenth Armies lost. It was a race against time as Kleist extricated his troops harrassed by partisans and Soviet aircraft, and nevertheless managed to slip through the Rostov gap, which Manstein kept open for him. On 6 February 1943 Hitler invited Manstein to a conference, at which Hitler not only accepted all the blame and responsibility for Stalingrad, but also gave him permission to withdraw to the Mius river line. Two years previously the mere suggestion of such a solution had cost Rundstedt his command. Moreover Kleist, after the completion of his successful retreat, received from Hitler the Field Marshal's baton.

Far left: **Another German submarine is launched to continue the Battle of the Atlantic.**
Left: **Grand Admiral Raeder was the head of the Kriegsmarine until his replacement by Karl Doenitz as the Battle of the Atlantic heightened.**
Right: **The petty officers' quarters on the** ***U-995*****, a late model built in 1943.**
Below right: **The depth regulator area on an early model U-Boat.**
Below: **The** ***U-203*** **as it left Brest for mid-Atlantic waters in 1943, when the Germans almost cut supply lines between Britain and America.**

Far left: **Men of *U-86* on the lookout for Allied shipping.**
Center left: **Wolf packs on the prowl.**
Left: **The Naval Hitler Youth attends a rally at Berlin's Sportspalast in 1943.**
Below: **American naval personnel capture *U-505*, which is now on display at Chicago's Museum of Science and Industry.**
Bottom: **Grand Admiral Karl Doenitz reviews U-Boat crews before they prowled the Atlantic waters.**

Apart from throwing away some 250,000 men Hitler lost initiative on the Eastern Front and never really regained it. By the end of February 1943 German front lines had moved some 200 miles west and Hitler could not even make his armies fight the same successful defense battles as in the previous winter. The Wehrmacht lacked men and armor for such a defense, while the Russians seem to have learned all the lessons of tank warfare: the fronts were very fluid and Hitler seemed lost, but all the same he allowed Guderian to control the armor in the south and fight defensive battles, to save Kharkov. On 21 February Hoth's armor attacked Popov and the 3rd SS Panzer Division equipped with new

Below: ***U-826*, flying the British white ensign, and *U-236* after they gave themselves up to the Royal Navy.**
Above right: **US aircraft drop bombs over Kassel as the air offensive over Germany heightened.**

Tiger tanks broke through the Russian line of advance. When their pincers closed, they captured some 9000 Russians, but still most of them escaped across the frozen Donets. But even this flexible defense failed to save Kharkov, which was evacuated without a fight, and the German front line came to rest almost exactly in the same place as it had been in 1942, when the Germans launched their summer offensive.

While the fronts stabilized until July 1943 the Germans could not relax. Large partisan armies increased their activity and the Wehrmacht instead of resting had to hunt for these enemies in its rear. In January and February 1943 Operations *Eisbär* I, II and III were launched against partisans in the areas of Bryansk, Dmitriyev and Mikhailovka. In these operations the Wehrmacht was aided by a Russian militia force commanded by a tough collaborator, Kaminsky. In Operations *Erntefest* I and II, police and SS formations had to help out in Belorussia. But in the area Kletnya and Mamyevka (Operations *Klette* I and II) the Wehrmacht had to do all the dirty work entailed by anti-partisan operations on its own. By March and May 1943 these large-scale operations were given more and more lyrical names [*Ursula* I, II; *Winterzauber* (Wintermagic), *Zauberflöte* (Magic Flute), *Zigeunerbaron* (Gypsy Baron), *Freischütz* (Magic Marksmanship)], but were the same depressing

Left: **The ball-bearing plant at Schweinfurt, which was a principal target for Allied aircraft in 1943. Some 400 Luftwaffe planes were shot down during the ten air raids over Schweinfurt.** *Right:* **Bombs drop over Schweinfurt during the October 1943 raids.**

reality: massacres of civilian population and the burning of villages. However the Wehrmacht's behavior on retreat did not much differ from these punitive expeditions – the Germans left behind utter and complete devastation.

In the meantime the Western Allies also prepared for a blow to the German military power. Though Stalin goaded them throughout the year 1942 to start a second front in France, they did not feel sufficiently strong to carry it out, especially after the British had been repulsed at Dieppe. Following Field Marshal Rommel's victories in Libya and Egypt Premier Churchill persuaded President Roosevelt to launch Operation Torch, which meant that British and American troops would land in Northwestern Africa: Casablanca, Oran and Algiers. The Free French were not told much and therefore there was initial resistance; in retaliation Hitler ordered German troops to occupy the rest of France and also seize airfields and sea ports in Tunisia. This act of German "perfidy" convinced the French, especially Admiral Darlan who was in Algiers by chance, that they must co-operate with the Allies. However before co-operation could proceed further Darlan was assassinated and General de Gaulle was able to take over: General Juin was to lead French armies into Tunisia with the Americans and British. Hitler also tried to seize the French fleet at Toulon but Admiral Laborde preferred to scuttle it. Although needing German troops in the USSR Hitler poured men into Northern Africa only to suffer another disastrous defeat.

Rommel launched his final offensive against Egypt on 1 July 1942, three days after Hitler's offensive on the Eastern Front. But there were no spectacular breakthroughs for Rommel at El Alamein: British defenses and then armor withstood the first assault and inflicted irreplaceable losses on him. For the rest of July fierce fighting continued while both sides were rushing reinforcements to El Alamein. General Auchinleck, who had numerical superiority over the Germans and Italians throughout, especially in tanks, only managed to halt Rommel's advance, but failed to defeat him. Premier Churchill then flew to Cairo and replaced Auchinleck with General Montgomery; however at the battle of Alam Halfa Montgomery delivered the same indecisive results as Auchinleck. Still the Royal Air Force began to blast Rommel's tanks which were handicapped by inadequate oil supplies, out of the desert; early in September 1942 Rommel started his tactical retreat. The British were in turn preparing their final offensive.

For this offensive the 8th Army mustered some 230,000 men, 1440 tanks and 1200 aircraft. By then Rommel only had some 80,000 men and 260 German and 280 Italian tanks with some 350 serviceable aircraft. However the Germans lacked oil, because their supply ships were being sunk and troops suffered from dysentery and jaundice – even Rommel was sick and returned to Germany for treatment. His replacement, General Stumme, died of a heart attack two days after the British offensive started. On 25 October 1942, the very day of the offensive, Rommel flew back from Austria to take charge of operations and soon had the British in trouble. But he had insufficient forces to resist the British assault, though even there Hitler ordered him not to withdraw. Only on 3 November did Montgomery's forces break through and they could have trapped the whole of Rommel's *Afrika Korps* had they exploited the advantage properly. Rommel was allowed to retreat successfully losing Benghazi on 20 November and Tripoli on 23 January 1943. By then he had reached General Jürgen von Arnim's Fifth Army which Hitler transferred to Tunisia to defend it against the Allies from Algeria.

After the successful Torch landings in November 1942 Allied armies intended to invade Tunisia: the British 1st Army along the coast to Tunis; while the American II Corps and French XIX Corps would move further south. The 1st Army was easily checked by the Germans who had only recently landed and enjoyed air superiority. In the south the French were heavily mauled while the inexperienced Americans were cut to pieces on 14 February 1943. However by now Rommel was at loggerheads with von Arnim and they failed to exploit this victory. Later in February and early in March 1943 Rommel unleashed his Fifth Army on the British 1st and 8th Armies, blooding their noses though suffering unacceptable losses in turn. Three days after his attack on the British at Medenine Rommel had to retire to Germany because of sickness, leaving Air Field Marshal Kesselring in command.

However both the British and Americans recovered from their surprise and launched attacks against the Mareth line, an improvized defense which protected the Germans and Italians in Tunisia. General Patton, who took command of the II Corps, attacked in the direction of Gafsa, while Montgomery's 8th Army tried to break the Mareth Line frontally. In the end New Zealanders outflanked the Germans who were forced to retire by the end of March. Next the Italian First Army was put under combined Anglo-American pressure and by 6 April 1943 it also withdrew towards Tunis. Throughout April 1943 the British 1st Army and the American II Corps pushed on towards Tunis which finally fell on 7 May. The Germans and Italians continued their resistance for another week, "until the last shot," when they surrendered: Hitler had thrown away another 275,000 men for no advantage at all.

Above: **Marienburg, Germany under air attack.**

Before the Western Allies could chastise Germany in the Mediterranean by landing in Sicily, Hitler was humbled by the Soviet armies on the Eastern Front. He now concentrated his attention entirely on the east, but this time without grandiose strategic plans. He thought most feverishly of new weapons and charged Guderian with revitalizing the Panzer forces. He no longer planned strategic offensives but did sanction the only large offensive in the summer of 1943, *Fall Zitadelle*. Paradoxically Hitler's very abstention from interfering in the planning condemned the offensive to failure, for in 1943 he was the only man who knew the complete strategic situation on the Eastern Front. *Zitadelle* or Citadel was a two-pronged attack on the Kursk salient and became the greatest tank battle of World War II. General Zeitzler planned the attack with two Army Groups under Field Marshals von Kluge and von Manstein, but General Jodl was against the offensive, for he wanted to preserve reserves in case they were needed in the Mediterranean area. General Guderian also wanted to wait until 1944 as he would have only some 324 Panther tanks for the offensive. Thus throughout the planning stage there was no unity of views, plenty of differences, hopeless hesitations and a complete lack of reliable intelligence on Soviet intentions.

The Russians could also see that the Germans would counterattack in the Kursk area and in contrast to the Germans they prepared well for the attack. Above all they were bringing in armor and guns at a greater speed than the Germans who were to attack. On the Central front under Rokossovsky's command there were five armies in the front line and the 2nd Tank Army behind them. Vatutin's Voronezh front also had five armies deployed and the 1st Tank Army to back them in the flank of the salient. Moreover the Stavka built

Left: **Armament Minister Albert Speer talks with a French colleague. Speer's organization of war production prolonged the war for at least a year.**

Above: **B-17s in the air battle over Bremen.**

up its strategic reserve there in the form of the Steppe front under the command of General Ivan Konev, who commanded three armies and the 5th Guards Tank Army. The salient was also well fortified with trenches in three zones and had extensive minefields. Thus the German Fourth Panzer Army, which was to attack in the south and the Ninth Army which was attacking in the north, were heading for the most terrifying rebuff ever administered to German armies. They would fall into a well-prepared trap.

On 4 July 1943 the Wehrmacht went on the offensive once again. Immediately many German tanks were immobilized by mines, but their wedge-like advance proved successful and the first line of Russian defenses was taken. However the Germans suffered heavy losses and Guderian's fears were proved right: the new Panther tanks were insufficiently protected and were easily set ablaze, because their crews were not properly trained. The Ninth Army used the Ferdinand self-propelled tanks which again the infantry could not protect and Soviet infantrymen managed to climb up on them and use their flamethrowers against engine ventilation slots. In any case Russian armor was moving up during the night and the Germans had to face the same odds as when they started. Still in the next five days they fought hard, especially the élite SS formations, *Grossdeutschland*, *Das Reich*, *Leibstandarte* and *Totenkopf*, which were best equipped, and succeeded in denting the Russian defenses both in the north and the south. However General Sokolovsky's Western Front then counterattacked on the extended left flank of the Ninth Army and forced it to withdraw. On 12 July the Stavka committed its 5th Guards Tank Army equipped with the latest SU85 guns, which collided with General Hoth's Fourth Panzers and swept them back. The following day Hitler can-

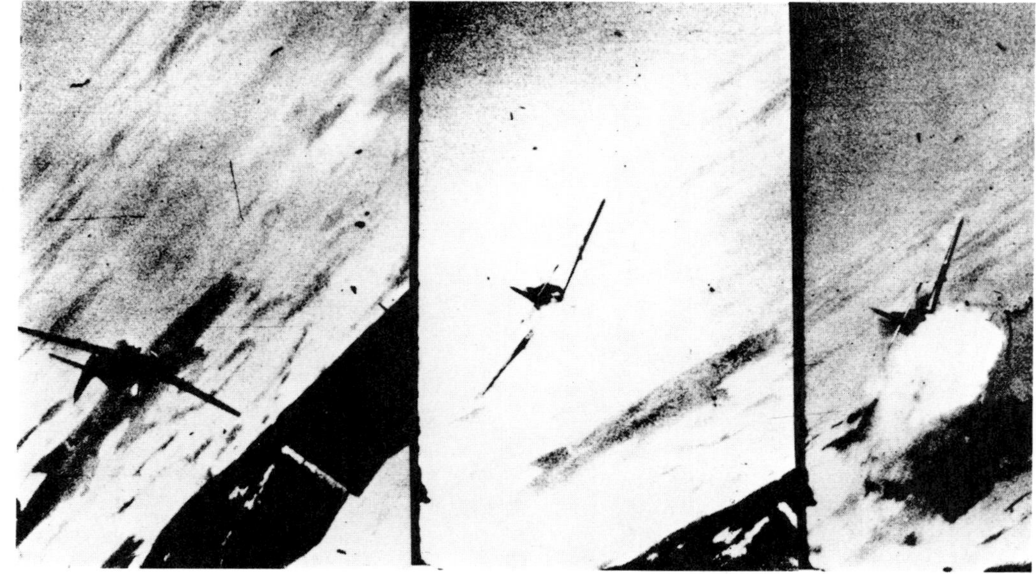

Right: **Three views of a Focke-Wulf 190 during an air battle with a North American P-51 Mustang in which the German aircraft was shot down.**

celled the offensive and henceforth defensive fighting was the order of the day.

The next menace developed in the south, where Manstein in anticipation struck across the Donets and Mius and forced Malinovsky's forces to retreat; he even took some 1700 prisoners, so unexpected was the blow and so chaotic the Russian retreat. Next Rokossovsky moved his 34th Army to a striking position some 350 miles northwest of Kursk. When German reinforcements failed to arrive in time, Rokossovsky poured his armor south and opened a 30-mile gap in the front. Subsequently Vatutin's attack west of Belgorod forced Manstein to abandon Kharkov, which he had recaptured in March. After that the Wehrmacht was steadily pushed back by the Russians; Hitler, seeing the inevitability of withdrawal, gave Manstein permission to fall back to the Dniepr. The retreat was confused and bloody, the Wehrmacht destroying everything as it withdrew. But even then the new front line on the river was out of balance, since Hitler insisted on so many bridgeheads to be held: Zaporozhe, Dnepropetrovsk, Kremenchug, Kiev. In the end Kiev was stormed on 6 November by the Russians, but the fronts were stabilized until the next Russian offensive in 1944.

While Hitler fought his July offensive in the USSR the Allied forces disembarked on the beaches of Sicily on 10 July 1943. For the invasion they assembled 140,000 men, carried them in 3000 ships and protected them with 3700 aircraft. Although the Italian and German forces were more numerous, it was quickly discovered that Italian fighting capacity was doubtful. By coincidence Hitler met Mussolini on 9 July; unknown to both of them Mussolini would be toppled from power within 2 weeks The subsequent armistice talks with the Allies would take Italy out of the war. As it was the Allies beat off the

Below : **Aerial view of the ruined Abbey of Monte Cassino, which cost thousands of Allied lives to capture, and finally fell in May 1944.**

first German counterattacks and then, by mobile maneuvering, unhinged the defense so that by 17 August they reached Messina and the straits dividing them from the mainland. The Germans skillfully ferried across some 100,000 men, but lost some 164,000, which they could ill afford.

On 3 September 1943 Montgomery's 8th Army invaded the Italian mainland and was skillfully held back by the 29th Panzer Grenadiers. A week later the 9th Panzer Grenadiers almost wrecked American landings in the bay of Salerno, but by the end of September the combined Allied drives reached the line between Naples and Termoli. By this time Italy and its army were paralyzed by the armistice talks and Field Marshal Kesselring had to do all the fighting with German troops. In the six weeks through which the armistice talks dragged on Kesselring managed to take control of two-thirds of Italy, all this with some 16 divisions. Nonetheless Hitler had to reinforce him and took the divisions from the Eastern Front. Kesselring then succeeded in stabilizing the front north of Naples, from Gaeta to Cassino and Ortona. Although Hitler rescued Mussolini from his prison, he failed to regain Italy, which was a deadly political blow to his prestige.

To complete the list of disasters for Hitler during these two decisive years of the war, 1942–43, he began to lose the Battle of the Atlantic. Admiral Doenitz who replaced Admiral Raeder in January 1943, lost some 87 U-Boats in four months, largely the consequence of aircraft cover of the convoys and radar detection of the escorts. When Doenitz wanted to withdraw his U-Boats from this unequal struggle he was ordered by Hitler to continue and promptly lost 64 more U-Boats within a month. The Allies were thus free to prepare ships for the invasion of France. In addition to losing the battle

Below : **Field Marshal von Kesselring masterminded the strategic withdrawal of German forces up the boot of Italy.**
Bottom : **Mussolini is kidnapped by Otto Skorzeny in a Fieseler-Storch glider.**

Far left: **Field Marshal Gerd von Rundstedt tried to strengthen the Atlantic Wall against the long-awaited Allied invasion.**
Left: **Mussolini with his captor, Otto Skorzeny, after their escape from the Gran Sasso and return to Germany.**
Below: **Mussolini's residence at Gran Sasso was over 7000 feet up, which forced the Germans to approach it by glider.**

on the high seas Hitler also lost it over Germany. The strategic bombing of German cities was proceeding on an unprecedented scale: in three months of 1943 the RAF dropped over 20,000 tons of bombs on Berlin only. Hitler had nothing left but the hope that the Allied alliance would break up, thus saving him and Germany from a final defeat which now began to stare him in the face. As if to deny Hitler this only hope the Allies (Stalin, Roosevelt and Churchill) met at their first summit meeting at Teheran in December 1943. Instead of quarreling they finally agreed on the second front, which was planned for 1944 and would take place in France. The combined pressures from the East and West would undoubtedly seal Hitler's and Germany's fate. All the same, by the end of 1943, though Germany had suffered a number of disasters, it still stretched from the Bay of Biscay to near Moscow, and from the fjords of Norway to Naples and Greece in the south; it had an experienced army in the field to protect it. However by now Hitler had run out of ideas and morale was low – only decline could follow.

1

2

3

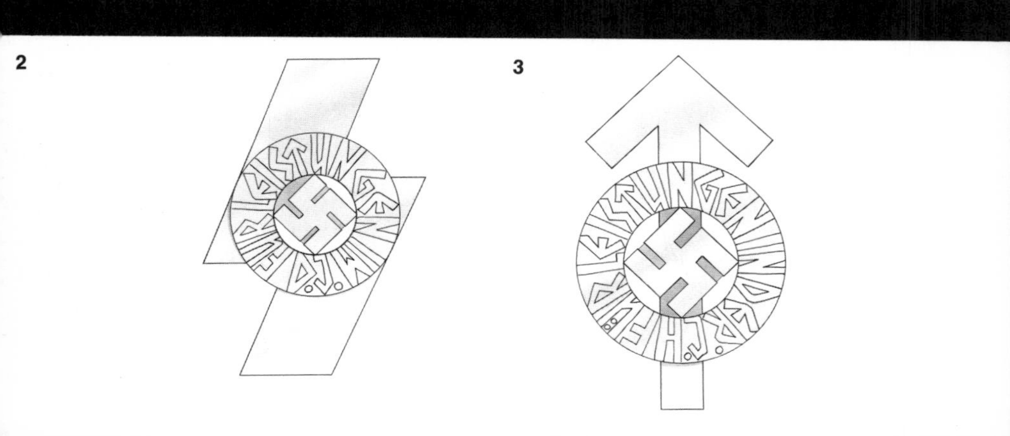

1. The Me-109 was the most useful combat aircraft of the Luftwaffe, and gained its reputation in the Battle of Britain.
2. Hitler Youth Proficiency Award, given to youths aged 10-14.
3. Hitler Youth Proficiency Award given to youths aged 15-18.
4. The flakvierling anti-aircraft gun used by the Wehrmacht late in the war, particularly during Operation Market Garden, the attempt to seize 'A Bridge Too Far' in the Arnhem Offensive.
5. Triumphant banner of the III Battalion of the Der Fuhrer Regiment of the Waffen SS.
6. SS Wreath Band honoring the death of the leader of the detachment of the Waffen SS in Flanders.

4

5

6

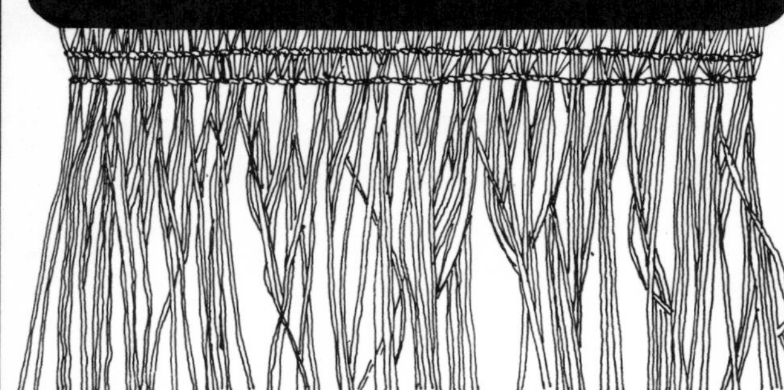

CONSPIRACY AND DEFEAT

At the end of 1943 Germany was heading towards the most obvious disaster in Russia, on the Eastern Front, where Hitler, instead of applying the successful mobile defense, insisted on holding onto strongpoints and bridgeheads on the Dniepr. On 24 December 1943 General Vatutin's 1st Ukrainian Front was launched against the German front in the Ukraine and cut it to pieces. His armored forces broke through, captured Zhitomir, Korosten and then swung south to encircle 10 German divisions in the area Kovel-Korsun. Field Marshal von Manstein had to send armored forces to relieve the encircled Germans, but instead of relief his force was checked, suffering some 20,000 casualties. Thus all his reserves had gone. On 5 February 1944 Vatutin captured Rovno and split Manstein's armies into two, reaching the foothills of the Carpathian mountains.

Further south the military situation looked equally desperate for the Germans. General Tolbukhin's 4th Ukrainian Front took Nikopol on 8 February and cut towards the Crimea; General Malinovsky's 3rd Ukrainian Front pushed forward to Krivoy Rog to meet Tolbukhin. By now the Ukraine was a cauldron of chaos where roving forces made themselves masters of whatever territory they fancied. Soviet and Ukrainian nationalist partisans were also fighting both among themselves and with the Germans and the Red Army. The Ukrainians succeeded in assassinating Vatutin whose place was taken by Zhukov. Notwithstanding, the Germans got the worst of this confusion: throughout March Zhukov and Konev maneuvered in the Ukraine, the one taking Tarnopol and then joining the other at Iassy on the Dniestr. Malinovsky also continued his progress westward taking Kherson and Nikolayev. On 30 March Field Marshal von Manstein was dismissed by Hitler and replaced by Field Marshal Model; Field Marshal von Kleist and General Hoth whose Fourth Panzer Army was separated from the First Army were also dismissed. Fortunately for the Germans the Russians then ran out of steam in the Ukraine and the front line stabilized a little.

In the far north, around Leningrad, which had been under siege for the past three years, the Russians were also able to gain ground. Throughout 1942–43 the Germans constructed deep defenses to prevent the Russians from breaking through into the Baltic provinces and while the Russians gained free access to the city in January 1943, they failed to break through the Northern wall, the defenses that the Germans relied on. The northern offensive to free Leningrad was launched on 14 January 1944; in two days the Russians broke through the Northern wall and by 1 March they had pushed the Germans some 200 miles from Leningrad. During

the summer the Germans and the Finns were forced to retreat to Karelia and on 30 June Vyborg was finally taken. Finland surrendered and was out of the war, while the offensive activity shifted to the German center front to which the Stavka transferred all its strategic reserves.

As a result the Belorussian campaign, Operation Bagration, proved to be one of the greatest disasters that the Germans suffered on the Eastern Front. Coming as it did two weeks after the Allied landing in France and timed to coincide with the anniversary of the German invasion of the USSR in 1941, the Germans were completely taken by surprise. Field Marshal Busch who was in command of the Army Group Center, thinned his troops in this sector as the newly created Field Marshal Model anticipated Russian thrusts in the Lvov area. The Russians concentrated some 118 infantry and 43 armored divisions, and placed their main thrusts north and south of Vitebsk. They easily broke through the thin German line and on 2 July the two thrusts met at Stolnbtsy. At Bobruisk some 30,000 Germans were encircled; at Minsk some 50,000 and there were smaller envelopments at Vitebsk and Vilna. The Army Group Center all but collapsed and Hitler transferred Model to replace Busch and restore the front. This excellent German warrior could do little, albeit Hitler continued to rush reinforcements to the East, despite the Allied breakthrough in Normandy. By the end of July 1944 the Red Army was deep in northeastern Poland: Lvov, Lublin and Brest-Litovsk fell in quick succession and the Russians netted some 200,000 Germans, 2000 tanks, 10,000 guns and 57,000 motor vehicles. Only when the Soviet armies reached the Vistula was the German Army capable of counterattacks. Still Field Marshal Model, frequently disregarding Hitler's directives, did succeed in extricating the remains of German Armies from the Byelorussian swamps. On 29 July Model counterattacked with three Panzer divisions in front of Warsaw and the Red Army became stuck on the Vistula for the next six months.

However disastrous the situation on the Eastern Front, Hitler now had to face a double danger, war on two fronts. On 6 June the Western Allies landed six infantry and three airborne divisions in Normandy. Hitler, who had some 58 divisions (10 of them were armored) in the West, could have dealt with the landing quite easily. However he was deceived into believing that the main strike and landing would take place in the Pas de Calais and hence refused to move his forces into the danger area. During these decisive 15 days Hitler and his generals on the spot did not see eye to eye and disputed each others' decisions vigorously. In any case none of them could make the quick decisions which the situation demanded, as they were dispersed: Rommel was away in Germany, the Commander-in-Chief West of the German Army was on exercise in Brittany, Hitler at Rastenburg. Only on 17 June did Hitler meet Field Marshals von Rundstedt and Rommel at Soissons, just to tell them that he was in charge and nothing could be done without his sanction. Thus tough and confused fighting continued throughout June and July, when the Allies finally managed to break through, particularly

Above: **Field Marshal von Rundstedt inspects a portion of the ill-equipped Atlantic Wall.**

Above: **Field Marshal von Richthofen had little success in preparing his already-weakened Luftwaffe for the Allied assault.**

Left: **Field Marshal Rommel is welcomed back to Germany by Keitel after his heroic defeat with the Afrika Korps. His next assignment was to help von Rundstedt prepare the Atlantic Wall.**
Right: **Early warning radar at Brest along the Atlantic Wall.**

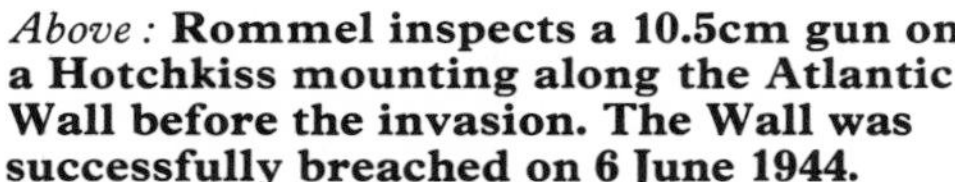

Above: **Rommel inspects a 10.5cm gun on a Hotchkiss mounting along the Atlantic Wall before the invasion. The Wall was successfully breached on 6 June 1944.**

after the assassination attempt on Hitler on 20 July. Thus ironically Hitler finally found an excuse for defeats and lost battles: the treason of his generals.

Conspiracies against Hitler and the Nazis started as soon as they took power in 1933. On the whole Hitler had been able to deal with them in anticipation, but he obviously underestimated the conspiracy hatched by his military leaders who began to plot in earnest as early as 1938. The animator was from the beginning Admiral Canaris, Head of the Abwehr, army intelligence. However, the conspiracy was widespread and included the Chief of Staff, General Ludwig Beck, the diplomat Ulrich von Hassell, the politician Karl Gördeler and even police officers Dr Hans Bernd Gisevius (Gestapo) and Artur Nebe. Still they all suffered from the old conspiratorial weakness, indecision: they wanted to seize power from the Nazis by a *coup d'état*, but could never fix a date. At first they wanted to exploit the war issue and topple Hitler from power under this pretext. But when he won the campaigns against Poland and then France so easily and brilliantly, they had to abandon this pretext. The only way Hitler could now be removed from power was by assassination and this discovery caused further divisions among the conspirators. The younger officers insisted on assassination, while the older conspirators, particularly Gördeler, never believed in using violence to achieve their political ambitions.

Below: **Walter Schellenberg arrives at the Führer-HQ in East Prussia. Hitler was convinced the Allied attack would take place near Calais.**

Despite indecision and division, the political and military conspiracies continued to flourish and in the winter of 1941–42 General Henning von Tresckow put pressure on Field Marshal von Kluge to force the Nazis and Hitler out of power in consequence of the defeat in the East. However this opportunity was not exploited either, because in turn it would have also meant the destruction of the Wehrmacht and the conspirators wanted somehow to avoid this dual demise. Admiral Canaris, who was in charge of relations with Spain, persuaded Generalissimo Franco to hedge and never really join Hitler in his military adventures; Gördeler was also busy recruiting allies in Germany, but was much less discreet than Canaris. In May 1942 Pastor Bonhöffer met the Bishop of Chichester, Dr Bell, in Sweden, but even then the German conspirators failed to establish direct contacts with Allied governments. It became apparent that even if the conspirators succeeded in assassinating Hitler (and this was far from easy), they had no guarantee that they would be treated better than the Nazis.

Above: **An example of German radar, which was insufficient to warn Hitler of the impending Allied naval and aerial invasion.**

Late in 1942 the Allied precondition for peace with Germany, namely unconditional surrender, was the most serious political blow to the conspiracy. However despite it the conspirators decided to carry on, though it now became extremely hazardous. Dr Müller, the negotiator with the Vatican, was under arrest and the Abwehr's Christian von Dohnanyi under suspicion. Out of the blue the Gestapo uncovered a parallel Communist espionage network, the *Rote Kapelle* and Hitler's attention was drawn to the number of officers who were willing to serve as spies for the USSR. A second blow to Hitler came from Munich, where the Gestapo discovered a student anti-Hitler conspiracy: Hans and Sophie Scholl together with some 100 more people were arrested and after a mock trial on 22 February 1943; the brother and sister were ruthlessly executed. Time was working against the conspiracy and the "young" conspirators began to press for decisive action.

The conspirators' best chance for the assassination of Hitler was to get him to the Eastern Front. Early in 1943 Canaris organized a conference of intelligence officers at Smolensk and firm decisions were made about the attempt on Hitler's life. On 13 March 1943 Hitler visited von Kluge's HQ, but the field marshal forbade any attempt at his headquarters. Thus instead von Tresckow gave Colonel Brandt, a member of Hitler's entourage, a package supposed to contain two bottles of Cointreau for General Stieff at GHQ Rastenburg. The bottles were, in fact, plastic bombs and were taken to the aircraft which conveyed Hitler back to East Prussia and although the conspirators in Russia alerted conspirators in Berlin with the codeword Flash, nothing followed. Tresckow dutifully pressed down the fuses in the bottles, but they failed to explode and stage two of the conspiracy, a coup in Berlin, had to be abandoned.

However by then several events rattled the conspirators. In May 1943 Gördeler went even as far as to suggest that he should go to Hitler and ask for his resignation. Later Gördeler toured bombed German cities and was so appalled by the devastation that he wrote a letter to Kluge urging him to take action immediately. Throughout 1943 the Abwehr was under investigation and in April 1943 many officers and their wives were arrested. Although incriminating documents were hidden in the intelligence safe at Zossen it was not searched and the conspiritors in the judicial branch of the Wehrmacht were even able to secure Christian von Dohnanyi's release from arrest. But something drastic had to be done soon, if the conspiracy was not to end in total failure. In September 1943 Field Marshal von Kluge met other resistance leaders at General Olbricht's house in Berlin and they made a definite decision to kill Hitler as soon as practicable and then carry out a *coup de force*.

Indecision gone they were haunted by bad luck. From October 1943 onwards Colonel von Stauffenberg was in Berlin and he personally carried out the planning of the coup most energetically. As it became apparent that Hitler and his entourage would not visit the Eastern Front again, he would have to be assassinated in his GHQ at Rastenburg: all other ways of eliminating Hitler proved either impracticable (suicide attempt using a greatcoat) or impossible, for Hitler kept his movements most secret. Before Stauffenberg could find a way, Dohnanyi was again interrogated, but this time by SS judges. Then in February 1944 Admiral Canaris was forced to retire and his Abwehr, which suffered several defections to the Allies,

Below: **Landing craft at Utah Beach, which was taken by the Americans.**

Above: **General Dwight D Eisenhower, Supreme Commander of the Allied invasion force on D-Day.**
Below: **US landing craft hit the beach on D-Day. Bad planning on the Omaha Beach attack almost caused a fiasco, although the three Anglo–Canadian landings went off without a hitch.**

and above all annoyed Hitler by accurate intelligence forecasting in the East, was dissolved, with Himmler's SS taking over its functions. Arrests of conspirators were occurring all the time – Count Helmut von Moltke, Julius Leber – and Kluge began to lose his nerve: he refused to take Tresckow with him to the Western Front whence he was transferred thus making his lack of enthusiasm clear. However in June 1944 the most significant step in the conspiracy was made: the energetic Stauffenberg was made Chief of Staff to General Olbricht, the Deputy Commander-in-Chief of the Reserve Army based in Berlin which gave Stauffenberg direct access to Rastenburg and Hitler himself.

On 3 July Stauffenberg received a special silent bomb from General Stieff at Berchtesgaden, but was unable to use it there. On 14 July Hitler moved to Rastenburg and the following day Stauffenberg had to abandon another attempt. Still fate had in store two bad blows for the conspirators: on 17 July Field Marshal Rommel was seriously injured in a car crash, after he had agreed to sign a separate peace in the West. On the next day Gördeler had to go into hiding leaving the terminally-ill General Beck in charge in Berlin. Then Stauffenberg was ordered to Rastenburg on 20 July to report to Hitler in person. This was to be the decisive day appointed by Hitler himself. Stauffenberg would place a bomb in the conference room and after it had exploded he would rush to Berlin to head the coup there.

Stauffenberg flew to East Prussia with a double bomb, while his assistant Häften carried another reserve bomb in his briefcase. They got through the SS screening without any mishap and shortly after the beginning of the conference Stauffenberg left the room to set the fuse. While setting the bomb he was disturbed by Corporal Vogel, sent to hurry him up: he only had time to set one part of the bomb. He took the briefcase to the conference room, placed it under the conference table and shortly afterwards was able to leave. On his way out he heard the explosion and saw the shattered hut and debris in the air. According to his estimation no one could have survived and he flew off to Berlin in the firm belief that Hitler was dead. It was probably unimportant whether Hitler was actually killed in the explosion, had the conspirators moved swiftly and carried out their coup, codenamed Valkyrie. Still they had to wait for Stauffenberg who arrived in Berlin at 1600 hours, some four hours later, to set the coup into motion.

Berlin was supposed to become the nerve center of the coup, but it seems that the conspirators were paralyzed by fatalism and were only keen to die. General Olbricht wrangled with superior officers and in the end a simple major thwarted them, after having spoken with the supposedly dead

Hitler on the telephone. Once General Fromm, the Commander-in-Chief of the Reserve Army, was released from arrest, he in turn arrested the conspirators and at midnight held summary court-martial. General Beck tried to commit suicide, but had to be shot together with Stauffenberg. Only in France was Operation Valkyrie successful: General Stülpnagel arrested all the senior SS and Gestapo officers, but then they heard of the debacle in Berlin and had to restore everything. Only two conspirators preferred flight. The rest stayed on to face Hitler's wrath. Himmler and the Gestapo struck immediately in

Top: **Aerial view of the landing craft at Gold Beach. Allied shipping would have been an easy target had the Luftwaffe been sufficiently prepared.**
Above right: **US LCIs land at Omaha Beach, where the fighting was fierce.**

the hours of confusion and as early as 21 July some 160 officers were executed. Hitler was confirmed in his mission by the "miracle" of his escape and was henceforth able to blame all the military reverses on treasonable generals. Reverses followed swiftly despite the miraculous escape.

On 25 July the American 1st Army launched Operation Cobra which finally resulted in a breakthrough in Normandy. A week later a large part of the German Army in Normandy was trapped in the Falaise pocket, but both the British and Americans failed to exploit this victory. German generals and armies were demoralized and hamstrung by Hitler's orders not to withdraw to a defensible line on the Seine. Still throughout August 1944 American 1st and 3rd Armies advanced deep into France taking Orleans on 17 August and liberating Paris on 25 August. The surrender of the Germans in Paris showed clearly that Hitler's orders were more and more disregarded, but Allied advance was still far from swift. It was only in September that Belgium was re-occupied with Brussels falling on 3 September. The

Above left: **German sniper surrenders in a French town near Toulon.**
Below: **Nazi prisoners are searched by US MP on Omaha Beach.**

Rhine in Holland was reached at about the same time, but the great leap forward to Arnhem on 17 September ended in failure, when the 1st Allied Airborne Army was cut off and forced to surrender after gallant fighting. In September the Americans also reached Nancy and Metz in eastern France, but then everybody seemed to have run out of steam and gasoline.

In the East catastrophic retreats and surrenders also continued, though there the German armies seemed to have been least affected by the assassination attempt. Previously in April the Russians stormed the Crimean peninsula and captured some 37,000 Germans. Sevastopol finally fell on 10 May 1944, while three days later some 30,000 Germans surrendered in the Kherson area. On 20 August the 2nd Ukrainian Front struck south of Iassy and the 3rd Ukrainian advanced west of the Dniestr. This was an obvious sign of end for the demoralized Rumanians. King Michael arrested his Prime Minister, Marshal Ion Antonescu, and on 23 August announced that he had changed sides. The Russians swept into Rumania and their armored formations reached the Yugoslav border:

Above right: **Allied armor presses northward after the landings in southern France in Operation Anvil in August 1944.** *Right:* **Troops of the First French Army use their .30 caliber machine gun to help liberate Belfort in Alsace.**

Right : **Hitler in his Wolf's Lair HQ is briefed by Generals Odebrecht and Busse.**
Below right : **Hitler says goodbye to Mussolini on the day of the bomb plot, 20 July 1944, as Goering and von Ribbentrop watch.**

Right : **Soviet troops cross the Oder River as the fighting pressed ever closer to Berlin.**

as a result the Germans lost some 20 divisions – 100,000 Germans went into captivity.

Russian penetrations into Poland during the month of July 1944 excited the Poles so much that they rose against the German garrison in Warsaw and by 6 August controlled most of the city. It seems that the Red Army genuinely ran out of steam in front of Warsaw, but Stalin also had ideological reasons for not making one more desperate effort to relieve the city: the uprising was organized from London and he had different political plans for Poland which obviously did not coincide with those of the London Poles. Hitler ordered the merciless suppression of the uprising and the destruction of the city; he transferred SS formations under SS Obergruppenführer Erich von dem Bach-Zelewski to the city and they hammered the city to smithereens. Former Soviet prisoners of war and German criminals on probation proved particularly ruthless and the uprising was quashed with terror. Still fighting continued for almost three months while the Russians seemingly did nothing. On 16 September 1944 the Polish division under General Zymierski was sent to relieve the city and though it reached the suburb Praga it could not move farther. As a result the Polish insurgents under General Bór surrendered to the Germans, who after their victory at Arnhem felt the surrender of Warsaw was another tremendous morale booster.

Despite these German victories the next collapse followed in the Balkans. By October 1944 the Russians aided by the Rumanian Army, cleared Transylvania of the Germans and prepared for the occupation of the Balkans by Malinovsky's and Tolbukhin's armies, some 38 divisions. While the 4th Ukrainian Front descended into Ruthenia and General Petrov's forces invaded Slovakia, Tolbukhin's armor crossed the Bulgarian border and on 11 September the new "patriotic front" government signed an armistice. At the same time the German front suddenly collapsed in Hungary and Malinovsky's 64 divisions drove fast to Budapest which they reached on 4 November 1944. Previously Belgrade was liberated and the Russian armies stood firm on the Danube.

It seemed clear that the German armies which were still in Greece and Yugoslavia would be cut off from Germany and destroyed. To extricate these precious troops from the Balkan trap Hitler sent Field Marshal von Weichs there, who only ordered the long retreat from Greece in November 1944. Throughout the winter months German armies defended themselves successfully against the various partisans and succeeded in breaking out from the Balkans. Another field marshal, Schörner, however, proved much less successful in the Baltic provinces and by the end of 1944 some 200,000 excellent German troops were isolated there. However the fronts again stabilized and Hitler quickly decided to

strike a deadly blow against the Allies in the West. Against the advice of his generals he concentrated some 20 divisions with 1000 tanks in the Ardennes area and decided to risk the outcome of the war on this desperate operation. In December 1944, when Hitler launched his offensive, the Russians were also ready to start their "usual" winter push forward, that front needed attention and required reserves which were being "wasted" in the West.

On 16 December the well-prepared Germans hurled themselves on the surprised 1st American Army. The Allies ignored intelligence reports of German concentrations in the area, for no one thought that the Germans were capable of an offensive on such a scale. Though Rundstedt was appointed Commander-in-Chief in the West, Hitler conducted this operation in person. He wanted to overwhelm the inexperienced Americans, separate them from the British in the north and then strike at their supply bases, even reach Antwerp. The Sixth SS Panzer Army was to play the vital role in this offensive although gasoline supplies were far from secure; after a while General Hasso von Manteuffel's Fifth Panzer Army inherited this rôle, when it had successfully broken the front. On 17 December Manteuffel's forces broke through in the Schnee Eifel area and captured some 8000 Americans. However, in the southern sector the Germans were checked and General Patton strengthened his front. In the north the advance was also checked after initial successes. Battle Group Peiper moved forward almost to the Meuse massacring American prisoners of war and Belgian civilians as it went. The deepest penetration was achieved in the central sector where Manteuffel's tanks cut off Bastogne on 10 December.

However 20 December seemed to have been the turning point of the offensive, albeit German armored advance still continued. It was on that day that General Collins's Americans turned south and checked the advance of the 15th German Panzer Grenadiers. Four days later, after the SS Panzers failed to reach the Peiper force, it had to abandon its tanks which ran out of fuel and retreat on foot back to the German line. On 26 December the Americans managed to relieve Bastogne and the Germans began to fall back all along the breakthrough. Dietrich's SS Panzers failed to help Manteuffel's Panzers as they both ran out of fuel, and since Hitler refused to give orders to retreat, he made quite sure that the offensive completely miscarried and needless heavy losses were incurred. Although the Allied advance was checked for months the Ardennes offensive insured the success of the Russian offensive, since by January 1945 Hitler had no reserves left with which to plug the holes which the Russians were going to punch in his eastern front.

Hitler's new Chief of Staff, General Guderian, anticipated the Russian offensive immediately after the Ardennes offensive and concentrated some twelve Panzer divisions to meet it. As early as 23 December Guderian requested that the Ardennes offensive be stopped and asked for the forces to be transferred to the East. Hitler refused all his requests, including tactical withdrawals in Poland and East Prussia so that a flexible defense could be put into

Left: **Soviet troops dance in the streets after the liberation of Lvov. After the Liberation Polish Communists tried to dominate the country and the Polish underground was involved in fighting until the Red Army suppressed them.**

Above: **US troops enter a Nazi stronghold in Germany in 1945.**

Below: **SS General von dem Bach-Zelewski greets his opponent in the Warsaw Uprising, General Bor-Komorowski, after resistance ended and the city was leveled in November 1944.**

operation. Guderian who toured the front in the first week of January 1945 was most impressed by the numerical increases of Russian forces all along this front: on the five fronts led by the best Russian generals, Chernyakhovsky, Rokossovsky, Zhukov, Konev and Petrov, Stalin had amassed some 225 infantry divisions and 22 armored corps and hoped to capture Upper Silesia and get to the river Oder. To face this mighty power Guderian had only twelve mechanized and some 50 infantry divisions.

On 12 January 1945 the Russians let loose their armies on Guderian's. Five days later Warsaw was finally taken, by

Left: **A German tank trap outside Berlin which was by-passed by the Soviets in the spring of 1945.**
Below: **A German woman looks at the ruins of her home as US troops pass through Bönnigheim in March 1945.**

which time Zhukov's armored spearhead reached Lódż and Krakow. By 19 January both cities were taken, the Red Army was on the threshold of Silesia and East Prussia: the Russian advance was 100 miles deep over some 400 miles. Within two weeks of fighting the Russians took 113,000 prisoners, invested Königsberg and finally fought on German soil. The long awaited Russian revenge was at hand, but Hitler still did everything his own way. He refused Guderian's request for the evacuation of 26 divisions in the Baltic states and diverted Dietrich's SS Sixth Panzer Army to Hungary instead of the Polish front. By now Zhukov had reached Pomerania and Brandenburg, Konev isolated Upper Silesia and the Red Army devastated the occupied East Prussia which was not properly evacuated.

By the end of February 1945 when the Russians again outran their supplies, Konev took Katovice, crossed the upper Oder, invested Breslau, reached Sommerfeld on his oblique way to Berlin and came to a halt on the Neisse river. Zhukov, who had as his objective the German capital, by-passed Poznań, took Landsberg, invested Küstrin and was checked on the Oder. On 23 February the Russians finally took Poznań, while ten days earlier they had taken Budapest with 110,000 German prisoners. The scale of Russian victories completely unhinged Guderian, who began to quarrel with Hitler. On 8 February Hitler almost hit his Chief of Staff, while five days later Guderian had to listen to Hitler's raging and ranting for two hours. Still he forced the Führer to allow General Wenck to assist Reichsführer Himmler in the preparation of a counterattack at Amswalde. Himmler without military experience was bound to bungle the job, but Hitler seemed to have boundless confidence in him. The six Panzer divisions which Guderian had ready for the offensive were too weak, especially since the tank crews were either exhausted or inexperienced. They also lacked air support and were counterattacking in the wrong place: the mass of the 47th Russian Army was farther back. Moreover Wenck, who had to attend Hitler's briefings, crashed on his way back to the front and being seriously wounded could not lead the

Below : **German women and children flee the blazing ruins of their homes in Kronach.**
Bottom : **German refugees flee westward to be liberated by the Western Allies.**

counterattack. After four days the Germans had to give up. Hitler subsequently sacked Guderian and replaced him with General Krebs, the erstwhile military attaché in Moscow.

By the end of February, after the Russians had ceased to hammer Germany, the Allies dropped their political superbomb on Germany from Yalta, where they were meeting to divide the world among themselves after the defeat of Germany, which now seemed a foregone conclusion. The principle of unconditional surrender was upheld, and the Russians were allowed a zone of influence in Eastern Europe as well as in Germany. The Germans, how-

Left: **German Prisoners of War are used to clear and reconstruct damaged airfields.**
Below: **British forces liberate a Dutch town prior to the Allied crossing of the Rhine.**

ever, only heard rumors of these proceedings which confirmed Hitler in his determination to fight to the last. Goebbels made a great propaganda coup with the leaked Morgenthau Plan which envisaged the dismantling of German industry after the war, but really needed no more to add to the horrors of Bolshevism, the specter which now haunted Germany itself. In this final phase Hitler turned to Goebbels, who, after General Guderian and Minister Speer had disappointed him, was practically the only Nazi leader sharing his Führer's belief in the hopeless alternative: victory or *Götterdämmerung*.

It was the turn of the Western Allies to

Right: **US "dogface" inspects a vehicle during the advance through Germany.** *Below:* **The "dragons' teeth" of a tank trap is by-passed by US troops near Roetgen as the "impregnable" Siegfried Line in penetrated.**

bring forward Hitler's death wish. The Russian winter offensive denuded the Western Front and the Allies prepared a veritable battering ram to get across the Rhine and invade Germany proper. The main rôle this time went to General Montgomery's group of armies, the 1st Canadian Army, the 2nd British Army and the 9th American Army. Still it was the Americans who had started the movements on the fronts. On 7 March General Patton's tanks broke through the German line in the Eifel hills and three days later reached the Rhine near Koblenz. Farther north at Remagen elements of General Bradley's armies captured a bridge across the Rhine intact, but failed to exploit it on the direct orders of Generalissimo Eisenhower. By 21 March a stretch of 70 miles on the western bank of the Rhine was clear of German forces, but the Americans waited for Montgomery's attack before plunging into Germany. On 23 March Montgomery launched his attack with 25 divisions against five dispirited German divisions and soon had bridgeheads on the other side of the Rhine; Germany's Western Front was ready to collapse.

In Italy German collapse was also imminent. In April 1945 when the 8th Army

Below: **US troops cross the Rhine in a "duck" barge specially constructed for the purpose.**

Above : **A bombed-out repair shop and hangar of the Dornier aircraft factory at Oberpfaffenhofen near Munich.**

Führer Order

Order of the Day 15 April 1945.

Soldiers of the German Eastern front!
For the last time our deadly enemies the Jewish Bolsheviks have launched their massive forces to the attack. Their aim is to reduce Germany to ruins and to exterminate our people. Many of you soldiers in the East already know the fate which threatens, above all, German women, girls, and children. While the old men and children will be murdered, the women and girls will be reduced to barrack-room whores. The remainder will be marched off to Siberia.

We have foreseen this thrust, and since last January have done everything possible to construct a strong front. The enemy will be greeted by massive artillery fire. Gaps in our infantry have been made good by countless new units. Our front is being strengthened by emergency units, newly raised units, and by the Volkssturm. This time the Bolshevik will meet the ancient fate of Asia – he must and shall bleed to death before the capital of the German Reich. Whoever fails in his duty at this moment behaves as a traitor to our people. The regiment or division which abandons its position acts so disgracefully that it must be ashamed before the women and children who are withstanding the terror of bombing in our cities. Above all, be on your guard against the few treacherous officers and soldiers who, in order to preserve their pitiful lives, fight against us in Russian pay, perhaps even wearing German uniform. Anyone ordering you to retreat will, unless you know him well personally, be immediately arrested and, if necessary, killed on the spot, no matter what rank he may hold. If every soldier on the Eastern Front does his duty in the days and weeks which lie ahead, the last assault of Asia will crumple, just as the invasion by our enemies in the West will finally fail, in spite of everything.

Berlin remains German, Vienna will be German again, and Europe will never be Russian.

Form yourselves into a sworn brotherhood, to defend, not the empty conception of a Fatherland, but your homes, your wives, your children, and, with them, our future. In these hours, the whole German people looks to you, my fighters in the East, and only hopes that, thanks to your resolution and fanaticism, thanks to your weapons, and under your leadership, the Bolshevik assault will be choked in a bath of blood. At this moment, when Fate has removed from the earth the greatest war criminal of all time, the turning point of this war will be decided.

Signed: ADOLF HITLER

Extract from H R Trevor-Roper *Hitler's War Directives, 1939-1945* (London, 1964). Quoted by permission of Sidgwick & Jackson Limited.

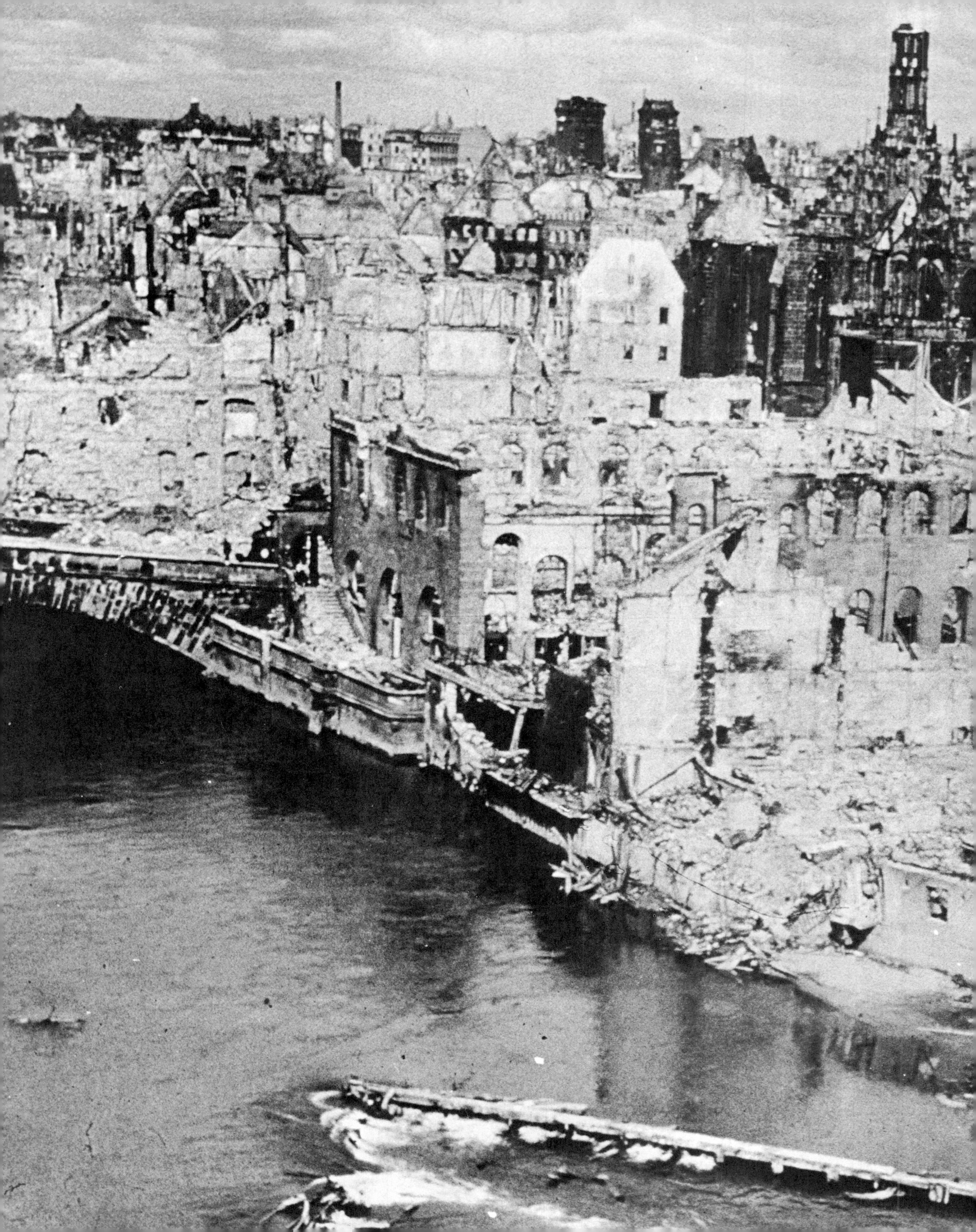

Below: **The remains of the walled city of Nuremberg, scene of Nazi rallies, after a series of Allied air raids.**

Top: **Dr Goebbels briefs the last defenders of Berlin. During the last months of the Third Reich he lived in the Bunker as part of Hitler's entourage.**
Above: **Heinrich Himmler visits some defenders of Berlin outside the city.**

began its final push it had at its disposal twice as many troops and artillery and three times as many armored vehicles as the Germans. In addition it had some 60,000 partisan irregulars helping it, absolute control in the air and plentiful gasoline supplies while the Germans were very short of fuel. Nevertheless the Germans fought well and Allied advance was slow. General Vietinghoff nonetheless saw the necessity of retiring behind the natural barrier of the river Po, but Hitler countermanded this order. By now Hitler's orders emanating from far away Berlin were generally disregarded and the Germans retreated just in time to avoid encirclement. On 26 April the Americans took Verona and the 8th Army penetrated the Venetian line. Italian partisan forces had blocked the Alpine passes so that the German Army in Italy was in reality trapped and at the mercy of Allied armies. In fact in February 1945 General Karl Wolff of the Waffen SS had opened negotiations with Allen Dulles (OSS Chief) in Switzerland about German surrender in Italy. However after the Allied offensive in April Himmler, who was kept informed, froze the negotiations. Still it was too late and the demoralized German troops were surrendering everywhere, although Wolff had negotiated surrender on 2 May 1945.

It was obvious that the last battle of the war would take place in the East and Hitler together with Himmler were feverishly preparing for it. It was at this desperate stage that Himmler and his SS finally took up the question of Soviet prisoners and decided to make use of them. As has been seen the Wehrmacht made use of these unfortunate captives in auxiliary capacity against Hitler's and Rosenberg's previous wishes. Pleading absolute military necessity some 3000 to 4000 Russians and Ukrainians made up every German division deployed in the East; often they had to fight, as many German divisions were practically devoid of German troops. However these hundreds of thousands of Russians and Ukrainians wanted to fight for their countries against the Stalinist régime rather than in the German armies. But the Wehrmacht, while recognizing their aims and respecting their desires,

Above : **The remains of an Me 109 at the Messerschmitt aircraft factory in Augsburg.**
Right : **Soviet artillery within Berlin fires at the Reichstag building.**

Left : **Soviet soldiers atop the Reichstag raise the hammer and sickle flag of Communism over the soon-to-be-divided city of Berlin.**
Right : **Berlin residents look for clothes and other essentials on a makeshift notice board (tree).**

never succeeded in persuading the politicians, especially Hitler, to enable them to fight their own battles.

In the summer of 1942, when General Andrey Vlasov was captured, the Russians even got themselves a capable organizer and leader who was willing to collaborate with the Germans in order to destroy the Stalinist régime with which he had become disillusioned. When previously the Smolensk Committee appealed to Hitler to raise a million-strong Russian National Liberation Army to fight against Stalin, he did not even bother to reply. Vlasov now took up this same cause and sponsored by the Wehrmacht he went round the prisoner of war camps, where he was received with certain enthusiasm. What was more significant were the requests of Soviet deserters, who as late as 1944 amounted to some 2500 to 3000 every day, to be enrolled in Vlasov's Liberation Army, which did not exist. Vlasov did impress Rosenberg who would have liked to help the Russian Liberation Movement, but as usual he failed to impress Hitler with his case, and therefore gave it up. However by 1943 Rosenberg was collaborating with Reichsführer SS Himmler and Himmler had more influence on Hitler than Rosenberg; in any case Himmler was prepared to go behind Hitler's back once he convinced himself that in the case of the Russian Liberation Movement, German national interests and his own coincided.

While the Wehrmacht, with the help of the Propaganda Ministry, could set up Vlasov and some 1200 propaganda specialists at Dahrendorf, Himmler could actually form these prisoners into military units and make them part of his Waffen SS. Quite cynically SS officers who saw fighting on the Eastern Front changed their ideas on the *Untermensch* theory and seeing the toughness and even enthusiasm of these *Untermenschen* recruited them for their SS units. Himmler swiftly gave permission and the SS recruited men from among the minor nationalities straight away and they quickly proved themselves to be as fanatical fighters as the SS themselves. Out of the 910,000 Waffen SS only 310,000 were Germans. The rest were non-Germans, mainly Slavs or "Germanic" volunteers. However by the fall of 1943 Hitler, who tolerated this "unofficial" recruitment, blamed the *Osttruppen* for minor Soviet successes on the Eastern Front, and insisted on having them all transferred to the West. Still seeing Hitler's acquiescence, the SS launched Operation *Skorpion* in the spring of 1944. Large Russian units were organized by the SS on the southern sector of the Eastern Front and the SS Standartenführer d'Alquen even wanted to issue a political declaration of the Russian Liberation movement. Though he was unable to do

Left : **Captured German general officers in front of the ruins of the Reichstag. It has since been restored by the East Germans.**
Right : **Soviet tanks enter Berlin in the final days of the Third Reich. Fighting more or less ceased on 2 May 1945.**

Left: **Soviet fighting men are addressed by an officer in front of the Brandenburg Gate on 2 May 1945. The Gate is now the awesome public symbol of the partition of the city.**

so at this stage, Hitler now charged Himmler with dealing with the Russians and their political aims.

In this hour of need for Germany Himmler finally condescended to meet Vlasov and discuss mutual problems. On 16 September 1944 they met in the GHQ in East Prussia and apparently reached an agreement: although in German uniforms the Russian liberation forces, some ten divisions, would be deployed on the Eastern Front with a view to liberating their homeland from the Bolsheviks. Vlasov was to be their supreme leader, while SS Obergruppenführer Berger was to act as Himmler's plenipotentiary and SS Oberführer Dr Kröger as liaison officer. As a result of this agreement the Germans formed the 1st Russian Division at Münsingen, which subsequently fought bravely at Frankfurt on the Oder as part of Himmler's Reserve Army. However nothing else came of this belated agreement but disillusionment. Soon it became clear that Himmler wanted only three divisions, not ten, and they were to fight under his command and not Vlasov's. Then it transpired that the Prague Manifesto, which Vlasov issued on 11 November 1944 and in which he invited not only all the freedom-loving Russians, Ukrainians, Cossacks, but also Czechs, Slovaks and Croats with Serbs to join him in his fight against Bolshevism, was not accurate. He apparently had no right to address himself to any other nationality and above all he could not even speak on behalf of all the Russians. Hopes and enthusiasm quickly evaporated, especially since the Red Army arrived at the gate of Berlin and was poised to pull down the edifice of the Third Reich. Vlasov's 2nd Division never became operational and in the spring of 1945 he concentrated all his forces in the area of Linz-Prague. Although the Liberation Movement would never substantially help the Germans, they proved more than willing to help the Czechs against the Germans. Early in May 1945 an uprising broke out in Prague and it was only thanks to the Vlasov Army that the SS formations did not suppress it in the same way they had in Warsaw. After this last good will gesture Vlasov and his forces retreated toward the Americans and surrendered to them.

Left: **German troops near Berlin's Anhalter Station watch the burning wreckage of a car and a truck. Many civilians tried to escape from the city but few succeeded.**

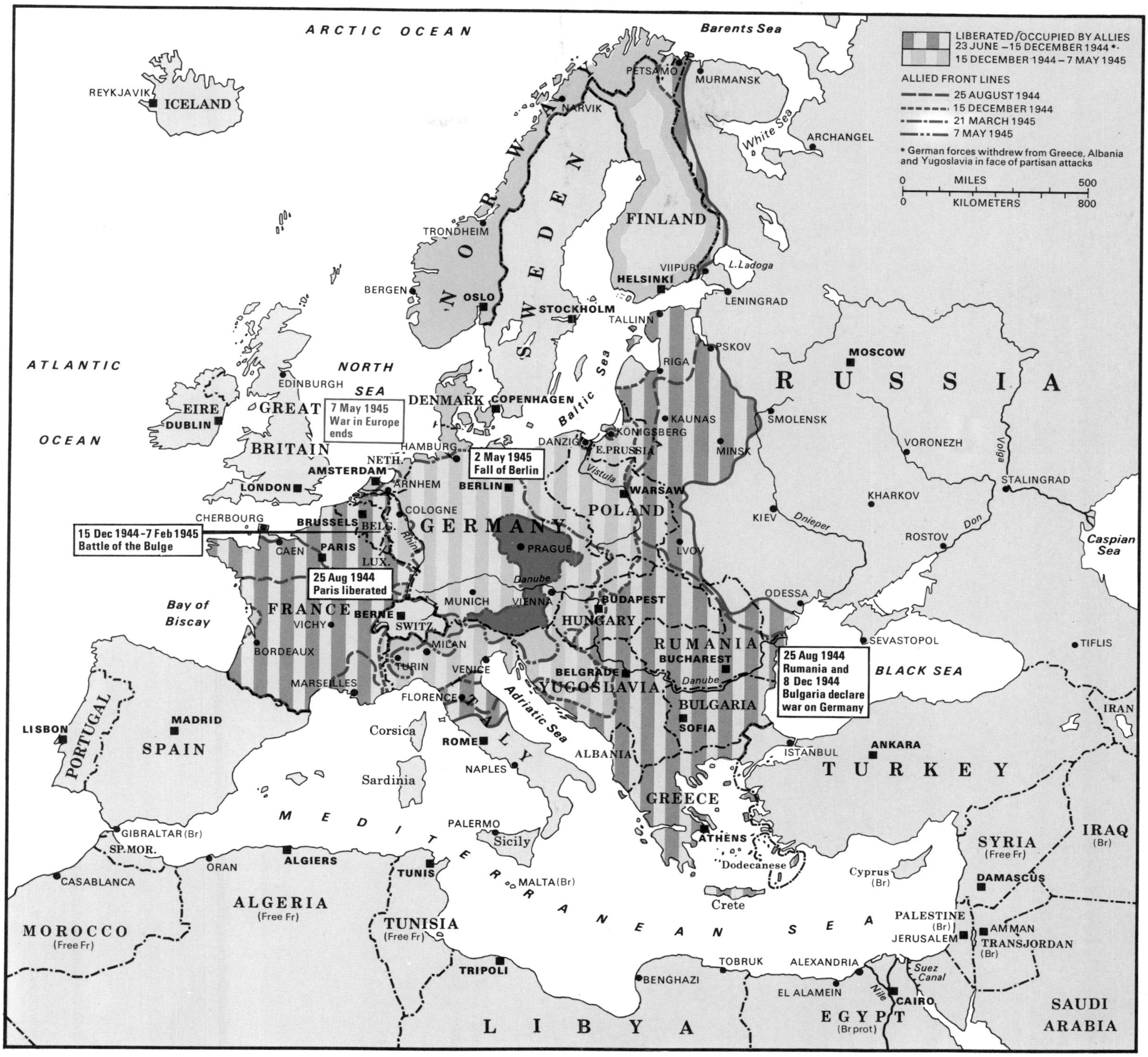

LIBERATED/OCCUPIED BY ALLIES
23 JUNE – 15 DECEMBER 1944 *
15 DECEMBER 1944 – 7 MAY 1945

ALLIED FRONT LINES
25 AUGUST 1944
15 DECEMBER 1944
21 MARCH 1945
7 MAY 1945

* German forces withdrew from Greece, Albania and Yugoslavia in face of partisan attacks

MILES 0–500
KILOMETERS 0–800

15 Dec 1944–7 Feb 1945
Battle of the Bulge

25 Aug 1944
Paris liberated

7 May 1945
War in Europe ends

2 May 1945
Fall of Berlin

25 Aug 1944
Rumania and
8 Dec 1944
Bulgaria declare war on Germany

Subsequently they were all handed over to Stalin, who after executing their leaders, reserved for them the same fate Hitler had offered: the deadly gulags.

While Hitler and the Nazis were making their last desperate moves the Western Allies began to exploit their breakthroughs on the Rhine. Although Hitler and his fellow Nazis resided in Berlin, thus making the capital the nerve center of Germany, the Allies changed their politico-military strategy, and instead of heading straight for the capital, decided on a different course by fighting envelopment battles in the Ruhr, or surging to take the mythical German National Redoubt in Bavaria and elsewhere. Thirty years after the war it is still not quite certain that the Allied Generalissimo, Eisenhower, was responsible for the change in strategy. As it was, Eisenhower made it clear to Montgomery that as soon as the German armies in the Ruhr were encircled the American 9th Army would be detached from his Army group and used in mopping-up operations in the Ruhr. Consequently Montgomery could not hope to reach Berlin before the Russians, if his armies could reach the capital at all. As before, in 1944, the Allied armies were to advance on the broadest

Right: **A wounded friend is carried away from the rubble inside Berlin. Thousands died in the house-by-house struggle to take Berlin.**

front and take Germany without the slightest regard to political aims. On 1 April 1945 Field Marshal Model's Army Group B was sealed in the Ruhr by the American 1st and 9th Army, whose armor then continued to reduce the pocket and capture its 320,000 demoralized combatants. Model committed suicide and Montgomery was fatally delayed in his dash to the Elbe.

Despite this useless battle the elements of the Allied armies reached the river Elbe on 11 April, which they wanted to cross and thrust on toward Berlin. But they were

Left : **Soviet troops dole out food, fuel and medical supplies to residents of Berlin after its capitulation.**
Below : **Russian troops move through Köslin, a town in Pomerania, which is now Koszalin in Poland.**

again stopped by General Eisenhower, who decided against taking Berlin. He was advised by his superior and by subordinate officers that the operation against Berlin would cause heavy casualties, (which in the view of the Wehrmacht's collapse sounded nonsensical) and would achieve only a doubtful prestige (which betrayed abysmal political ignorance). Thus it was that the Allied armies halted their victorious joyrides up and down Germany, and waited for the Russians to complete their military victories by taking Vienna, Prague and Berlin, all capitals of Central Europe, the centers of power in any post-war political settlement.

In Berlin Hitler and the Nazi leaders were hoping for such strategic errors to be committed by the Western Allies, though at this late hour they also tried to resist the Russian advance as best they could. However their situation was quite hopeless: Hitler had been in the bunker under the New Chancellery since 20 November 1944, when he evacuated Rastenburg. He still imagined that he commanded the German armies, as he in fact did for a short time while conducting in person the Ardennes counterattack. But he also imagined that supernatural forces were on his side and that they would save him and Germany. While busy planning offensives he dreamt of Frederick the Great of Prussia who had been saved in Berlin from the Russian armies by the death of Empress Elisabeth. When Goebbels gave him the news of President Roosevelt's death, they were both elated for a while. On 20 April, his birthday, Hitler was again overwhelmed by the hopeless reality and agreed to share the command of his hypothetical forces with Admiral Karl Doenitz in the north and Field Marshal Albrecht von Kesselring in the south; after all he still had some 6,000,000 men under arms. However, shortly afterwards his closest political associates, Himmler, Goering and Ribbentrop, left him forever and let him organize the defense of Berlin. The garrison of Berlin amounted to some 25,000 men and obviously could not stand up to the double attack which the Russians finally mounted on 16 April 1945. But to the last moment Hitler insisted on commanding phantoms: on 21 April he ordered General Steiner to counterattack with his "army," and when Steiner could not be found and the counter-

Above: **Soviet troops engaged in house-to-house fighting outside Berlin. More than two and a half million Soviet soldiers were involved in the battle for Berlin. The "city" fighting involved children and old men and left the populace without any amenities.**
Below: **A Berlin organ-grinder entertains women and children in the ruins of Berlin. By the time the Soviet troops entered the city the basic amenities of life, food, water, heat and the like were non-existent.**

Left: **A demobbed German soldier sits on the rubble of the Reichstag.**
Right: **General Jodl on his way to Rheims to sign the document of surrender in the presence of General Eisenhower. The surrender was unconditional. Jodl was tried at Nuremberg and executed.**
Far right: **The first issue of the new** *Communist Berliner Zeitung* **is sold to Berliners hungry for news as well as food.**

attack never materialized Hitler went into the longest rage of his life. General Wenck's relief army never arrived either, by which time Hitler was completely unhinged by disappointments, and chose the easy way out of his predicament: suicide.

In those seven days of life that Hitler had left after the final Soviet onslaught, he had to taste bitter political disappointments. Goering who was in Bavaria suddenly seized the initiative and proposed to negotiate an armistice. Hitler was beside himself and ordered Martin Bormann to have him arrested. Then his favorite Minister Speer confessed that he was not implementing the scorched earth order, but Hitler found it possible to forgive Speer. However when he heard that his faithful Heinrich (Himmler) was negotiating terms of surrender with the enemy, he finally decided on self-destruction. On 28 April with the Russians near the Potsdamer Platz, Hitler married his mistress Eva Braun and wrote his last testament. In the testament, apart from pious claptrap, he appointed Admiral Doenitz as his successor, and Goebbels and Bormann to head the state and party administration. Then he only had enough time to hear of his friend Mussolini's death before dispatching himself.

The Third Reich's fate was sealed on 16 April, when Generals Zhukov and Konev launched their assault on Berlin. With reserves they had some 2,500,000 men concentrated on this 40 mile front with more than 42,000 guns, 6250 tanks and 7500 aircraft to support them. By 25 April Berlin was isolated and the German Army Groups Vistula and Center were simply disappearing; Steiner's and Moser's reserve forces melted away and Berlin was being reduced in tough street fighting by such specialists as General Chuikov and his 8th Guard Army, lately of Stalingrad. Only on 2 May 1945 did the German garrison surrender.

Below: **Rubble is cleared away from the Reichstag after the Soviet occupation of Berlin.**
Right: **Soviet troops in the devastated streets of Berlin.**

The final act of dissolution, however, was played elsewhere. When Goebbels and Bormann failed in their approaches to the Soviets, initiative passed to Admiral Doenitz, who swiftly agreed to surrender unconditionally. His plenipotentiary, Admiral Hans von Friedeburg, surrendered to General Montgomery all German forces in Holland, Northwest Germany, Schleswig-Holstein and Denmark on 4 May. On 7 May General Jodl surrendered to General Eisenhower on behalf of the Wehrmacht at Reims and two days later a general surrender was ratified in Berlin with the Russians. By this time the principal Nazi leaders, who had dragged Germany into the war, were either dead or in captivity; and with them had died more than ten million German soldiers and civilians. Germany was devastated, leaderless, occupied by the armies of Soviet Russia, the USA, Britain and France; its cities in ruin and its economy non-existent. Apart from this *Götterdämmerung* the Third Reich which was to insure German hegemony for a thousand years could boast the following achievements: some 6 million Jews were killed together with 16 millions of Soviet citizens (all approximate figures) which made it the bloodiest war in human history. At the time of dissolution some 40,000 SS *Totenkopf* men guarded some 714,211 humans in concentration camps; countless millions of other foreign slaves (Russians, Ukrainians, Poles, Czechs, Frenchmen, Italians) were scattered all over Germany thus giving Hitler's *Götterdämmerung* a distinctly international flavor. In the fateful hands of the unhinged Führer German nationalism became the greatest nihilist force ever to engulf the German nation.

Above: **General Jodl signs the unconditional surrender for Germany at Reims on 7 May 1945.**
Below: **Marshal Zhukov signs the instrument of surrender on 7 May 1945.**
Right: **The Instrument of Surrender signed by Field Marshal Montgomery.**

Instrument of Surrender

of

All German armed forces in HOLLAND, in

northwest Germany including all islands,

and in DENMARK.

1. The German Command agrees to the surrender of all German armed forces in HOLLAND, in northwest GERMANY including the FRISIAN ISLANDS and HELIGOLAND and all other islands, in SCHLESWIG-HOLSTEIN, and in DENMARK, to the C.-in-C. 21 Army Group. This to include all naval ships in these areas. These forces to lay down their arms and to surrender unconditionally.

2. All hostilities on land, on sea, or in the air by German forces in the above areas to cease at 0800 hrs. British Double Summer Time on Saturday 5 May 1945.

3. The German command to carry out at once, and without argument or comment, all further orders that will be issued by the Allied Powers on any subject.

4. Disobedience of orders, or failure to comply with them, will be regarded as a breach of these surrender terms and will be dealt with by the Allied Powers in accordance with the accepted laws and usages of war.

5. This instrument of surrender is independent of, without prejudice to, and will be superseded by any general instrument of surrender imposed by or on behalf of the Allied Powers and applicable to Germany and the German armed forces as a whole.

6. This instrument of surrender is written in English and in German.

The English version is the authentic text.

7. The decision of the Allied Powers will be final if any doubt or dispute arises as to the meaning or interpretation of the surrender terms.

B. L. Montgomery
Field-Marshal

4 May 1945
1830 hrs

v. Friedeburg

Kinzel.

G. Wagner

[illegible]

[illegible]

GLOSSARY

Useful German titles and terms

Agrarpolitischer Apparat	AA	Office of Agriculture (Nazi section).
Abschnitt	Abs	a subdivision.
Abteilung	Abt	Branch or subdivision of a department also military unit up to a battalion.
Abwehr	Abw	Defense, specifically Espionage, Counter Espionage and Sabotage Service of the German High Command.
Allgemeines Wehrmachtsamt	AWA	German Armed Forces Office in OKW.
Amt		a main office branch.
Armee-Oberkommando		an Army Headquarters.
Auslandorganisation		Organization of Nazi party members living outside the Reich.
Barbarossa		Codename for German attack on the USSR, 22 June 1941.
Bund Deutscher Mädchen	BDM	League of German Girls.
Chef des Generalstabes des Heeres		Chief of General Staff, Army.
Chef der Sicherheitspolizei und des SD		Chief of Security Police and Security Service.
Chef der Zivilverwaltung		Head of Civilian Administration of an Occupied territory.
Deutsche Afrika Korps	DAK	German Afrika Korps.
Deutsche Arbeitspartei	DAP	German Workers' Party.
Deutsche Arbeitsfront	DAF	German Labor Front, largest of NSDAP's affiliated organizations.
Deutscher Frauenorden		Order of German Women.
Deutsches Jungvolk	DJV	German Young People.
Deutschnational Volkspartei	DNVP	German Nationalist People's Party, a leading conservative party in the Weimar Republic.
Deutsch-Sozialistische Partei	DSP	German Socialist Party, anti-Semitic party merged with NSDAP in 1923.
Deutsche Volkspartei	DVP	German People's Party, liberal.
Deutschvolkische Freiheitspartei	DVFP	German People's Freedom Party, anti-Semitic splinter group of DNVP.
Donnerschlag		Codename for the breakout of the Sixth Army from Stalingrad.
Einsatzgruppe		operational group of Sipo and SD for special invasions into occupied territory.
Einsatzkommando		a detachment of Sipo and SD, part of an *Einsatzgruppe*.
Ersatzheer		Replacement Army.
Freikorps		Volunteer units brought in by the German government in 1918 to protect it from left wing coups.
Freiwilligen		a volunteer.
Frontbann		Front union, important illegal organization of the old SA members still active after the 1923 putsch.
Führer		a leader, commanding officer, chief.
Führerhauptquartier		Hitler's field Headquarters.
Gau		main territorial unit of the Nazi Party, which divided Germany into 42 Gaus.
Gauleiter	GL	highest ranking NSDAP officials below Reichsleitung.
Geheime Feldpolizei		Secret Field Police-executive arm of the Abwehr for security tasks in the Armed Forces.
Geheime Staatspolizei	Gestapo	Secret State Police.
Gelb, Fall		Plan for the invasion of France, Belgium and Holland, 1939.
Generalstab des Heeres		The General Staff, Army.
Gliederung		an organization, a collective name for para-military groups and other sections of the NSDAP.
Heer		an army.
Heeresgruppe		army group.
Hitler Jugend	HJ	Hitler Youth.
Kampfbund		Militant Association of Bavaria for the right, formed to organize the 1923 Putsch.
Kommunistische Partei Deutschlands	KPD	Communist Party of Germany.
Kreis		administrative district, subdivision of a *gau*
Kriegstagebuch		a war diary.
Kriminalpolizei	Kripo	Criminal Police.
Landbund		Farmers' Union.
Lager		a concentration camp.
Leibstandarte SS Adolf Hitler		Bodyguard Regiment, the oldest of SS militarized units.
Nationalsozialistische Deutsche Arbeiter Partei	NSDAP	National Socialist German Workers' Party
Nationalsozialistische Freiheitspartei	NSFP	National Socialist Freedom Party, union of NSDAP and DVFP in 1924–26.
Oberbefehlshaber des Heeres		Commander in Chief of the Army.
Oberkommando des Heeres	OKH	Army High Command.
Oberkommando der Wehrmacht	OKW	High Command of the Armed Forces.
Organisation Todt		Semi-military government agency established in 1933 to construct strategic highways and military installations.
Parteikanzlei		Hitler's chancery as leader of the NSDAP, directed by Bormann.
Politische Organisation	PO	Political Organization described the NSDAP's party administration during the Strasser crisis of 1932.
Reichsarbeitsdienst		National Labor Service, compulsory for both sexes.
Reichsführer SS		Reich leader of the SS, Himmler's title.
Reichsgau		one of the 11 regions formed of annexed territories in 1939.
Reichsleitung		Reich leadership, top level bureaucratic decision-making of the NSDAP.
Reichskommissar	RK	Reich Commissioner, of occupied territories.
Reichskommissriat fur das Ostland		German administration of Soviet territories.
Reichsmarschall		Reich Marshal, Goering's title.
Reichsministerium des Innern	RMdI	Ministry of Interior (Frick until 1943 then Himmler).
Reichsministerium für die besetzte Ostgebiete	RMO	Reich Ministry for Occupied Eastern territory (1941 Rosenberg).
Reichsministerium für Enährung und Landwirtschaft	RMEuL	Reich Ministry of Food and Agriculture (Darré until 1943 then Backe).
Reichspropagandleitung	RPL	Reich Propaganda Leadership (Goebbels).

Reichssicherheitshauptamt		Special Security Service for the Nazi leadership.
Reichssicherheitshauptamt	RSHA	Central Security Department of the Reich, formed in 1939 combining Gestapo, Kripo and SD.
Reichstag		Parliament or legislative assembly of the Weimar Republic.
Reichswehr		The 100,000 Army allowed Germany by the Treaty of Versailles. 1935 became the Wehrmacht.
Rotfrontkämpferbund	RFB	Red Front Association, para-military group of the KPD.
Schutzpolizei		Auxiliary police in the Eastern territories.
Schutzstaffel	SS	Protection Department, became the most powerful para-military group in the Reich under Himmler.
Seelöwe		Operation Sealion to invade Britain, 1940.
Sicherheitsdienst des Rfss	SD	Security Service of the SS, formed in 1932 under Heydrich became central organ of RSHA.
Sicherheitspolizei	Sipo	Security police comprising Gestapo and Kripo under Heydrich.
Sozialdemokratische Partei Deutschlands	SPD	Social Democratic Party of Germany.
Staatspolizei		Formerly Prussian Political Police became Nazi Political Police.
Stahlhelm		Steel helmets, Nationalist ex-servicemen's organization.
Stammlager	Stalag	Permanent prisoner of war camp.
Sturmabteilung	SA	Brownshirts or Stormtroopers. Purged in 1934.
Tannenbergbund		Tannenberg Association, rightist group led by General Ludendorff.
Volkssturm		People's Storm, military units of old men and young boys used in the last months of the war.
Waffen SS		fully militarized combat formations of the SS.
Wehrmacht		Armed Forces.
Wehrmachtbefehlshaber		Commander in Chief of Occupied territory.
Weserübung		Invasion of Denmark and Norway, April 1949.
Zitadelle		Attack on the Kursk salient, July 1943.

Some second rank Nazi Party officials

Backe, Herbert	State Secretary in the Reich Ministry of Agriculture 1933–42; acting Minister of Agriculture 1942–45.
Best, Werner	Reich Plenipotentiary in Denmark, 1940–45.
Bürckel, Josef	Gauleiter of the Palatinate, 1933–44; Reich Commissioner of the Saar, 1935; Reich Commissioner for the reunification of Austria and Germany, 1938–39; Reich Commissioner in Lorraine, 1940–44.
Daluege, Kurt	Administrative assistant to Göring, 1933–34; head of the *Ordnungspolizei,* 1936–45 in Czechoslovakia at end of the war.
Darré, R. Walther	Reich Minister of Agriculture, 1933–42.
Dietrich, Otto	Reich Press Chief, 1933–45.
Epp, Franz von	Reich Governor in Bavaria, 1933–45.
Frank, Hans	Bavarian Minister of Justice, 1933–45; Governor-General in Poland, 1939–45.
Freisler, Roland	State Secretary in the Reich Ministry of Justice, 1933–42; President of the People's Court, 1943–45, tried the July 1944 Conspirators.
Frick, Wilhelm	Reich Minister of the Interior, 1933–43; Reich Protector in Bohemia-Moravia, 1943–45.
Funk, Walther	Reich Minister of Economics, 1938–45.
Globocnik, Odilo	Gauleiter of Vienna, 1938–39; SS leader in occupied Poland, 1940–41.
Henlein, Konrad	Gauleiter of the Sudetenland, 1938–45.
Henningsen, Harry	Deputy Gauleiter of Hamburg, 1933–41; leading official in the Reich Ministry for Occupied Eastern Territories, 1941–43.
Heydrich, Reinhard	Head of the SS Security Service (SD), 1933–40. Reich protector in Bohemia-Moravia, 1940–42;
Hildebrandt, Friedrich	Gauleiter of Mecklenburg, 1933–45.
Holz, Karl	Editor of *Der Stürmer*, 1933–45; deputy Gauleiter of Franconia, 1933–40; acting Gauleiter of Franconia, 1940–45.
Kerrl, Hans	Prussian Minister of Justice, 1933–35; Reich minister for religious affairs, 1935–41.
Klemm, Hans	State Secretary in the Reich Ministry of Justice, 1942–45.
Koch, Erich	Gauleiter of East Prussia, 1933–45; Reich commissioner in the Ukraine, 1941–45.
Krüger, Friedrich W.	Leading SA official, 1933–34; head of the SS in occupied Poland, 1941–45.
Kube, Wilhelm	Gauleiter of Kurmark, 1933–36; Commissioner in Belorussia, 1941–43.
Lammers, Heinrich	Head of the Reich chancellery, 1933–45.
Lauterbacher, Hartmann	Deputy Head of the Hitler Youth, 1933–40; Gauleiter of Hanover, 1940–45.
Lohse, Heinrich	Gauleiter of Schleswig-Holstein, 1933–45; Reich commissioner in the Baltic, 1941–44.
Lutze, Victor	Head of the SA, 1934–43.
Meyer, Alfred	Gauleiter of Westphalia-South, 1933–45; State Secretary in the Ministry for Occupied Eastern Territories, 1941–45. . .
Ruberg, Bernhard	Head of the *Auslandsorganisation* in Holland, 1940.
Sauckel, Fritz	Gauleiter of Thuringia, 1933–45; Reich Plenipotentiary for Labor Allocation, 1943–45.
Schepmann, Wilhelm	Head of the SA, 1943–45.
Schirach, Baldur von	Head of the Hitler Youth, 1933–40; Gauleiter of Vienna, 1940–45.
Seyss-Inquart, Arthur	Prime Minister of Austria, 1938; Deputy Governor-General in Occupied Poland, 1939–40; Reich Commissioner in Holland, 1940–45.
Simon, Gustav	Gauleiter of Koblenz-Trier, 1933–45; chief of Civil administration in Luxumbourg, 1940–45.
Streicher, Julius	Gauleiter of Franconia, 1933–40.
Stürtz, Emil	Gauleiter of Kurmark, 1936–45.
Terboven, Josef	Gauleiter of Essen, 1933–45; Reich Commissioner in Norway, 1940–45.
Thierack, Otto	Reich Minister of Justice, 1942–45.
Tiessler, Walter	Liaison official of the Party Chancellery to the Reich Ministry of Propaganda, 1940–45.

The Nuremberg Laws

The Reich Citizenship Law of 15 September 1935

The Reichstag has adopted by unanimous vote the following law which is herewith promulgated.

Article I (1) A subject of the state is one who belongs to the protective union of the German Reich, and who, therefore, has specific obligations to the Reich.

(2) The status of subject is to be acquired in accordance with the provisions of the Reich and the state Citizenship Law.

Article II (1) A citizen of the Reich may be only one who is of German or kindred blood, and who, through his behaviour, shows that he is both desirous and personally fit to serve loyally the German people and the Reich.

(2) The right to citizenship is obtained by the grant of Reich citizenship papers.

(3) Only the citizen of the Reich may enjoy full political rights in consonance with the provisions of the laws.

Article III The Reich Minister of the Interior, in conjunction with the Deputy to the Führer, will issue the required legal and administrative decrees for the implementation and amplification of this law.

Promulgated: 16 September 1935. *In force:* 30 September 1935.

The Law for the Protection of German Blood and Honor, 15 September 1935

Imbued with the knowledge that the purity of German blood is the necessary prerequisite for the existence of the German nation, and inspired by an inflexible will to maintain the existence of the German nation for all future times, the Reichstag has unanimously adopted the following law, which is now enacted:

Article I (1) Any marriages between Jews and citizens of German or kindred blood are herewith forbidden. Marriages entered into despite this law are invalid, even if they are arranged abroad as a means of circumventing this law.

(2) Annulment proceedings for marriages may be initiated only by the Public Prosecutor.

Article II Extramarital relations between Jews and citizens of German or kindred blood are herewith forbidden.

Article III Jews are forbidden to employ as servants in their households female subjects of German or kindred blood who are under the age of 45 years.

Article IV (1) Jews are prohibited from displaying the Reich and national flag and from showing the national colors.

(2) However, they may display the Jewish colors. The exercise of this right is under state protection.

Article V (1) Anyone who acts contrary to the prohibition noted in Article I renders himself liable to penal servitude.

(2) The man who acts contrary to the prohibition of Article II will be punished by sentence to either a jail or penitentiary.

(3) Anyone who acts contrary to the provisions of Articles III and IV will be punished with a jail sentence up to a year and with a fine, or with one of these penalties.

Article VI: The Reich Minister of Interior, in conjunction with the Deputy to the Führer and the Reich Minister of Justice, will issue the required legal and administrative decrees for the implementation and amplification of this law.

Article VII: This law shall go into effect on the day following its promulgation, with the exception of Article III, which shall go into effect on 1 January 1936.

First Supplementary Decree of 14 November 1935

On the basis of Article III of the Reich Citizenship Law of 15 September 1935, the following is hereby decreed:

Article I (1) Until further provisions concerning citizenship papers, all subjects of German or kindred blood who possessed the right to vote in the Reichstag elections when the Citizenship Law came into effect, shall, for the present, posses the rights of Reich citizens. The same shall be true of those upon whom the Reich Minister of the Interior, in conjunction with the Deputy to the Führer, shall confer citizenship.

(2) The Reich Minister of the Interior, in conjunction with the Deputy to the Führer, may revoke citizenship.

Article II (1) The provisions of Article I shall apply also to subjects who are of mixed Jewish blood.

(2) An individual of mixed Jewish blood is one who is descended from one or two grandparents who, racially, were full Jews, insofar that he is not a Jew according to Section 2 of Article V. Full-blooded Jewish grandparents are those who belonged to the Jewish religious community.

Article III Only citizens of the Reich, as bearers of full political rights, can exercise the right of voting in political matters, and have the right to hold public office. The Reich Minister of the Interior, or any agency he empowers, can make exceptions during the transition period on the matter of holding public office. These measures do not apply to matters concerning religious organisations.

Article IV (1) A Jew cannot be a citizen of the Reich. He cannot exercise the right to vote; he cannot occupy public office.

(2) Jewish officials will be retired as of 31 December 1935. In the event that such officials served at the front in the World War either for Germany or her allies, they shall receive as pension, until they reach the age limit, the full salary last received, on the basis of which their pension would have been computed. They shall not, however, be promoted according to their seniority in rank. When they reach the age limit, their pension will be computed again, according to the salary last received on which their pension was to be calculated.

(3) These provisions do not concern the affairs of religious organizations.

(4) The conditions regarding service of teachers in public Jewish schools remain unchanged until the promulgation of new regulations on the Jewish school system.

Article V (1) A Jew is an individual who is descended from at least three grandparents who were, racially, full Jews . . . .

(2) A Jew is also an individual who is descended from two full-Jewish grandparents if:

(a) he was a member of the Jewish religious community when this law was issued, or joined the community later;

(b) when the law was issued, he was married to a person who was a Jew, or was subsequently married to a Jew;

(c) he is the issue from a marriage with a Jew, in the sense of Section I, which was contracted after the coming into effect of the Law for the Protection of German Blood and Honor of 15 September 1935;

(d) he is the issue of an extramarital relationship with a Jew, according to Section I, and born out of wedlock after 31 July 1936.

Article VI (1) Insofar as there are, in the laws of the Reich or in the decrees of the National Socialist Labor party and its affiliates, certain requirements for the purity of German blood which extend beyond Article V, the same remain untouched. . . .

Article VII The Führer and Chancellor of the Reich is empowered to release anyone from the provisions of these administrative decrees.

Editor's Note: Article V could be used by Hitler's security agencies to define as Jewish those they wished to prosecute but many half Jews (even those with Jewish mothers and thus technically Jews according to Jewish Law,) escaped the Nazi holocaust.
Extract from *Reichsgesetzblatt*, 1934, No.89.

BIBLIOGRAPHY

Bracher, Karl-Dietrich	*Die Deutsche Diktatur* (Cologne, 1969, Eng.ed, New York 1970)
Buchheim, Hans	*Anatomie des SS-Staates* (Olten und Freiburg, 1967)
Bullock, Alan	*Hitler – A Study in Tyranny* (New York, 1962)
Fest, Joachim	*Das Gesicht des Dritten Reiches* (Munich, 1964)
Heiber, Helmuth	*Joseph Goebbels* (Berlin, 1962, Eng. ed, New York, 1972)
Hilberg, Raul	*The Destruction of the European Jews* (Chicago, 1961)
Hillgruber, Andreas	*Hitlers Strategic, Politik und Kriegsführung* (Frankfurt/M, 1962)
Lewy, Gunther	*Catholic Church and Nazi Germany* (New York, 1964)
Liddell Hart, Basil	*History of the Second World War* (London, 1970).
O'Neill, Robert	*The German Army and the Nazi Party* (London, 1968
Peterson, Edward	*The Limits of Hitler's Power* (Princeton, NJ, 1969).
Schleunes, Karl	*The Twisted Road to Auschwitz* (Urbana, Illinois, 1970)
Schirer, William	*The Rise and Fall of the Third Reich* (New York, 1960)
Speer, Albert	*Inside the Third Reich*
Trevor-Roper, Hugh	*The Last Days of Hitler* (London, 1947)
Weinberg, Gerhard	*Nazi Foreign Policy* (Chicago, 1970)
Wright, Gordon	*The Ordeal of Total War:* 1939–1945 (New York and London, Harper & Row, 1968)

INDEX

Abwehr, 169, 220, 221
Abwehr des Faschismus, 59
Air Pact (1935), Anglo-German, 103
Alam Halfa, Battle of, 208
Aleksandrov, Georgi F, 184
All-German Congress of Workers' and Soldiers' Councils, 18
Allied Forces, 212
Allied Supervisory Commission, 36
Allies, 36, 123–24
Altmark, 121
Anglo-French Allies, 128
Anschluss, 108
Anti-Bolshevism, 48
Anti-Comintern Pact with Japan, 103, 104, 112
Antonescu, Marshal Ion, 225
Appeasement policy (1938), 109
Arbeitsdienst (Labor Service), 85
Ardennes Offensive, 229; Counter offensive, 245
Armament industries, 35
Armistice (Franco-German), (1940), 135
Armistice Negotiations (1918), 11
Armistice talks, British-Italian, 212–13
Arnim, General Jürgen von, 208
Aryans, 48
Athenia, 120
Atlantic, Battle of the, 213
Auchinleck, General Claude, 208
Austrian Nazis, 100, 106–107
Axis, 103

B

Bach-Zelewski, Obergruppenführer Erich von dem, 227
Bagration, Count, 171
Bagration, Operation, 219
Balck, General Hermann, 201
Baltic states, 150
Bandera, Colonel, 169
Barbarossa, Operation, 147, 155–58, 169
Barth, Emil, 16
Barthou, Louis, 108
Battle of Britain, 141–42
Bauer, Gustav, 26, 34
Bauhaus, 40
Bavarian Diet, 14–15
Bavarian Left, 20
Bavarian Nationalist Party, 38
Bavarian People's Party, 78
Beck, Colonel Jozef, 109, 112
Beck, General Ludwig, 75, 109, 220, 222–23
Beer hall *putsch* (1923), 46
Belgian Army, 124, 126, 128
Bell, Dr George, 220
Beneš, Dr Eduard, 108–109
Berger, SS Obergruppenführer, 242
Berlin, Defense of, 241
Berlin Police HQ, Occupation of, 18
Berlin Sportpalast, 64, 111
Billotte, General Gaston, 130
Bismarck, Chancellor Otto, 20, 38
Black Day of the German Army, 8, 11
Black *Reichswehr*, 29
Blaskowitz, General Johannes von, 116
Blitzkrieg (against Poland), 113, 116, 157
Blitzkrieg tactics, 121
Blomberg, General Werner von, 69, 75, 87, 89, 93, 103, 104, 106
Blum, Léon, 108
Bock, General Fedor von, 116, 132–33, 159, 167, 168, 169
Bodin, Lieutenant General Piotr I, 184
Bolsheviks, 14, 154, 242
Bolshevism, 17, 20, 103, 105, 112, 172, 242
Bonhöffer, Pastor Dietrich, 220
Bor, General Tadeusz, 227
Bormann, Martin, 246, 247
Bosch, Robert, 62
Bose, Herbert von, 90–91
Bradley, General Omar, 234
Brandt, Colonel, 221
Brauchitsch, General Walter von, 109, 140, 153, 167
Braun, Eva, 246
Brecht, Bertolt, 40
Bredow, General von, 90
British Alliance Treaty with Poland, 113
British Army, 147; 1st, 208; 2nd, 234; 8th, 208, 213; Divisions, 133
British Expeditionary Force (BEF), 124, 126, 130, 132
British Fleet, 11, 120
British Navy, 130, 132
Brown Movement, 100
Brüning, Heinrich, 53, 56, 60, 76, 84
Bürgerbräukeller, 46
Busch, General Ernst, 140, 219

C

Canadian Army, 1st, 234
Canaris, Admiral Wilhelm, 169, 220, 221
Catholics, 20, 79: Center Party, 76; Church, 79; Trade Union, 78; Youth Association, 83
Center Party, 20, 36, 38, 43, 53, 56
Chamberlain, Sir Neville, 106, 109, 111, 113
Chernyakhovsky, General Ivan, 230
Christian Churches, 79
Christians, German, 79, 81
Christian Trade Unions, 78
Chuikov, General Vasiliy, 186, 188, 192–94, 196, 246
Churchill, Sir Winston, 130, 135, 136, 143, 196, 208, 215
Civil Service Act, 83
Cobra, Operation, 224
Collins, General, 229
Communist Party, 15, 18, 20, 34, 36, 38, 43, 69, 76, 78, 95; Soviet, 185;
Communists, 75, 79
Compiègne (1940), 135
Concentration camps, 78–9
Concordat, 79
Conservatives, Ultra-, 69
Corap, General, 128
Councils: All-German Congress of Workers' and Soldiers', 20; Sailors', Soldiers', Workers', 11, 14
Courageous, 120
Crystal Night (1938), 79
Culture purges, 81
Cuno government, 38
Czechoslovak-Soviet Treaty (1935), 108

Daladier, Edouard, 111
Daluege, Kurt, 74
Danzig, Annexation of, 112, 116
Darlan, Admiral, 208
Darre, Walter, 85, 87, 100
Dawes Plan, 38
Defense Pacts with Baltic States, 112
Delbos, 108
Democratic Party, 20
Denmark and Norway, Occupation of (1940), 121–23
Derousseaux, General, 128
Deutscher Kampfbund, 45
Diels, Rudolf, 74
Dietrich, Otto, 89
Dietrich, Colonel General Sepp, 229–30
Diktat, Munich, 111, 136
Dimitrov, Georgi, 76
Dirksen, Herbert von, 104
Doenitz, Admiral Karl, 213, 245, 246, 247
Dohnanyi, Christian von, 220, 221
Dolchstosslegende, 26
Dollfuss, Engelbert, 100
Dorrenbach, Lieutenant, 17
Drang nach Osten (March in the East), 105
Drexler, Anton, 30
Dunkirk, 130, 132, 136
Dulles, Allen, 238
Dutch Army, 124, 126

E

Eastern Campaign, 120
Eastern Pact, 108
Ebert, Friedrich, 15–18, 20, 24, 26, 34, 40
Economy, 84–5; Plans, 84
Eden, Anthony, 103, 107
Education purges, 83
Eher Verlag, 83
Ehrhardt, Arthur, 50
Eichorn, Emil, 18, 20
Eisbär, Operations I, II and III, 207
Eisenhower, General Dwight, 234, 243, 244, 247
Eiserne Republikanische, 59
Eismann, Major, 201
Eisner, Kurt, 14, 20
Enabling Act, 76
Epp, Franz Ritter von, 76
Erntefest I and *II*, Operation, 207
Erzberger, Mattias, 36
European Economic Conference, Genoa, 36

F

Falkenhorst, General Nikolaus, 121
Fall, see Operations
Fehrenbach government, 36
Festung Stalingrad, 201
Final Solution, 79
Foch, Marshal Ferdinand, 135
Fort Eben Emael, Surrender of, 124, 126
Four-Power Conference, Munich, 111
France, Battle of, 128; Invasion of, 213, 219
Franco, General Francisco, 103, 142, 220
Franco-Soviet Mutual Assistance Pact (1935), 103, 108
Franck, Hans, 120
Free French, 208
Freemasons, 56
Freikorps, 20, 26, 34–6
Freischütz (Magic Marksmanship), 208
Fremde Heere Ost, 173, 178
French Army, 38, 124, 132–33: 1st, 130, 132; 2nd, 128; 7th, 126; 9th 128; XIX Corps, 208
French Front, 133
French Popular Front, 108
Frick, Wilhelm, 53, 69, 95
Friedeburg, Admiral Hans von, 247
Fritsch, General Werner von, 89, 104, 106
Fromm, General Fritz, 223
Funk, Walter, 85

G

Gamelin, General Maurice, 128, 130
Gaulle, General Charles de, 128, 208
Gehlen, General Reinhardt, 173, 178, 181
Gelb, Operation, 120, 124
Geneva Convention, 156
Geneva disarmament conference, 100
Geneva Protocol, 108
German Armed Forces, 121
German Army, 11, 20, 26, 29, 30, 35, 64, 75, 89, 93, 100, 101, 103, 106, 116–17; General Staff, 95, 152, 120, 128, 130, 132, 140, 141, 147, 150, 155–58, 160, 161, 167, 168, 177, 188, 219, 227, 238; Second Army, 173; Third Army, 116–18; Fourth Army, 116–18, 160, 167; Sixth Army, 124, 126, 140, 177–78, 185, 186, 188, 201; Eighth Army, 116–18; Ninth Army, 140, 160, 211; Tenth Army, 116–18; Eleventh Army, 173; Fourteenth Army, 116–18; Sixteenth Army, 116–18, 136; Eighteenth Army, 124, 134, 181; Army Group North, 158, 166; Army Group Center, 159, 161, 166, 181, 219, 246; Army Group South, 159, 173; Army Goup Vistula, 246; Afrika Korps, 145, 208
German Foreign Ministry, 104
German High Seas Fleet (Mutiny of), 11, 14
German Labor Front, 78
German Navy, 75, 140–42
German Republic, 16, 60
German Workers' Party, 29–30
Gessler, Otto, 34
Gestapo, 74, 161, 220, 223
Giraud, General Henri, 126
Gisevius, Dr Hans Bernd, 220
Gleichschaltung (Streamlining), 78–9, 81, 83, 93, 108
Gleiwitz Incident, 113
Goebbels, Paul Josef, 64, 75, 76, 81, 87, 89, 95, 233, 245, 246, 247
Goering, Hermann, 46, 48, 62, 69, 72, 74, 78, 87, 89, 95, 101, 104, 111, 132, 135, 141, 171, 178, 201, 245
Golikov, General Filipp, 188, 201
Golovanov, General Aleksandr, 190
Gördeler, Karl, 220–22
Gordov, General V N, 184, 186, 188
Gort, Lord, 126, 130, 132
Graziani, Field Marshal, 145
Green shirts, 29, 78
Groener-Ebert Pact, 24
Groener, General Wilhelm, 17, 18, 24, 26
Gropius, Walter, 40
Grün, Operation, 108
Guderian, General Heinz, 93, 118, 130, 159, 166, 167, 168, 206, 210, 211, 229, 230, 231–33

H

Haase, Hugo, 16
Habsburgs, 108
Hácha, President Emil, 111–12
Häften, Lieutenant Werner von, 222
Hague Convention, 156
Halder, General Franz, 109, 128, 161, 178, 181
Halifax, Lord, 105–107
Harrer, Karl, 30
Hasse, Ernst, 62
Hassell, Ulrich von, 104, 220
Heim, General, 199, 201
Heines, Edmund, 90
Held, Heinrich, 48, 76
Henderson, Sir Nevile, 109
Henlein, Konrad, 108, 109
Hentsch, Lieutenant Colonel, 8
Hereditary Farm Act, 85
Herrenvolk, 171
Hertling, Prime Minister, 11
Hess, Rudolf, 48, 87, 95, 108, 135
Heydrich, Reinhard, 89, 108, 120
Himmler, Heinrich, 89, 120, 153, 156, 171, 222–23, 231, 238, 239, 241, 242, 245, 246
Hindenburg, Marshal Paul von, 11, 24, 26, 40, 53, 60, 62, 64, 69, 93
Hitler, Adolf, *passim*
Hitler Jugend (Nazi youth movement), 83–4
Hodža, Milan, 108
Höpner, General Erich, 126, 159, 167
Hossbach memorandum, 105
Hoth, General Hermann, 128, 159, 166, 167, 177, 191, 206, 211, 218
Hugenberg, Alfred, 50, 53, 64, 69, 78, 87
Huntziger, General, 128, 135, 136
Hurricane airplanes, 142

I

IG Farben, 101
Imperial Army, 20
Imperial Germany, 15
Independent Socialists, 14–16, 18, 20, 34
Insurrections: Bavarian Republic, 20; Düsseldorf, 20; Mannheim, 20; Nuremberg, 20
Intelligence, 178, 181
Italian Army, 145, 147; First, 208; Eighth, 181, 201

J

Jesuits, 56
Jews, 48, 56, 78–9, 81, 83, 93, 120, 154, 161, 247
Jodl, General Alfried, 140, 155, 210, 247
Judeo-Bolshevism, 171
Juin, General, 208
Jung, Edgar, 90–91
Junkers airplanes, 89

K

Kaas, Monsignor, 76
Kahr, Gustav von, 29, 46, 93
Kandinsky, Wassily, 40
Kapp, Dr Wolfgang, 29
Kapp *Putsch*, 26, 34
Katyusha mortars, 166
Keitel, General Wilhelm, 106, 108, 111, 135, 136, 156
Kessel, 160
Kesselring, Field Marshal Albrecht von, 208, 213, 245
Khrushchev, Nikita, 173, 188
Khryukin, General, 190
Kiel, Mutiny, 11, 14; Sailors' People's Naval Division, 17
Kirdorf, Emil, 53
Klausener, Erich, 91
Klee, Paul, 40
Kleist, General Ewald von, 128, 134, 159, 173, 178, 181, 201, 218
Klette I and *II*, Operations, 207
Kluge, Field Marshal Günther von, 116, 167, 168, 210, 220–22
Knilling, Premier Eugen von, 45
Koch, Erich, 171–73
Kolpachi, Major General, 184, 186
Kommissar Ordnung, 156, 161, 169
Konev, General Ivan, 211, 218, 230–31, 246
Krasovsky, General, 199
Krebs, General, 232
Krofta, Professor, 108
Kröger, Dr, 242
Krosigk, Count Schwerin von, 69, 93
Krupp factory, 35, 101
Krupp, Alfred, 62
Küchler, General Georg, 116, 124, 134
Kühlmann, Foreign Minister von, 8
Kuznetsov, General Vasily, 184

L

Laborde, Admiral, 208
Labor Service (*Arbeitsdienst*), 85
Laval, Pierre, 108
Lang, Fritz, 40
League of Nations, 40, 100
Lebensraum, 103, 150, 153, 155
Leber, Julius, 222
Ledebour, Georg, 15, 18, 20
Leeb, General Wilhelm von, 76, 159, 167
Leibbraut, Dr Georg, 171
Leipart, Theodor, 76
Lemmgen, Petty Officer, 20
Lenin, Vladimir, 20
Leningrad, Siege of, 218
Leopold, King of the Belgians, 126, 128, 130
Leventzow, Admiral von, 74
Ley, Dr Robert, 62, 95
Liberals, 20
Liberation Movement, 242
Liebknecht, Karl, 15–18, 20
List, General Wilhelm von, 116, 169, 181, 201
Little Entente, 103, 108
Litvinov, Maxim, 108, 112
Locarno, Treaty of, 40, 103, 108
Lohse, Heinrich, 62, 171
Lopatin, General, 191
Lossow, General Otto von, 46
Lubbe, Marius van der, 75
Ludendorff, General Erich, 8, 11, 15, 46, 48, 50
Luftwaffe, 101, 116–17, 124, 132, 140–42, 160, 168, 178, 186, 188, 199, 201
Luther, Martin, 81
Lutze, Victor, 89
Luxemburg, Rosa, 18, 20

M

Machtergreifung und Evolution, 87
Maginot Line, 128, 134
Majority Socialists, 14–16, 18, 20, 26, 34
Malenkov, Georgi, 188
Malinovsky, General Rodion, 212, 218, 227
Malyshev, V A, 188
Manstein, General Erich von, 124, 128, 173, 201, 210, 212, 218
Manteuffel, General Hasso von, 229
Manuilsky, General Josif, 184
Marburg University, 89–90
Mareth Line, 208
Mark, Collapse and stabilization of (1923), 38
Marxism, 30, 56
Mathausen concentration camp, 108
Max, Prince of Baden, 11, 15
Mein Kampf, by Adolf Hitler, 48, 79, 81, 91, 98, 103, 104
Meissner, Dr Otto von, 62, 64
Mekhlis, Leonid, 184
Melnyk, Colonel, 169
Mercury, Operation, 147
Michael, King of Rumania, 227
Miklas, President, 108
Ministries of Defense, 106; Economy, 87; Finance and War, 107; Food and Agriculture, 87; Interior, 95, 107; Propaganda, 81, 241; Propaganda and Culture, 87; War, 20
Model, Field Marshal Walther, 218, 219, 243
Molotov, Vlachislav, 112, 113, 150, 154
Moltke, Count Helmut von, 8
Montgomery, General Bernard, 208, 213, 234, 243, 247
Moral relaxation in Germany, 40, 42
Morgan, General Frederick, 35
Morgenthau plan, 233
Moser, General, 246
Moskalenko, K S, 186, 190
Müller, Dr, 220
Müller, Hermann, 26, 34, 36
Munich: Diktat, 111; Four-Power Conference, 111; HQ, 53; House of German Art, 81
Mussolini, Benito, 89, 100, 103, 104, 107–108, 111, 112, 134, 135 142–43, 145, 212, 213, 246
Mutinies, 11, 14
Mutschmann, Martin, 62

N

Narvik Operation, 122–23
Nationalism, 48, 64, 69
Nationalist Bavarian Peoples' Party, 20
Nationalist Party, 78
National Reich Church Program, 79
Nazification of Germany, 87
National socialism, 172
National Socialist German Workers' Party (formerly German Workers' Party); Nazi; 30, 34, 38, 43, 45–6, 48, 50, 53, 56, 59, 60, 62, 69, 72, 74, 75, 76, 78–9, 81, 84–5, 87, 93, 95, 171, 220, 243, 245; Propaganda, 64; Students' Union, 56
Naumann, Dr Werner, 161
Naval Pact, Anglo-German (1935), 103
Nazi Youth Movement (*Hitler Jugend*), 83–4
Nebe, Artur, 220
Neurath, Baron von Konstantin, 69, 74, 93, 95, 103
New York Stock Exchange, 43
Niemöller, Pastor Martin, 81
Night of the Long Knives, 89
NKVD, 166, 169, 188; 10th Division, 194
Non-Aggression Pact with Poland, 112–13
Noske, Gustav, 14, 20, 34
November traitors, 56
Novikov, General Aleksandr, 190
Nuremberg Laws, 79; Rally, 109

O'Connor, General Richard, 145
Ohlendorf, Dr, 161
OKW (*Oberkommando der Wehrmacht*), 95, 106, 113, 116, 121, 155–56
Olbricht, General, 221, 222
Operationsbefehl No 1, 194
OSS, 238
Oster, General, 124
Ostpolitik, 169, 171
Otto, Operation, 104, 107
Oven, Lieutenant General von, 20

P

Pact of Steel (German-Italian), 112
Palatinate government, 38
Panzer Armies: First Panzer Army, 173, 177–78, 181, 201, 218; Fourth Panzer Army, 173, 177–78, 186, 188, 201, 211, 218; Fifth Panzer Army, 229; 1st Panzer Group, 159; 2nd Panzer Group, 159; 3rd Panzer Group, 159, 161; 4th Panzer Group, 159, 161, 211;
Panzer Divisions, 118, 124, 133, 140, 158, 191, 219, 229, 231; 2nd Panzer Division, 130; 6th Panzer Division, 181; 7th Panzer Division, 128; 11th Panzer Division, 201; 14th Panzer Division, 194; 22nd Panzer Division, 178; 24th Panzer Division, 194
Papen, Franz von, 60, 62, 64, 69, 74, 84, 87, 90–91, 101, 104, 106
Partisans: Italian, 238; Nationalist, 173, 218; Non-Nationalist, 173; Soviet, 156, 161, 173, 177, 218; Ukrainian, 218
Patton, General George, 208, 229, 234
Paulus, Field Marshal, 173, 186, 188, 190, 192–94, 201
Peace Treaties: March 1918, Germany /Soviet Russia (Brest-Litovsk), 8; May, 1918, Germany/Rumania, 8
People's Naval Division, 20
People's Party, 78
People's Security Forces, 20
Pétain, Marshal Philippe, 135, 142
Petrov, General, 227, 230
Phony War, 120
Pius XI, Pope, 79, 136
Poland, Invasion of (1939), 117–19
Polish Army, 116–17, 227
Popov, Lt General Markian, 76, 206
Popular Front (France), 108
Prague Manifesto, 242
Press, Left wing, 81; purges, 81
Preuss, Professor Dr Hugo, 20
Prisoner of War (POW) Camps, 161
Protestant churches, 79, 81; Conference (1933), 79
Purges: Armed Forces, 106; Army, 89–90; Church, 91; Culture, 81, 91, 93; Education, 83; Government, 90–91; Press, 81
Putsch, Beer Hall (1923), 46, 93

Q

Quisling, Vidkun, 121

R

Radek, Karl, 20
Radu, General, 201
Raeder, Admiral Erich, 120, 140, 213
Rearmament, 101, 103
Red Air Force, 166
Red Army, 150, 178, 181, 196, 218–19, 227, 230, 242
Red Army (German), 20, 34
Red Cross, 156
Reich, 15, 20, 38, 46, 81, 112; Thousand year, 48
Reich Chamber of Culture, 81
Reich Colonial Association, 103
Reich Food Estate Act, 85
Reichenau, General Walther von, 116, 124, 126, 140, 168
Reichsbanner, 59
Reichskomissariat, 155
Reichsministerium für die besetzten Ostgebiete, 171
Reichsrat, 24
Reichstag, 11, 24, 34, 36, 38, 43, 45, 53, 56, 59, 60, 62, 69, 75, 76, 78, 87, 93, 120
Reichswehr, 29, 34–6, 38, 46, 53, 74, 75, 87, 89, 93
Reinhardt, Max, 40
Reparation Commission, 36
Reparations bill, 36; payments, 38, 40, 50
Reynaud, Premier Paul, 134–35
Rhineland, Occupation of, 103; separatist republic, 38
Ribbentrop, Joachim von, 95, 103, 104, 105, 107, 108, 113, 171, 245
Richtlinien, 156
Ripka, Dr, 108
Rodimtsev, General, 191
Röhm, Ernst, 50, 59, 87, 89–90
Rokossovsky, General, 194, 199, 201, 210, 212, 230
Romanenko, General, 201
Rommel, Field Marshal Erwin, 117, 128, 145, 208, 219, 222
Roosevelt, President, F D, 112, 136, 208, 215, 245
Rosenberg, Alfred, 79, 95, 157, 171, 239, 241
Rot und Grün, Operation, 104
Rote Front, 59
Rote Kapelle, 220
Royal Air Force, 128, 140–42, 208, 215; radar stations, 141
Royal Oak, 120
Rudenko, General Sergey, 190, 199
Ruhr, Occupation of (1923), 36; Treasury, 53; Uprising in, 34
Rumanian Army, 227; 1st Armored Division, 201, Third, 181, 199; VI Corps, 199, 201
Rumanian oil fields, 150, 153
Runciman, Lord, 109
Rundstedt, General Gerd von, 116, 124, 128, 132–34, 136, 159, 161, 167, 201, 219, 229
Russian Liberation Movement, 241
Russian National Liberation Army, 241
Rust, Bernhard, 62, 83, 95
Rydz-Smigly, Field Marshal, 116

S

SA (*Sturm Abteilung*), 29, 45–46, 50, 56, 59, 64, 69, 72, 74, 75, 78–79, 87, 89–90, 93
Sarayev, General, 188
Sas, Colonel, 124
Saturn, Operation, 196, 201
Saxony Uprising, 34, 38
Schacht, Dr Hjalmar, 62, 84–85, 95, 104
Scheidemann, Phillip, 15, 20, 26
Schirach, Baldur von, 83
Schlabrendorff, Colonel Fabian von, 171
Schleicher, General Kurt von, 53, 62, 75, 90, Government, 64
Schmid, Dr Willi, 93
Scmitt, Dr Kurt, 87
Schmundt, General, 194
Schneidhuber, Major, 90
Scholl, Hans and Sophie, 220
Scholz, Wilhelm von, 20
Schörner, Field Marshal Friedrich, 227
Schröder, Kurt von, 62, 64
Schulenberg, Count Friedrich von der, 171
Schulze, Archbishop of Cologne, 79
Schuschnigg, Dr Kurt von, 103, 106, 108
Schwender, General von, 194
SD (*Sicherheitsdienst*, Security Division), 156, 165, 169, 177
Sea Lion, Operation, 136, 142
Sedan, 128
Seeckt, General Hans von, 29, 34–35
Seisser, Colonel Hans von, 46
Seldte, Franz, 87
Sergeyevich, Nikita, 184
Sevastopol, Fall of, 225
Seyss-Inquart, Artur von, 107–108
Shamil, Said, 171
Shirer, William, 120
Shumilov, General M S, 194
Siegfried Line, 103
Sicily, Invasion of (1943), 212–213
Simon, Sir John, 101, 103
Skorpion, Operation, 241
Smolensk Committee, 241
Social Democrats, 38, 43, 53, 56, 62, 76, 78, 107
Socialists, 26, 29
Sokolovsky, General Vasily, 211
Somme, 134
Soviet Air Force: 16th Air Army, 190, 199; 17th Air Army, 199
Soviet Armed Forces, 160
Soviet Army: Central Front, 210; Don Front, 199; Southeastern Front, 184; Southern Front, 184; Southwestern Front, 161; Steppe Front, 211; 1st Ukrainian Front, 218; 2nd Ukrainian Front, 225; 3rd Ukrainian Front, 218, 225; 4th Ukrainian Front, 218, 227; Voronezh Front, 210; Western Front, 211, 234; 1st Guards Army, 188, 190, 199; 21st Army, 186, 199; 24th Army, 188, 190, 199; 47th Army, 231; 51st Army, 186, 199; 57th Army, 186, 199; 62nd Army, 184, 186, 191; 63rd Army, 184; 64th Army, 184, 186, 199; 66th Army, 188, 199; 1st Tanks, 156, 210; 2nd Tanks, 210; 5th Tanks, 181, 199, 201
Soviet-Finnish War, 120
Soviet-German Pact (1939), 150
Spanish Civil War, 103, 104, 108
Spartacists, 15, 18, 20, 34
Speer, Albert, 233, 246
Spitfires, 142
Sprenger, Jacob, 62
SS (*Schutz Staffeln*), 29, 50, 74, 78, 87, 89–90, 93, 106, 120, 156, 169, 171, 177, 221–23, 227, 239, 241
SS formations: *Grossdeutschland*, 211; *Das Reich*, 211; *Leibstandarte*, 211; *Totenkopf*, 211, 247
SS (*Einsatzgruppen*), 117, 156, 161, 169
SS Panzers, 6th Army, 229, 230
Stahlecker, Dr, 161
Stahlhelm, 29, 36, 59, 69, 74
Stalin, Josef, 112, 118, 120, 166, 173, 184, 185, 186, 188, 190, 199, 208, 215, 230, 241, 242
Stalingrad, 184–201 *passim*
Stauffenberg, Count Claus, von 171, 221–23
Stavka, 196, 210, 211, 219
Steiner, General Felix, 245–46
Stempfle, Fr, 91
Stepanov, General, 190
Stieff, General Helmuth, 221, 222
Strasser, Otto and Gregor, 50, 59, 62, 90, 100
Bombing of German cities, Strategic, 215
Strauss, General, 140
Streicher, Julius, 50, 78
Stresa, Front, 103
Stresemann, Gustav, 38, 40
Stufenplan, 98
Stukas, 124, 128, 141, 192, 193, 196
Stülpnagel, General Karl Heinrich, 223
SU 85 guns, 211
Sudeten Party, 108–111
Stumme, General Georg, 208

T

Tanks: Ferdinand self-propelled tanks, 211; Panther, 210, 211; T-34, 181; Tiger, 207
Teheran Conference, 215
Ten-year Non-Aggression Pact with Poland, 100
Thuringia, Uprising in, 34, 38
Thyssen, Fritz, 53
Times, The, 109
Timoshenko, Field Marshal Semyon, 173, 186
Tiso, Monsignor Josef, 111–12
Tolbukhin, General Fedor, 186, 218, 227
Torch, Operation, 199, 208
Trade Union movement, 30, 78
Tresckow, Henning von, 75, 220–22
Twenty-five Point Program, 30
Typhoon, Operation, 166

U

U-Boats, 213
U.29, 120
U.30, 120
Udet, General Ernst, 168
United States' Army: 1st Army, 224, 229, 243; 3rd Army, 224; 8th Army, 238; 9th Army, 234, 243, 244
Untermensch, 169, 241
Uprisings: Ruhr, 34; Saxony, 34, 38; Thuringia, 34, 38
Uranus, Operation, 196, 199
Ursula, Operations, 207

V

Valkyrie, Operation, 222–23
Vasilievsky, Colonel General Aleksandr, 185–86, 188, 196, 199
Vatican, 79, 220
Vatutin, General Nikolay, 199, 210, 212, 218
Versailles, Treaty of, 26, 35, 36, 85, 100, 101, 103
Viethinghoff, General Heinrich von, 238
Vlasov, General Andrey, 241, 242
Volkischer Beobachter, 48, 83, 89, 108
Volsky, General V T, 199, 201
Voronezh Front, 201
Vorwärts, 20
Vossische Zeitung, 81, 83

W

Waffen SS, 95, 238, 241
Wagner, General Eduard, 171
Wehrmacht (formerly *Reichswehr*), 95, 106–109, 111, 112, 113, 116, 128, 136, 147, 154, 169, 171, 184, 194, 196, 199, 206–207, 208, 211, 212
Weichs, Field Marshal Maximilian von, 227
Weimar: Constituent Assembly, 20; Republic, 20 26, 29–30, 34, 36, 38, 43, 45, 53, 62, 69, 74, 76;
Weiss, Operation, 112, 116
Wels, Otto, 17, 76
Weltanschauungen, 154, 156
Wenck, General Walter, 231, 245
Western Allies, 112–13, 120, 124, 208, 210, 219, 229, 233–34, 243, 245
Western Powers, 109, 113
Weygand, General Maxime, 130, 133–35
Wietersheim, General von, 194
Wilhelm II, Emperor of Germany, 8, 11, 15, 17, 136
Wilhelmina, Queen of the Netherlands, 124
Wilson, President Woodrow, 11
Wilson, Sir Horace, 111
Winkelman, General H G, 124
Winterzauber, (Wintermagic), 207
Wirth, Joseph, 35
Wittenberg Synod, 81
Wolff, General Karl, 234

Y

Yeremenko, Colonel General Andrey, 186, 188, 194, 196, 199, 201
Young Plan, 50, 53
Youth Association, 83

Z

Zauberflote, (Magic Flute), 207
Zeitzler, General Kurt, 181, 196, 210
Zhdanov, Andrey, 184
Zhukov, General Georgi, 166, 188, 190, 196, 199, 218, 230–31, 246
Zigeunerbaron, (Gipsy Baron), 207
Zitadelle, Operation, 210
Zymierski, General, 227

Acknowledgments
The author would like to thank the following people who helped in the preparation of this book: Catherine Bradley, who edited it; David Eldred, who designed it; Richard Natkiel, who drew the maps; and Susan Piquemal, who prepared the index.

The author would also like to thank the Bundesarchiv which provided the majority of the photographs. The remaining photographs were supplied by the following libraries:

Bison Picture Library: p 41 (top 2), 42 (right), 42–43 (all 3), 44–45 (all 4), 46–47 (all 5), 49 (top right), 57 (bottom), 61 (top), 62 (top right), 65 (all 5), 70–71, 73, 74 (top left), 75 (below), 76 (below), 77 (top right and below left and right), 78 (top right), 79 (both), 80 (both), 81 (top center and right), 82–83 (top 3), 84 (top left), 86–87 (all 5), 90–91 (below), 92, 93 (center and below), 94 (top right and center and both below), 95 (both), 98–99 (top 3), 100 (center), 114–115, 118 (top), 119, 122–123 (all 3), 126 (left), 127 (top), 130–131 (all 4), 138 (bottom), 139 (top left, center left and below), 142–143 (all 4), 150–151 (below), 154–155 (all 4), 158–159 (all 3), 162–163, 166 (top right and below left), 167, 170–171 (all 5), 174–175 (all 4), 178, 179, 186, 186–187 (top), 187 (top right), 191 (top right), 206–207.
Robert Hunt Library: p 48 (bottom left), 48 (top right), 101, 104 (top), 105 (top left), 124–125 (all 4), 127 (below), 128 (both), 129 (top left), 132 (below), 133 (both), 134 (top and bottom), 136–137 (all 4), 140, 141, 151 (top left), 160–161 (all 5), 165 (top left), 166 (top left), 168, 169, 172–173 (all 4), 176–177 (all 3), 181 (top), 184 (below), 188 (top left), 190–191 (below), 191 (top left), 193 (top), 194–195 (below), 194 (top), 198 (top right), 202 (top right), 205 (below right), 206 (top), 208, 209, 210 (below), 213 (below), 214–215 (all 3), 218, 219 (top both), 221, 222–223 (all 4), 225 (all 3), 228, 229 (both), 230 (below), 231 (both), 232 (below), 233 (both), 234–235 (below), 238 (top both), 241 (both), 242 (below), 246 (below left), 246–247 (top), 248–249 (all 3).
Novosti Press Agency: p 164–165 (below), 184–185 (top), 185 (below), 187 (below), 188 (top center), 188–189 (below), 192–193 (below), 196–197, 198, 199 (top left), 199 (below), 200–201 (all 3), 226–227, 230 (top), 239 (right), 240 (both), 242 (above), 243, 245 (both), 246 (top left), 247 (top and below).
USAF: p 182–183, 210 (top), 211 (both), 212, 232 (top), 235 (top), 236–237, 238–239.
Orbis Publishing: p 72 (top), 75 (top), 77 (top left), 135, 139 (top right), 144 (top), 151 (top right), 224.
Masami Tokoi: p 150 (top left and center), 156–157, 157 (top both), 164.
K W Krause Collection: p 105 (below), 149 (top left), 227 (center).
Keystone Press Agency: p 22 (below).
Foto-Schardt: p 203 (top right).